The Leisure Society

JEREMY SEABROOK

The Leisure Society

Basil Blackwell

Copyright © Jeremy Seabrook 1988

First published 1988
First published in USA 1989

Basil Blackwell Ltd
108 Cowley Road, Oxford, OX4 1JF, UK

Basil Blackwell Inc.
432 Park Avenue South, Suite 1503
New York, NY 10016, USA

British Library Cataloguing in Publication Data

Seabrook, Jeremy, 1939–
    The leisure society
    1. Leisure. Social aspects.
    I. Title
    306′.48

    ISBN 0–631–14543–5
    ISBN 0–631–16365–4 Pbk

Library of Congress Cataloging in Publication Data

Seabrook, Jeremy, 1939–
    The leisure society / Jeremy Seabrook.
        p.   cm.
    ISBN 0–631–14543–5.   ISBN 0–631–16365–4 (pbk.)
    1. Social history.   2. Leisure.   3. Service industries workers.
4. Leisure class.   I. Title.
HN16.S43   1988   88–14576
306′.48–dc19   CIP

Typeset in 9½ on 11½ pt Plantin
by Joshua Associates Ltd, Oxford
Printed in Great Britain
by Billing and Sons Ltd, Worcester

Contents

1

Introduction

The overwhelming experience of most people in the industrial era has been of the appropriation of time by work. Leisure has been something won in the interstices, something precious and insufficient. For the majority of working people, time spent not working had to be as unlike the conditions under which they laboured as possible; which is why the men of the forges, foundries and mines speak so tenderly of the walk to the allotment when work was finished, the catching and cherishing of song-birds, the release of the pigeons from their pens, the visit to the wind-scoured hills overlooking the colliery; or of stumbling with relief into the pub which, it was always said, was the quickest way out of Wigan or Glasgow or Hartlepool. (There are more subtle forms of exit from these places now.)

The leisure of women was of a different order, although it meant time stolen also, from domestic labour. It was spent often with other women from the family or neighbourhood, examining the vast patchwork of relationships of all those close to them, knitting and unpicking it with the same tireless gestures that they used in the sewing and mending and darning of more material fabrics. The idea of a leisure society would be as incomprehensible to these people as the necessity for industrial discipline must have appeared to those accustomed to the slower – though equally inflexible – rhythms of the year, of sowing and harvest, of sunshine and rain, of spring and fall.

Perhaps this is why the disappearance of workplaces from the old industrial areas has not given rise to universal celebration. Quite the reverse: a growing sense of dislocation and anxiety can be found in those regions where, for six generations or more, people's lives were marked, indeed often deeply scarred, by the demands of labour. The reasons for this absence of enthusiasm are not difficult to imagine: the principal consequence of technological change in the last quarter of the twentieth century has been the re-emergence (after such a short interval of relief) of mass unemployment; and the one thing that has been worse in popular experience than work has been the lack of it, whether caused by variations in the trade cycle, the pulse of boom and slump, or by the more sombre rhythm of the constant decay of old skills and the summoning forth of new ones, excluding, depressing, eclipsing groups of workers who had once felt themselves to be powerful and secure in possession of their craft or skill. The promise of leisure to those whose destiny had always been to labour is perhaps the most disconcerting of all the many adaptations that have been demanded of them since the early industrial period both shaped and was shaped by the sensibility of the new working class. The loss of the familiar is always painful, even when what is held out in its place is offered as a deliverance.

Leisure as time taken from work, as occupation entered into in contrast to it for relaxation and pleasure, is far from the proposition that leisure may become a primary purpose in our lives. Our natural suspicion of this sudden reversal is intensified by the exhortations that we must also work harder, increase productivity, become competitive in the markets of the world. The leisure society – with all its aristocratic associations – belongs securely to the future. The three groups (apart from children) who have the most leisure now are the rich, the retired and the redundant; and not all of these bring back travellers' tales from the country of the future calculated to make the rest of us yearn to get there. Those for whom leisure is a central life-purpose are the very rich; and, as we shall see, they have very powerful reasons for insisting, not on their lack of occupation, but on the pressing importance of it. In other words, the prospect of leisure is necessarily subordinate to wealth. 'You can't do anything without money', the young tell us; not even do nothing, not even muck about or hang around, those traditional and bitter-sweet disoccupations of adolescence. The main experience of leisure in our society is of a particular absence of work, with minimal income; a caricature of the ease and comfort which the fluent proponents of the leisure society hold out to us.

The word 'leisure' comes from the same Latin root which gives us the English word licence, meaning to permit or to allow. It implies, therefore, that one group of people will do the allowing and another group will be the beneficiaries of the permission. This suggests continuing patterns of subordination and dependency which characterized the culture of labour, now at such an advanced stage of decay. Perhaps it is worth looking at the terms on which the leisure society is going to be conceded.

For one thing, it remains conditional on Britain getting richer. Now, it is already clear that as we get more money, many of the activities and pursuits which once cost very little or nothing can no longer be carried on without tribute being paid to someone for the privilege of continuing to engage in them. Some of these are obvious – the 'need' for special clothing or equipment, often stamped with particular brand names, before we can participate in certain sports; the falling into disuse of the ability to 'make our own fun', as an older generation still remembers, although ridiculed now as they remember how much they could do without money by those who have acquired the superior wisdom of knowing how little can be done without a lot of it; the transformation of homely and commonplace sports – darts and snooker, for instance – into big business, with the result that star status is visited upon even the most unlikely individuals, Jocky Wilson or Alex Higgins, as they promote what was formerly a mild and unaggressive diversion into a nationally competitive activity, in which the young will take part, partly for the delight of the game, but partly in the hope of gaining recognition, celebrity status, distinction. On the other hand, it is essential to take account of the extraordinary energy and passion, the commitment and skills that people in Britain give voluntarily: whether this is in the form of gift-work – from nature conservation to sitting on committees for the NSPCC or running Oxfam shops – or whether it is the devotion to the growing of fuchsias, breeding dogs or collecting butterflies. There exists a vast reservoir of knowledge and expertise, much of it highly specialized, often recondite and obscure, which creates a world of detailed specialisms which mean nothing to outsiders. There is a vast channelling of altruism and enthusiasm into activities undertaken for their own sake or for the sake of those who share the same, ordinary passions. Leisure remains an ambiguous idea; what makes it interesting is that it represents both an intensifying of marketed experiences on the one hand, and growing individual autonomy on the other. This book is about that tension.

Leisure, then, is often discussed as though it were anticipated free time: certainly for those in work there has been little decrease in the actual number of hours worked. The promise of the leisure society acts as a comfort and distraction in a present that is often hard to bear; it eases painful transitions and, more important, gains our acquiescence in necessary changes. One of the most salient features of our culture is our preoccupation with both the future (you must have something to look forward to) and the past (you must have something to look back on). Simultaneously, we eagerly anticipate the future and hoard our memories. Is it an elaborate avoidance of the here-and-now that sends out the winter holiday brochures in midsummer and the summer holiday suggestions on Boxing Day? Enjoyment of the present is always contaminated by the belief that the future is going to be much better or is spoilt by longings profitably moulded by the nostalgia industries. Crossing the desert of the present (which is, after all, where we live) requires vast enterprises devoted to escape. What is it that so many of us feel such a pressing need to escape from? It certainly cannot be that we suffer a surfeit of reality for we already live in the most escapist society the world has ever known. It may well be that the need for escape is the wish to avoid an absence of significant activity, a lack of function and purpose: it is a way of mourning the loss of those very things which we are constantly being urged to greet as the source of our liberation. Of course, it is sometimes argued, we are now going through a period of adjustment. We shall get used to it, just as people accustomed themselves to the new environment of an industrial landscape superimposed upon that of fields and commons. The contemporary uncertainties are merely the unavoidable frictions of transition; nothing more than the grumbles of characteristically British recalcitrants who have always lamented change as deterioration and loss.

It is worth noting that the most persuasive advocates of the leisure society are themselves in little danger of finding themselves suddenly bereft of function. These are, for the most part, busy economists and futurologists, entrepreneurs who have considerable stakes in leisure industries, as well as those whose time is both usefully and enjoyably spent as well as being highly rewarded. It is clear that in 'our' workless future, work is going to belong to the privileged, to those fortunates who declare 'I'm only doing what I would be doing anyway, and getting paid for it'. These get the best of all worlds. For them, demarcation between work and leisure is blurred; they constitute a considerable force – media people, designers, planners, consultants in a vast range of practical and abstract expertise, entertainers, advertisers, researchers, communicators of all kinds. (It is not without significance that they frequently borrow the language of more primitive forms of labour to express themselves, admiring each other's 'work', attending endless 'workshops', discussing their 'skills', 'crafts', referring to themselves as 'workaholics'; indeed, they often inhabit former places of far cruder toil: disused and converted warehouses and factories, with bright green rails, iron ladders, red-painted windows and decorative remnants of the building's original function left as ornamentation.) The path-finders of a leisure-dominated future are in no danger themselves of being overwhelmed by an excess of it. (There is a more extended discussion of their role in chapter 1.)

Leisure is full of paradox. On the one hand is the possibility of setting ourselves freely chosen goals and purposes in which we can express ourselves in ways that work never permitted most people; and, on the other, a growing and always extending marketing of experience which is, in important ways, in contradiction to these possibilities. As we get richer, more and more areas of our lives become monetized. This means that the freedoms we gain from toil are increasingly the object of attention of the markets – even those lowly and unspectacular activities that belonged to back parlour or church hall or working men's club. Leisure in this context suggests accelerated spending, a succession of marketed interests, fads and whims, distractions succeeding each other, being ousted by more urgent and recent ones, making demands on money that must never rest but agitates people in its unquiet dance. Continuous movement, serial and fragmented experience: a process that bears an extraordinary resemblance to the feverish activity of capitalist labour – the very scourge to which leisure is proposed as an answer and relief. This leisure speaks of a restless search for entertainment and escape; a full-time occupation which in many ways suggests a perpetuation of the never-completed task of work in mine, mill or factory. Nor should this similarity surprise us. For the forms of labour that have, to a considerable degree, deserted the 'developed' world have not been suppressed. It is simply that basic manufacture, the production of both necessary and useful things which gave coherence and readily apprehended meaning to the lives of people in the industrial regions of Britain, has been transferred to places where it can be accomplished more cheaply and efficiently. And we continue to live in the shadow of that labour, both in time – invited to contrast our leisure-rich present with a work-laden past – and in space, as it continues to live on, even though spirited from our sight, in the newly industrialized countries of the South. We are still compelled by the rhythms and the logic of that labour, however curtailed our direct experience of it may be.

The resemblance between our former work and our future leisure does not end here. For most of us, the actual work we do provides little sense of function and significance. (All the research suggests that the greatest satisfactions gained at work are by means of the relationships and contact with fellow-workers; our ostensible reason for our attendance there is secondary.) A consequence of this is that we increasingly seek in leisure the purposes that elude our labour. It is observable that many leisure activities become the focus of ambitions beyond anything suggested by the idea of leisure: they seek to transcend themselves by, for instance, going professional, becoming an expert, perfecting certain skills and techniques that will then be marketable. Leisure, in this way, strives to re-enter the world of labour from which it is supposed to offer relief: making the big time, winning the competition, becoming a famous musician, a gymnast, an ice-skater, an actor. Even those occupations that seem most capable of resisting this process – growing flowers, breeding birds – get readily caught up in the kind of competitiveness that has nothing to do with the old-fashioned and unthreatening rivalries of leek-growing or pigeon-racing. They become intense specialisms, the reward for which, more often than not, turns out to be big money or at least substantial cash prizes.

Much of leisure is haunted in more obvious ways by the earlier age of labour; that which is given over to the exploration of our industrial and pre-industrial past; the time devoted to seeking out the conditions in which people lived and worked, discovering the roots of family identity, recreating the artefacts and products of earlier times. In this sense, model railways can be seen as nostalgia for the days of steam, sailing is a sublimation of centuries of naval history; the interest in crafts, pottery, embroidery, sewing, weaving, the creation of working museums where the reason for existence of so many industrial towns and cities has its last resting place, all suggest a powerful impulse to escape. I have been struck by the numbers of people who during their free time pretend they are someone else – not only in amateur dramatics, but those who live out in fantasy the lives of people from another time and place, often meticulously reconstructing the costume and re-enacting the customs of the period with complete authenticity – medieval England, the Wild West of the nineteenth century, the Civil War, the Roman Imperial Army, the Crusades, the French Revolution. And yet, as though to undermine any simple idea that people are merely trying to get away from it all (when it all has quite obviously gone away from us), it is extraordinary to see how many of these activities are for charitable purposes: much of the dressing up and the pretending and the escaping are done in order to give to others – whether for Sunshine Coaches, the elderly, for kidney units or spastics or for some vital piece of hospital equipment or to contribute to the expenses of a sick child who has to go to the United States for a rare operation. It may seem a rather roundabout and cumbrous way of helping, but at times Britain seems to be full of people entertaining each other for charity.

There is another function yielded by leisure activity which is not normally sought there and was perhaps formerly provided by work. In the absence of continuous shared experience at work, leisure readily becomes the principal focus of solidaristic activity; so that the club, the group or the team, or simply the shared interest, takes on many of the attributes associated with comrades, the community, even the family. The space which the communal endeavour of the activity provides is a shelter, a place of resistance, even defiance against the outside world – a world which to many seems both incoherent and menacing. It provides a site for choice and self-determination, where the 'real world' makes us feel both powerless and bewildered. ('What can you do about it?' 'You'll never change the world.') Whereas in the specialized area of freely chosen activity, it is impossible not to be moved by the dedication of people to shared discovery, knowledge, forms of self-education far beyond the confines of official structures; the joy of young people making music together, the intensity of the friendships, the depths of feeling of people *working together* on a shared endeavour. The separation and self-containment of so many of these occupations may involve a narrowing of experience, but they deepen it also; and in this become the contemporary equivalent of a kind of village life. Everyone in, say, the world of growing dahlias will know each other, in the same way that everyone in small towns used to know each other; and will offer a source of comparison, gossip, emulousness, resentment and pleasure.

There is one other remarkable, and troubling, feature which emerges from people's discussion of their chosen activity, and this is that many of them speak as though it drove them. It is, they tell you, addictive. You get obsessed, it takes you over, you get hooked, it becomes a way of life, it gets out of control. This kind of expression recurs too frequently to be ignored in people's accounts of how they spend their time. It seems to be related to the need for function; the surprise with which we respond when a stranger hasn't heard of some luminary in our field of interest for a moment breaks the collusive and supportive understanding that binds us to those who share our overriding interest, our narrow specialism. These have to be elevated, given an independent significance that validates the fascination they hold for us. But the sense of not being quite in control suggests something far from the self-determination and freely chosen occupation we like to think it is: the needs which leisure activities are called upon to answer are perhaps far more profound than the words themselves suggest.

2

From leisure class to leisure society

When Thorstein Veblen was writing his elegant and critical essay on the leisure class at the end of the nineteenth century, he maintained that such a class must at all times demonstrate its remoteness from physical labour, its exemption from useful employment and its non-productive use of time.* All activity undertaken by this class – their occupations, their social life, the appearance of their dependants and servants (which included their wives), their homes – was designed to serve this end of ostentatious superfluity. Veblen's description of their archaic fashions indicated that even their dress was unfitted for any significant function:

> The pleasing effect of neat and spotless garments is chiefly, if not altogether, due to their carrying the suggestion of leisure – exemption from physical contact with industrious processes of any kind. Much of the charm that invests the patent leather shoe, the stainless linen, the lustrous cylindrical hat, and the walking stick, which so greatly enhance the dignity of a gentleman, comes of their pointedly suggesting that the wearer cannot when so attired bear a hand in any employment that is directly and immediately of any human use.

If this passage has a singularly old-fashioned sound, this is not simply because the clothing described has long passed out of customary wear. Veblen's assertion was that the 'leisure class' evolved out of a post-predatory culture, where the functions of the ruling class – warfare, plunder and hunting – had been, for the most part, superseded, such activities having been sublimated in a pecuniary and emulative culture, in which conspicuous waste and show replaced earlier and more primitive displays of physical prowess.

The idea of a leisure class has dissolved in our time. This is (perhaps mistakenly) believed to be the result of a more democratic and egalitarian

---

* Thorstein Veblen, *The Theory of the Leisure Class* (Unwin, 1970; first published 1899).

sensibility. As J. K. Galbraith observed, 'Nearly all societies at nearly all times have had a leisure class – a class of persons who were exempt from toil. In modern times and especially in the United States, the leisure class, at least as an easily identifiable phenomenon, has disappeared. To be idle is no longer considered rewarding or even entirely respectable.'*

The existence of such a class has been replaced in recent years by the promise of a more generalized 'leisure society'. This implies that the advantages that were once the prerogative of a small minority are now going to be extended to all the people. 'We must be educated for leisure' it is claimed; just as, little more than a century ago, it became of great urgency to train our people for more sophisticated forms of labour under the impulse of competition from Germany and the United States; just as in the first industrial era, a recalcitrant peasantry had to be 'educated' to the more regular and coercive rhythms of industrial production. We must now learn to adapt to the fact that work will be an only intermittent, less salient feature of our lives than hitherto. We can no longer expect 'a job for life'. Instead of continuous employment, we should be prepared to work for no more than 50,000 hours, according to Charles Handy, while André Gorz estimates the labour of a lifetime at no more than 20,000 hours for each individual (approximately ten years of working a 40-hour week).†

The requirement to be educated for leisure suggests that the model for such an education already exists. It will, presumably, be a suitably modified version of that of the former leisure class, whose lifestyle (or at least a mass approximation of it) will be more and more widely diffused. The leisured will no longer be an exclusive and wealthy caste whose privilege has been won at the expense of the necessities of the people. This exciting vision, and how it is to be realized, has not been defined. All that we can do, pending its advent, is to prepare ourselves, to remain attentive and flexible, above all, not hinder this benign evolution which is already occurring. It will be self-fulfilling, as long as we do not place unnecessary obstacles in its path, such as those set by conservative elements of labour, who insist upon maintaining obsolete and outworn forms of work in the name of traditional skills or time-honoured customs, or even for the sake of keeping people at work. In other words, it requires of the people a great act of faith.

Although it is true that there has been no marked redistribution of wealth from rich to poor in the Western democracies, the vast increase in production in these economies has extended to the majority of people goods and services that had once appeared far beyond their reach; and this -

---

* J. K. Galbraith, *The Affluent Society* (Penguin, 1982).

† Charles Handy, *The Future of Work* (Blackwell, 1984); André Gorz, *Paths to Paradise* (Pluto, 1984).

strong impulse towards progressive material advance, with its labour-saving possibilities and its invitations to a more relaxed life of ease and inabstinence, has created a pervasive impression of movement towards a form of leisure society. If this has not, in the main, been accompanied by a significant increase in free time – one of the most vital attributes of the leisured life – except for the most disadvantaged (the unemployed), this discrepancy has not disturbed the feeling of irresistible and necessary forward movement. This process has helped to blur older antagonisms between the privileged and those formerly known as the labouring poor; indeed, has made class conflict appear to many an archaic and fruitless undertaking. For does not the way the rich live serve as model and pattern to shape the hopes and dreams of more and more people? In this context, we may well wonder what a man such as Veblen can have to say to us about a leisure class when that seems so remote and redundant now, a curiosity of social history, written by an unrecognized and possibly embittered man almost a hundred years ago. How can 'The Theory of the Leisure Class' be of more than historical interest?

It has been a matter of much comment in Britain that a great deal of the industrial base on which the wealth of the country was created has been severely eroded during the space of the past generation or so. Another way of putting this would be to say that much useful and productive activity has been removed from the reach of the people. The echo of what Veblen wrote could not be more clear: only whereas it was at the turn of the century the mark of the leisured that they emphasized their distance from the industrious processes, now it is the industrious processes themselves that have been withdrawn from the daily experience of the people. Are we to assume that it is from that very distance that a mass leisure society is expected to evolve? For it is perhaps this development that lies at the heart of all the speculation and the promises about the shape of post-industrial society. What is to fill the space evacuated so recently by industrial manufacture?

The most obvious factor in this altered climate is that to disdain productive employment would be quite unnecessary, to say the least, because fewer and fewer people are contaminated by its disagreeable compulsions. Indeed, quite the reverse may be happening. With the rise of the service industries, the prominence of banking, merchandising, credit, insurance, retailing, tourism, travel, catering, we are dealing with far more nebulous activities than when it was a question of the stern materialities of mining, manufacture or engineering. So much of present-day economic endeavour is connected with impalpables – consultancies and public relations, the making and changing of images, the play of appearances, the adding of value, the selling of ideas, the marketing of abstractions, the importance of 'invisibles' – that labour, sheer hard work, becomes something not to be scorned by the privileged, but rather to be appropriated by them. And there is considerable evidence that this is the case. The work ethic, far from having been discarded, has merely been re-shaped by the rich for their own purposes; not this time, to serve as a model of iron discipline to the workers in industry, but as a kind of decoration, an impressive and plausible façade for themselves, which will conceal the uselessness or even the downright noxious nature of their avocations. They proclaim themselves dedicated to work in such a way as to maintain the fiction that the distribution of labour in the contemporary world falls most onerously upon them.

It may well be that the work to be done – the significant work or at least that which can be presented as such – has become both too important and perhaps too scarce to be left to the working class. It is no accident that in this age the rich have developed a hitherto well-concealed talent for making great public display, not of the idleness and vacuity of their pastimes, but of their own functional and indispensable role in society, their exhaustless devotion to work, the seriousness of their purposes, their service to the nation. Princes are no longer playboys, but hard-working and energetic servants of the people. Prince Andrew, for instance, is not only a war hero, but has an important naval career to pursue; and his bride expressed her desire to continue her work in publishing despite her elevation to the position of Duchess of York. Princess Anne regularly demonstrates her dedication to the poor of Africa by means of her work for the Save the Children Fund; the Prince of Wales's concern for the fate of the inner city, the deprived and disadvantaged is deeply felt, something far more than a piece of astute public relations; and this is before any of the burdens of official duties which claim so much of their time and energy.

These illustrious public activities are only the most dramatic efflorescence of a far more widespread and deeply rooted assumption of a burden of labour by minor royals and major celebrities who leave their names on all those tablets commemorating ceremonial openings of mainly undistinguished modern buildings – new civic centres and shopping precincts, stretches of motorway and sheltered accommodation for the elderly. The same commitment to work may be seen in the conspicuous 'punishing schedules' of business people and executives, those unwearying commuters of transnational corporations whose budgetary responsibilities are said to exceed those of many sizeable nation states, in the ills attendant upon the disorientation induced by a series of identical luxury hotels, the jet-lag and hang-overs from the unavoidable intensity of that hospitality which is part of their duty of selling British, showing the flag, boosting exports, chasing up orders, opening up markets, clocking up sales. Their weary attendance at expensive restaurants where so much vital work is done; the obligatory nights in the opera boxes which their company reserves for the season; the millions of pounds for which they are personally accountable to the last penny; the entertainment of irksome and mannerless foreign buyers on their yacht and in their mansion behind screens of rhododendron and conifer in the Thames Valley; the indulgence of the whims of potential customers on rain-swept golf courses or in discreet and expensive sex parlours; the vast expenditure of energy in the futures and commodity and stock markets which burn people out before they reach 35; the six-figure salaries justified only because nobody can work at that pitch for more than a few years and which must compensate for the long years afterwards spent nursing the heart condition or in the vain search for relief from the disordered digestive system – all this amounts to an oppressive excess of labour, a sacrifice to command the awe and the compassion of those called to perform no such exalted task in the world. Perhaps most glaringly of all, the new votaries of labour are the pop, TV and movie stars, discussing their 'work' in breathless media interviews, as they extort public sympathy for their high-speed, coast-to-coast appearances, for a life that is no longer their own, pursued as they are from pillar to post by both fans and journalists; an unstinting giving of themselves to insatiable audiences that can lead only to nervous exhaustion and collapse. It is perhaps only to be expected that politicians should also have surrendered themselves to the same gruelling surfeit of labour. Their busy attendance at summit meetings is only the most visible aspect of this – the sessions prolonged into the early hours, the rumours of tensions and irreconcilable differences, the breakthrough at the eleventh hour, the officials working on an agreed communiqué, the press conference at dawn delivered in the insomniac style of those celebrated for needing no more than four hours of sleep a night; how taxing, yet how selfless it all is.

Nor is this remarkable weight of function confined to those in whom it has been traditionally to a remarkable degree absent. A clamorous and aggressive self-justification penetrates quite deeply into the employment structure. Never in the history of labour – so much of it backbreaking and destructive of life and limb, so much of it that drained the last ounce of energy from muscle and sinew – has there ever been such a competitive claim for recognition, for the tribute due to such feats of toil as are undertaken today. We have only to consider all the voluntary 'workaholics' in our society, those who don't know what to do with themselves when they're not working, those striving to wrench or coax a sense of purpose out of the most unpromising circumstances: the self-important and the inflated self-worth of the media people, the performers and the journalists, as well as those devoted to 'working with people', and whose work in consequence is never finished, the social and community workers, the architects and planners, all those experts and professional people committed to the running of other people's lives, the teachers and academics, not to mention the salespeople and advertisers whose mission it is to rouse some slumbering whim and elevate it into insatiable desire for some commodity; those on crusades and quests to promote some supremely marginal and dispensable product; those processors of words and generators of ideas and masters of information and possessors of knowledge, the custodians of the labyrinths of impenetrable but vital bureaucracies – all those whose lonely and unacknowledged self-immolation to labour means that at the end of the day they find it impossible to turn off, to wind down, to relax, to sit down and take stock, and who spend their leisure time colluding with each other that theirs is the most supremely exigent and necessary contribution to the work of society. One result of all their efforts is, of course, real suffering. These are the people most liable to tension, worry and stress, to heart disease, ulcers and breakdown, as they valiantly brave intolerable tube journeys and interminable tailbacks on the M25, with nothing but the cassette of Nina Simone or *Carmina Burana* for company and the endless newsflashes telling them to avoid the congestion they are trapped in. They struggle into work even though they have a temperature of 103° and have been told by their doctor that he or she will not answer for the consequences if they don't take a couple of weeks' complete rest. Their heroic commitment to customers, clients, employees or colleagues is perhaps prompted by an obscure sense that their absence, even for a day, might not only fail to result in the collapse of the firm, company or department but, on the contrary, might not even be noticed; indeed, an even greater worry, that the whole enterprise might actually proceed more smoothly without them underlies the defensive insistence that they must at all costs put in an appearance. Cynical friends sometimes strike a painful chord by pointing out that if they fell under a bus tomorrow (always a bus, never the more likely agent of their annihilation, the car), this would not be the end of the world for those who employ them.

Many of these people are part of that group identified by Galbraith as members of the New Class, often in origin far from anything resembling a leisure class. They 'take it for granted that their work will be enjoyable. If it is not, this is a legitimate source of dissatisfaction, even frustration. No one regards it as remarkable that the advertising man, tycoon, poet or professor who suddenly finds his work unrewarding should seek the counsel of a psychiatrist.' Galbraith points out that 'the New Class is not exclusive. While virtually nobody leaves it, thousands join it every year.' But what he didn't mention – or perhaps it was too early in the 1950s to perceive one of its distinguishing traits – was its defensive self-importance and self-attributed heroics: 'I have to be in Brussels on Tuesday, then I've a meeting in Manchester, and there's the conference in Stockholm next weekend'; the fluttering of the leaves of diaries, the frowns and bitten Faber-Castell pens and the adamant declaration that it is impossible to fix up anything before the end of November. 'I can't make it, I'm busy, I haven't a free moment, I've got meetings, engagements, commitments.' People book appointments with each other at many months' distance that call for the movement of sheaves of papers across the city – or even across continents – by document-bearers on motorcycles called Hermes or Mercury, delivering scripts, outlines, plans, blueprints, briefings, portfolios, curricula, drafts, agendas that are required to have reached their destination yesterday. They engage upon campaigns and strategies to discuss market research at solemn, even portentous, meetings, where projects of vast triviality take on the allure of a major military manoeuvre: 'For many long-standing advertisers, television advertising has been transformed from a matter of saturation bombing to something resembling guerrilla warfare' (*Campaign* magazine). There is a deep displacement of emotion poured into the committee meeting, the planning group or the advisory panel, where the question 'Well, what is it all for?' must never be asked in all the hyperactive intensity that goes into discussions about the promotional merchandise or the layout of the new magazine, the format of the half-hour programme that involves such a vast expenditure of energy and money in order to attract a few stray moments of attention in off-peak time from a jaded and indifferent public. They invoke the regrettable necessity of living in the real world, that increasingly eccentric construct of fantasy. Many women are expected to find satisfaction in the borrowed lustre of those they serve in the guise of personal assistant or person Friday to the big white chief, the managing director, the principal, the king pin, he who must be obeyed. They spend whole days talking things through, looking at a project from all angles, sleeping on it, wrestling with problems of presentation and differences of emphasis, deciding whether a re-vamp or a shake-up is required, making lightning raids, planning mergers and take-overs, pooling resources, exchanging views, acting as a sounding-board, floating an idea, thrashing things out, getting hyped up to meet a deadline, to land a contract, to deliver on time, to make a killing, to go for broke. If so many people admit, in their less defensive moments, that what makes their work worthwhile is the people they work with, this may be because these have often become the primary purpose, and the ostensible reason for their labour is seen for what it is – an elaborate and collusive suspension of disbelief.

In support of their heroic role, the new martyrs to labour can often be heard wishing they had a humdrum nine-to-five job, expressing their envy of those who work merely for the wage-packet at the end of the week and can forget all their worries the minute they walk off the premises. Such carefree employees do not lose sleep fretting about some particularly intractable problem of office management, wondering how on earth they are going to tell the most recent employee that her contract cannot be renewed when you know she is a single parent with three small children; *they* don't wake up in the early hours with parched throat, trembling with responsibility of having to face all those people in the morning; *they* aren't up at dawn, writing down a few notes, an outline of a lecture, a few selling points, some ideas on a new creative thrust that will keep some brand fresh, relevant and motivating; and *they* don't get up feeling like nothing on earth, but knowing that they must be at their sparkling best in time for that 10.30 meeting, and ransacking an inadequate wardrobe for something to give them that extra lift, that little touch of distinction.

Sometimes these people go even further, using their exploited and disregarded substance in order to lay claim to self-administered rewards and treats as an extra consolation for salaries which are, in general, not inconsiderable, but are never quite enough to compensate for the stresses and strains that go with the job. 'I must get some sun', they say passionately, leafing through the brochures that advertise discreet private villas in Tuscan hill-towns; or, more regularly, 'I need a drink.' 'I must have some space, some time, some room to think', 'I must have a break', 'I shall have to get away', 'I must get out from under', 'I can't stand the pressure.' And the self-pity which is never far from the surface seems to be allied to a gnawing and subjective feeling of poverty, in spite of a parallel awareness of great privilege. They are always hard up, regretting the things they can't afford, wondering how they are going to get through to the end of the month, snowed under with bills and demands, terrified of facing the bank manager, wondering how on earth they will survive without the phone-answering service or the domestic help; and because they are, on the whole, so well-rewarded, their sense of impoverishment must be taken as metaphor, and as arising from causes other than insufficient money. If they dwell at such length on their unique importance, their vital role, this is perhaps less because of the indispensable nature of their specialized and infinitely subdivided labour than because they suspect its marginality, its expendability and, above all, its growing remoteness from any detectable human purposes. As Veblen observed in 1899:

The strain is not lightened as industrial efficiency increases and makes a lighter strain possible, but the increment in output is turned to use to meet this want [i.e. that of conspicuous consumption], which is infinitely expansible, after the manner commonly imputed in economic theory to higher or spiritual wants. It is owing chiefly to the presence of this element in the standard of living that J. S. Mill was able to say that 'hitherto it is questionable if all the mechanical inventions yet made have lightened the day's toil of any human being.'

It is perhaps the further development of this process that makes the rich societies of the late twentieth century create an artificial busyness (claimed by the most privileged), which is sometimes more akin to the make-work tasks of the occupational therapy ward than to the more direct service of human need (the therapy in question being, of course, the servicing of autonomous economic processes to which our interests are increasingly subordinated). It is perhaps the fatigue that comes from spinning fantasies around a ruined sense of function that makes such a real burden of so many forms of contemporary labour which are, in themselves, much mitigated. Murray Bookchin described this development almost 20 years ago:

> Much of the social 'complexity' of our time originates in the paper-work administration, manipulation and constant wastefulness of the capitalist enterprise. The petty bourgeois stands in awe of the bourgeois filing system – the rows of cabinets filled with invoices, accounting books, insurance records, tax forms and the inevitable dossiers.* He is spellbound by the 'expertise' of industrial managers, engineers, stylemongers, financial manipulators, and the architects of market consent. He is totally mystified by the state – the police, courts, jails, federal offices, secretariats, the whole stinking sick body of coercion, control and domination. Modern society is incredibly complex, complex even beyond human comprehension, if we grant its premises – property, 'production for the sake of production', competition, capital accumulation, exploitation, finance, centralization, coercion, bureaucracy and the domination of man by man. Linked to every one of these premises are the institutions that actualize it – offices, millions of 'personnel' forms, immense tons of paper, desks, typewriters, telephones, and of course, rows upon rows of filing cabinets. As in Kafka's novels, these things are real but strangely dreamlike, indefinable shadows on the social landscape. The economy has a greater reality to it and is easily mastered by the mind and senses, but it too is highly intricate – if we grant that buttons must be styled in a thousand different forms, textiles varied ￿

---

* Information technology which has swallowed up this outdated (though at least tangible) paraphernalia of bureaucracy only makes the mystifying 'complexity' more overwhelming.

endlessly in kind and pattern to create the illusion of innovation and novelty, bathrooms filled to overflowing with a dazzling variety of pharmaceuticals and lotions and kitchens cluttered with an endless number of imbecile appliances. If we single out of this odious garbage one or two goods of high quality in the more useful categories and if we eliminate the money economy, the state power, the credit system, the paperwork and the policework required to hold society in an enforced state of want, insecurity and domination, society would become not only reasonably human but also fairly simple.*

In the interests of maintaining the fiction that we still live in a society of scarcity, and must therefore continue to produce more of everything that makes money, the rich have breathed new life into a work ethic which serves their purpose of concealment. But there is another element in their resuscitation of a defunct ideology of work. For they have also appropriated the heroic myth of labour, a myth belonging traditionally to a working class that has, to a considerable extent, recently been relieved of its sustaining purpose. The refurbishing of this collective myth is, as must be expected in its new guise as the property of the rich, in the form of individual and personal achievement and enterprise. Listening to the new bearers of Herculean workloads, it would seem that the rigours of mill or mine were not more oppressive than the pressure of that perpetual mobile of constant travel, of boardroom marathons, of conquering new markets, of a restless life fuelled by a 'potent mixture of adrenalin and high-octane energy' (*Campaign* magazine), of rushing all over the globe to the joyless interchangeability of Holiday Inns, in which you can discover exactly where you are only from the motif embossed on tasselled menus in the curtained and sequestered enclosures of the restaurants. The vast and self-protective activity which surrounds the contemporary rich occurs in the wake of the departure of much productive and necessary labour from the heart of Western industrial societies, labour which for 200 years had been their primary purpose. The work that has been suppressed in the rich countries has not disappeared from the face of the earth. Much of it has merely been transferred elsewhere, following a new international division of labour, whereby a great deal of manufacture can be carried out more cheaply and more efficiently in the slums of the cities of Asia and South America or in the industrializing countries on the rim of the Pacific. The vacuum in which all the talk of 'leisure societies' is possible in the West is that left by the removal of a great deal of essential work; it depends upon the extent to which the poor of the earth are willing – or can be coerced

* Murray Bookchin, *Post-scarcity Anarchism* (Wildwood House, 1974).

into – underwriting the declining sense of function of the people in the West, notably of the Western working class. The politics of fantasy readily springs up to occupy the evacuated spaces; and this is how the privileged can plausibly project themselves as the true embodiment of necessary labour while, paradoxically, at the same time promising the millennarian coming of the leisure society to the people. In the meantime, leisure – not the easy opulence that is associated with past aristocratic castes or that which is to be achieved in an indefinite future, but actually existing leisure, leisure as a full-time activity (if that is not an indelicate word in the context) – devolves chiefly upon the most dispossessed in society, the unemployed, the retired and the young adults for whom no work is available. Needless to say, all the mysterious occupations of an antique privileged class are transformed in this devolution from being a mark of distinction, worth and breeding into a burden scarcely to be endured. Such are the cynicism and rapacity of those who have that they will not even leave to the poor their function as workers, the dignity which they formerly conceded of humble toil, but have arrogated to themselves the apparent onerous weight and the glory of a labour which they and their forebears not only imposed with the utmost equanimity and the most hardened callousness on those they despised and rewarded insufficiently, but from which they themselves made great show of their own moral and material distance.

If the wealthy have become even more exalted by this historic act of plunder, it is not to be supposed that those left with more homely and trivial occupations should be left to go about their diminished business in peace. It would not do, for instance, for groups who have always been regarded as the 'aristocracy of labour' to remain in undisputed possession of such distinction. Sober industry, the sweat of thy brow, honest toil, even a fair day's work are too rare and ennobling concepts to be associated any longer with the working class. In consequence, the remoralizing of the rich in our time has gone forward simultaneously with the disgracing of the workers. This may well be the deeper meaning of the long miners' strike in 1984–5 in Britain, which was declared by the Conservative government to have been such a good investment. In what precisely, one may wonder, were the authorities investing? During the prolonged public spectacle, the miners were transformed, before our very eyes, from the mythic heroes who bring out into the light the mysterious treasures of the earth, into thugs, hooligans and wreckers – the dangerous classes; resuming, incidentally, a role assigned them at an earlier stage of the industrial era, that of half-wild barbarians whose savage manners and customs rendered them fit for nothing more than a life of concealment under the ground. Of course, attempts to diminish and disgrace workers have always been part of the persistent struggle between capital and labour; but in the late twentieth century, it takes on a new vibrancy. Those who appear to cling to super-seded practices and outmoded forms of labour can be represented as obstacles in the way of progress towards the benign and universal reign of leisure. The steel workers and railwaymen, the print workers and car makers have all, in their time, been subject to the same obloquy, as have the public service workers who were so emphatically discredited during the 'winter of discontent' in 1978–9. As the workers in the old heavy industries are reduced to permanent minority status (there are now less than one-eighth of the miners there were in 1914; more people are employed in the tourist industry in Britain now than ever worked in the pits; and by the end of 1988 there will be no more than 5.25 million people employed in manufacturing industry), they are being tarnished by a kind of delayed social revenge by those whose position they once threatened, as well as being consistently disparaged in order that the importance of their labour may be taken over by their betters. It is perhaps this consistent denial of the worth of workers that leads to what have appeared to outsiders as recalcitrant and arbitrary withdrawals of labour over trivia: the only way that people can impose themselves is by ceasing work rather than by continuing to perform it. In this way, they gain attention, not through the positive application of their skills, but by the withholding of them. They see no reflection of their value in any of the official channels of information by which we are kept 'informed'; they recognize themselves in the media, not as affirmation, but at best as an absence and, at worst, as a force for destruction.

It is because of this seizure by the powerful of the important work that all that is on offer to the working class in even the most hopeful forecasts about the future is 'jobs'. The idea of 'jobs' – promised in even greater profusion by the leaders and defenders of labour – suggests the kind of occupation that irresistibly attracts the adjective 'odd'; implies activities that are devitalized, requiring neither energy nor skill, and promising neither permanence nor satisfaction. Jobs are precisely what the homely term conveys, something desultory and intermittent, certainly not calcu-lated to call upon real human powers and possibilities. They evoke the mind-numbing ennui of the service sector, that sprawling institutionalized servitude for which the young are being prepared by means of unemploy-ment and inactivity to be grateful. The use of the word 'jobs' occludes ideas of work, of labour, let alone of career, function or purpose. Such notions are doubtless too exalted for mere workers to be granted access to them. (The shallowness of political discussion about unemployment is only one aspect of a more general diminishing of debate over a wide area of social and political concerns which is achieved through selective use of language. For instance, 'information technology' is becoming a major source of economic expansion. The need for 'information' is considered self-evident. In the process, 'knowledge' is mysteriously spirited away beyond our horizons, while 'wisdom' has become too abstract and hence unmarketable and has therefore been suppressed. In the same way, whole industries have been devoted to discovering the 'opinions' of the people: opinions, instantly evolved, become congealed and are solemnly discussed as though they revealed something essential about the state of the nation. In this way, we are securely sheltered from the upsetting possibility that we might be capable of something more than opinions – judgements, for instance, thoughts, not to mention that absolute taboo on ideas; which follow function and wisdom into a remote empyrean, and which belong securely to those who will, no doubt, in due course find ways of selling them back to us as commodity.)

The privileged have colonized the language of work and made it their own. Who but they talk now of getting their shoulder to the wheel, of being in harness, of the fruits of their labour, of working like galley-slaves or Trojans, until they are finally put out to grass? Theirs is a lexicon of drudgery before which the work of the labourers of the industrial revolution looks inconsequential: their daily grind, their position on the tread-mill, in the rat race, their reluctant inclination to the laws of the jungle as they burn the candle at both ends, strain every sinew, leave no stone unturned, go at it hammer and tongs, for all they're worth, heart and soul, give it all they've got; as they seize time by the forelock, strike while the iron is hot, never letting the grass grow under their feet in an attempt to steal a march upon rivals and competitors in order to keep the pot modestly boiling at home. And, as if repossessing the language of labour were not enough, they have, with even greater effrontery, filched the vocabulary of poverty. It is they who are always declaring that there are no free lunches, that the world owes nobody a living, that they must pinch and scrape to eke out a living, to feather their own nest and turn an honest penny, yet live like church mice for all their efforts. It is they who have to stint themselves, go short, scrimp and save, scrape up the deposit, can scarcely make ends meet, must take the bread out of their mouths, are having a hard time, fall on evil days, don't know which way to turn, risk finishing up in queer street, who are strapped for cash, in the red, in hock, in debt, have neither brass farthings nor red cents. They alone, it seems, fear the poorhouse, for they are already absolute paupers, on their uppers, on their beam ends. The vocabulary of the well-to-do is far richer in expressions of poverty than of wealth.

This is not, of course, the whole story. For one thing, it would be false to conclude that the showy assumption of an onerous workload has led to the disappearance of the leisure class. It was only as an 'easily identifiable phenomenon' that Galbraith observed its absence from contemporary society. These new and heavy responsibilities which the rich now bear carry with them certain advantages, not the least of which is that these legitimate the conspicuous use of their leisure, not now by virtue of caste, breeding or station, but by virtue of their indispensable contribution to the labour of society. In fact, this may well be the principal reason for the extravagant display of seriousness and high purpose on which they have been engaged in recent years. The yachts, the fur coats, the villas in unspoilt Costas Verde and Dorada, all the paraphernalia of wealth can be flaunted, not as evidence of their disoccupation or leisure but, on the contrary, as the well-earned rewards for their indefatigable toil. The 'idle rich' is a phrase that has been expunged even from the vocabulary of the politics of envy – that maligned and powerful sense of the injustice of the way the world is, and which was, not so long ago, as Caroline Steedman has suggested, such a significant component of radical politics.*

The objects and appurtenances of the good life do not change. One has only to consider the sequence of symbols and images displayed at the beginning of American soap-operas – diamonds, caviar, champagne, Rolls-Royce cars, private jets, *haute couture*, mansions, paintings, horses, roulette wheels – to understand the paralysis which appears to seize the imagination of those who have money, and for whom it is turned, Midas-like, into a predictable and preordained panoply of goods and services. But these symbols no longer lend themselves to the sinister interpretation that they are the usurped fruits of the labour of others but, on the contrary, have taken on the patina of just and merited desserts. Perhaps it is the very audacity of such claims that seems to have reduced to silence the workless and the more humble labourers of our age; at any rate, these seem to have retreated into a kind of speechless acquiescence in this version of the way things are, conceding perhaps that it is indeed 'nice work if you can get it'.

It may well be that the expropriation of function is the least remarked and most subtle of all the manifold expropriations of the poor. It is, of course, presented as though it were doing the working class the greatest favour imaginable. The reason for this is not far to seek. Because, as E. P. Thompson says, the shadow of relentless labour fell across the lives of the people more darkly than any other of the afflictions of industrialism, those who offer deliverance from such a curse are, understandably, likely to be welcomed as those who might come to relieve the inhabitants of a city long under siege.† Experience might prompt the more sceptical to wonder at

* Caroline Steedman, *Landscape for a Good Woman* (Virago, 1986).
† E. P. Thompson, *The Making of the English Working Class* (Penguin, 1970).

the motives of those newly concerned for the liberation of the very people who had so recently been their 'wage slaves': after all, precedent suggests that those earlier enemies of formal slavery did not find 'free labour' a notable impediment to their continuing enrichment. Altruism has rarely been a major determinant in what has always rigorously been referred to as economic necessity. That it should make so urgent and spectacular an appearance at this moment might have set us on guard; the more so, since its most enthusiastic proponents are the same people (or their representatives) who have sought throughout the industrial era to resist every advance of the labour movement in the same direction, and who have been so lavish in their expenditure of both money and, where necessary, blood also, to demonstrate why even the slightest rise in the standard of living, even the most modest piece of legislation aimed at abridging the long hours of labour of working people, must lead immediately to the ruin of all trade and the collapse of the nation.

It has been both convenient and plausible to issue the promises of leisure to the people as compensation for the burdens of labour of the past, rather than as a response to the economic exigencies of the present. That this should occur at a time of renewed mass unemployment, that 'social death' as André Gorz calls it, makes it the more remarkable that even those who claim to be the defenders of labour seem to accept the terms and conditions on which it is currently being extended to more and more of the (former) working class.

For it is by means of such strategies of mystification that, in spite of all the social and economic upheavals of recent generations, stability and continuity have been assured. Indeed, it is precisely the true meanings of those upheavals that have to be concealed. These have all been in the interests, not of lessening inequalities, but of sharpening them, not of modifying the structures of wealth and power, but of preserving, even strengthening, them. All talk of 'change', of 'progress', even of 'revolution', turns out to refer to nothing more than patterns of consumption, of taste, of the forms of subordination (i.e. work or the lack of it) to which people will be subjected. The surface of things is constantly re-worked only in order that the substance may remain untouched. The leisure society that is anticipated remains tied to the control of the rich, and is far removed from the kind of autonomous activity in which people genuinely liberated from labour could, given the possibilities of technology, freely engage. It is a leisure dedicated to the service of commodities, 'a kind of forced labor or industrial serfdom in the service of commodity-intensive economies', as Ivan Illich describes it.* The closer the leisure society

---

* Ivan Illich, *The Right to Useful Unemployment* (Marion Boyars, 1978).

comes, the more desirable work seems, as can be seen both in the conspicuous busyness of the well-to-do and the despair of the long-term
unemployed. In *The Right to Useful Unemployment*, Illich says:

> In an advanced industrial society it becomes almost impossible to
> seek, even to imagine, unemployment as a condition for autono-
> mous, useful work ... Work done off the job is looked down upon if
> not ignored. Autonomous activity threatens the employment level,
> generates deviance, and detracts from the GNP, therefore it is only
> improperly called 'work'. Labour no longer means effort or toil but
> the mysterious mate wedded to productive investments in plant.
> Work no longer means the creation of a value perceived by the
> worker but mainly a job, which is a social relationship. Unemploy-
> ment means sad idleness, rather than the freedom to do things which
> are useful for oneself and one's neighbour. An active woman who
> runs a house and brings up children and takes in those of others is
> distinguished from a woman who 'works', no matter how useless or
> damaging the product of this work may be. Activity, effort, achieve-
> ment, or service outside a hierarchical relationship and unmeasured
> by professional standards, threatens a commodity-intensive society.
> The generation of use-values that escape effective measurement
> limits not only the need for more commodities but also the jobs that
> create them and the paycheques needed to buy them.

What Illich is evoking is another kind of leisure from those kinds actually
available to capitalist society – on the one hand, unproductive unemployment and, on the other, leisure that must be purchased and that can be
permitted only through continuous growth and expansion. Those futurologists who, like Charles Handy, persuade us that the leisure society will
allow us to engage upon all the voluntary and non-market sector activities
usually associated with such freedoms are silent on how this can be made
compatible with the intensifying market penetration of all human activity,
on which growth and the leisure society that evolves in its shadow will
depend.

Veblen observed 'The prescriptive position of the leisure class as the
exemplar of reputability has imposed many features of the leisure-class
theory of life upon the lower classes; with the result that there goes on,
always and throughout society, a more or less persistent cultivation of
these aristocratic traits.' And the patterns of social behaviour, the
responses and the activities of the former leisure class are so much part of
the iconography of our culture, are so deeply inscribed on the consciousness of the people, that the well-off, their imitators and flatterers, and the
aspirants to their position know exactly what to do with any access of

riches, however modest; we obligingly follow the broad paths beaten by our superiors; the scenario has long been written, and all that remains is for us to play out the roles that devolve upon us.

Perhaps it is this bold seizure of functions formerly associated with lowlier castes – and ceded by them virtually without contest – that has made the rich so much more assertive in recent decades. For a brief moment, in the middle years of this century, they had become decidedly cautious; so prudent, in fact, as to deny that they even existed. This was when they could be heard proclaiming that their spirit of enterprise was being stifled by Labour goverments, that they were being crucified, taxed to extinction, that they were brought to the brink of beggary. But their more confident declaration today is that 'we are all working class now', an assertion which not only betrays the nature of their usurping of the function of others, but also releases them, as it were, from their vow of poverty, no longer compels them to concealment. Indeed, this unnatural discipline, while it lasted, must have been extremely irksome, for the enjoyment of wealth in secrecy must be savourless indeed: the consumption of the good things must be, as Veblen perceived, highly visible. ('It is for this class to determine, in general outline, what scheme of life the community shall accept as decent or honorific; and it is their office by precept and example to set forth this scheme of social salvation in its highest, ideal form.')

The extension of conspicuous consumption to more and more people, including those from whom the necessities of life had for generations been withheld, has been the mechanism whereby, not only the values and customs of the rich prevail, but also the illusion can be maintained that we still live in a society of scarcity. This is what Murray Bookchin indicated when he said 'In the industrialized Western world, scarcity has to be enforced, so great is the productive potential of technology.' By an ever more wanton and profligate using up of resources, the need for more becomes, as it were, self-evident, built as it is into the very psychic structures of the people in the Western world.

Veblen saw this development even before the twentieth century had begun:

> Goods are produced and consumed as a means to the fuller unfolding of human life; and their utility consists, in the first instance, in their efficiency as means to this end. But the human proclivity to emulation has seized upon the consumption of goods as a means to an invidious comparison, and has thereby invested consumable goods with a secondary utility as evidence of relative ability to pay. This indirect or secondary use of consumable goods lends an honorific character to consumption and presently also to the goods

which best serve the emulative end of consumption. The consumption of expensive goods is meritorious, and the goods which contain an appreciable element of cost in excess of what goes to give them serviceability for their ostensible mechanical purpose are honorific. The marks of superfluous costliness in the goods are therefore marks of worth – of high efficiency for the indirect, invidious end to be served by their consumption; and conversely, goods are humilific, and therefore unattractive, if they show too thrifty an adaptation to the mechanical end sought and do not include a margin of expensiveness on which to rest a complacent invidious comparison.

The elaboration of this process in our time, no longer confined to the wealthy, has become the principal motor of a social and economic system that has always been dedicated to growth and expansion. At an earlier phase of industrial society, the promise was that this growth would one day end poverty; now the promise is that it will usher in the universal reign of leisure.

The only practicable means of impressing one's pecuniary ability on ... unsympathetic observers of one's everyday life is an unremitting demonstration of ability to pay. In the modern community there is also a more frequent attendance at large gatherings of people to whom one's everyday life is unknown; in such places as churches, theaters, ballrooms, hotels, parks, shops and the like. In order to impress these transient observers, and to retain one's self-complacency under their observation, the signature of one's pecuniary strength should be written in characters which he who runs may read. It is evident, therefore, that the present trend of the development is in the direction of heightening the utility of conspicuous consumption as compared with leisure.

This last observation helps to account for the mirage-like quality of the leisure society, tantalizing, yet out of reach: the energy required to make the money which alone will enable us to enjoy it defers it as effectively as the everlasting feast was deferred for the toilers in mines and factories of the early industrial period.

Such developments are not confined to our culture, as may be seen, for instance, in Ruth Benedict's account of the lives of the Indians of the North West Coast of the United States:

Manipulation of wealth in this culture has gone far beyond any realistic transcription of economic needs and the filling of those needs. It involved ideas of capital, of interest, and of conspicuous waste. Wealth had become not merely economic goods, even goods put away in boxes for potlatches and never used except in exchange, but even more characteristically prerogatives with economic functions. Songs, myths, names of chiefs' house-posts, of their dogs, of their canoes, were wealth ... The manipulation of wealth on the North West Coast is clearly enough in many ways a parody of our own economic arrangements. These tribes did not use wealth to get for themselves an equivalent value in economic goods, but as counters of fixed value in a game they played to win.*

Nor is conspicuous waste a recent phenomenon. Tawney wrote of its tragic consequences in the sixteenth century:

Mankind, it seems, hates nothing so much as its own prosperity. Menanced with an access of riches which would lighten its toil, it makes haste to redouble its labours, and to pour away the perilous stuff, which might deprive of plausibility the complaint that it is poor. Applied to the arts of peace, the new resources commanded by Europe during the first half of the sixteenth century might have done something to exorcise the spectres of pestilence and famine, and to raise the material fabric of civilization to undreamed-of heights. Its rulers, ecclesiastical and secular alike, thought otherwise. When pestilence and famine were ceasing to be necessities imposed by nature they re-established them by political art.†

This unhappy experience has a vibrant contemporary ring. It has been repeated once more in the industrial era by means of the arms race and of the conjuring of abject poverty – indeed, even major famines – out of unparalleled plenty. Hunger and want in the countries of the South have gone hand in hand with the spread of conspicuous waste to wider and wider sections of the people in the rich countries (as well as to the elites of the poor ones).

This process has been a major source of interest to social scientists and commentators throughout the twentieth century, but particularly since the Second World War. In the 1950s, Vance Packard set out to discover what happens to class distinctions between people when most of them have been enjoying a long period of material abundance.‡ He found that the search for status through the possession of certain estimable goods produced at least one consequence which was of enormous benefit to the rich, in that it clouded and weakened class consciousness. The leisure class, in such a context, was saved from the danger that it might become redun-

* Ruth Benedict, *Patterns of Culture* (Mentor Books, 1951).
† R. H. Tawney, *Religion and the Rise of Capitalism* (Penguin, 1961).
‡ Vance Packard, *The Status Seekers* (Longman, 1960).

dant, by the even greater demand placed upon it that it should serve as model and inspiration to all those who were so understandably eager to better themselves. Its even greater prominence and self-advertisement than before seemed desirable. Clearly delighted with this new role, and discovering that it was no longer an object of resentment, the leisure class was not content to rest there; but, on the contrary, set about the appropriation we have seen of even more vital roles and functions.

Not that the one it already had was negligible. For what the privileged have to offer the rest of us is essentially an education; or, in the case of those considerable numbers of people whose previous instruction had consisted principally, if not solely, in the fundamental lesson that they were born to labour, a re-education; something which, as all the re-moulders of human sensibilities well understand (mostly those involved in the many and varied forms of brainwashing practised in the world), cannot be accomplished without pain. As one elderly and bewildered worker put it, 'We used to have spare time, now we have leisure.'

The idea of spare time connotes inactivity, idleness, but of a very particular kind. It suggests an amiable passing of the hours, without special aim or direction; perhaps what the Italians call *dolce far niente*; in English, messing out, doing nowt, pottering, passing time, as it were, through the easy filter of a long summer afternoon. But time that is spare in an avid and market-hungry world is meagre and profitless indeed. By being demarcated as 'leisure', such time is defined and enclosed, taken over by others in preparation for being turned into a commodity for sale – bottled like wine, fenced off like commonland, gift-wrapped like sugar-candy. And, as Illich suggests, 'Each new commodity degrades an activity by which people so far have been able to cope on their own; each new job takes away legitimacy from work done so far by the unemployed. The power of professions to measure what shall be good, right and done warps the desire, willingness and ability of the "common" man to live within his measure.'

Leisure is one of the most spectacular commodities to have appeared in Western society in this generation; and as such, it has drawn large numbers of people into its service. 'Spare-time wear' would be a strange idea; leisure-wear commands a whole industry, indicates ceremonial robings that must be gone through before spending time which is akin to (and often coterminous with) money. In the same way, pastimes or hobbies have an archaic sound. There is something homely and fumbling about them, something messy and inexpert. By being transformed into leisure pursuits, these become institutionalized, gain higher definition, become self-conscious, achieve an added legitimacy. Indeed, the notion of 'leisure pursuits' is an interesting and evocative expression, hinting perhaps at the chase, a restless movement after (possibly) elusive satisfactions; something, at any rate, not to be captured by the pursuer, but more likely to remain firmly in the possession of a proprietor or professional. Indeed, leisure is seen as a kind of unexplored continent, ripe for colonizing: 'With spending on leisure in 1984/5 exceeding £50,000 million, five times greater than car sales, the potential for expansion is enormous. But these figures do not just happen. They are the result of large and small companies and individuals having the foresight and courage to do their thing' (*Leisure Management*, October 1986). In this way, abstractions are made material, commodities appear out of thin air. Freely provided open spaces and recreation grounds become invisible and are supplanted by leisure parks, which contain 'events areas' and 'riverside walks', 'water activities centres', custom-designed retractable enclosures, soft-play environments, leisure inflatables, theme parks; learning to avail ourselves of these new commodities is an arduous business, and cannot be left to chance. It is what Veblen called the 'quasi-sacerdotal office' of the rich to teach us.

Thus the role of the rich and their relationship to leisure are somewhat more complicated than when Veblen was writing. For one thing, they have had to re-insert into their lives something of the heroics and prowess which Veblen had associated with an earlier and more primitive phase of social development. There has been no curtailment of conspicuous consumption; quite the contrary. Only now it must be seen as the reward for equally conspicuous achievement, a recompense for feats of labour which more modest workers in retail outlet, fast-food store or hotel kitchen could never hope to rival. Highly visible expenditure as a reward for prodigious effort remains a legitimation and a model for millions of imitators and aspirants to riches; it is simply that most of these fall hopelessly short of the examples of perfection held up to them.

In *this* epic of labour, the myth that belonged to a whole class is fragmented into the lives of thousands of individuals: the celebrities and the stars, the personalities and the experts, the performers and prominent figures who pass before our eyes every day in the popular press and on TV. Not only are they granted permission to dilate freely upon their formidable attainments in the world, but this activity has the vast advantage of diminishing the confidence of the onlookers in their own powers and abilities. This taking on of an Atlas-like labour of sustaining the world on their shoulders confuses and humbles those to whom leisure is being promised in such profusion; and a modest and becoming gratitude is the only proper response for the Stakhanovite heroics of the famous which fill the ample leisure of those without work and provide entertainment and distraction to those many more millions trapped in routine and tedious jobs. In truth, one of the less fantastic functions of the notabilities of sport and show-business is to conceal perhaps the greatest contradiction at the heart of all the promises of a leisure society – that this means the emergence of patterns of work that are exploitative, ill paid, de-skilled, despised and unrewarding in every way. The people who work in the restaurants and the beauty salons and the theme parks don't see it as glamorous at all – they are only too aware of the backache, the varicose veins, the dermatitis, the long hours and the poor pay.

The stars and celebrities are the real 'educators for leisure', not the pedagogues, social scientists and specialists in the subject (although these professions have also multiplied in recent years); least of all is it the function of those practitioners of education whose thankless task it is to promote all the official versions of education. (This helps to explain, incidentally, why the educational system is held in such low esteem. It is too easily bypassed by other channels of communication, whose far more beguiling and insistent messages easily eclipse the offerings of mere teachers, however entertaining and inventive these may strive to be.)

It is essentially to the recent rich that the high calling of leisure education is entrusted. It is their function to reconcile the excluded, the poor, and especially those whose burden of work is no fantasy, to the extreme wealth of others. This they do by great public show of their arduous accomplishments and unique talents. Those to whom this exalted mission has fallen are, in the main, former members of the working class who have been projected spectacularly upwards. In this way, they can be relied upon to share many of the tastes, values, hopes – and weaknesses – of the majority of the people. They are essentially individuals thrust into stardom by virtue of some successfully marketed attribute – whether musical ability or sporting skill, a gift for being comic, for distinguishing themselves by some recondite knowledge, or by acting in a popular TV series. They occupy a glaring and unblinking limelight. They are constantly in the papers and on TV chat shows, confiding their plans, their career ambitions, describing the extravagances on which they will spend their rewards, buying 'something I've always dreamed of', claiming sympathy for roles that have been so draining emotionally and physically, dwelling upon the anguish and the penalties of their restless martyred lives. Most of them are people like us, upon whom fortune – that significant transformer of destinies in capitalist society – has smiled. The day before yesterday, they too were at home in Dagenham or Newton-le-Willows with nothing but a dead-end job and a burning ambition; and today, there they are, a household name because they hit number one in the charts, won the big prize in the darts or the table tennis, came first in the beauty contest, or were selected to play the star role – out of 5,000 applicants – in the smash Broadway musical when it opens in London.

The significance of their being 'people like us' lies in the fact that they do with their money exactly what we would do; and indeed, in our modestly emulous way, attempt to do. That is to say, they spend it; lavishly, generously, without restraint. Not for them the stocking under the mattress, or the hoarded pence in the burial club, or the few pounds set aside for a rainy day. Indeed, there aren't going to be any more rainy days. For it is their function – given the dominant values of the society, one could almost say their predestiny – to live as though there were no tomorrow. They follow a by now well-worn trajectory upwards; not the antique path beaten by the sons (and more rarely, daughters) of successful nineteenth-century entrepreneurs, as they shed their regional accents and passed through the public schools (those powerful re-formers of sensi-bilities, those engineers of human souls who prefigured the more drastic reconstructors of the twentieth century in Josef Skvoresky's novel, *The Engineer of Human Souls*); no longer part of that 'consolidation of a gentri-fied bourgeois culture, particularly the rooting of pseudo-aristrocratic attitudes and values in upper middle-class educated opinion, which shaped an unfavourable context for economic endeavour'; but a far more dazzling and dramatic ascent in the world, that is of a piece with the accelerated tempo of the age and requires no radical change in the social persona. This shows itself in the rapid acquisition of wholly contemporary emblems of wealth – the personalized numberplate, the heart-shaped swimming pool, the gold-plated stretch limo, the love-nest in LA, the surprise party for the latest girlfriend, which involves flying out a few hundred intimate friends to Acapulco. The lives of these people are not, it goes without saying, all roses. The very publicity that creates them is also their undoing. Their tragic divorces are chronicled in great detail, as they go their separate ways from those they imagined they loved only two brief years before, with the amazing disclosures of the other's cruelty, kinkiness and venality in the press soon afterwards; their dating of new celebrities, models and racing drivers in exclusive night-spots round the world are all faithfully recorded. The stormy scenes in airport lounges – those transparent acres which might have been specifically constructed as an arena for their dramas – are played for all they're worth, as tragic figures clutch their duty-free drink and orange teddy-bears, and face the reporters in furs and dark glasses, while the true story of their heartbreak is signed up for a six-figure sum.

Their lives form a kind of morality play – in three acts. The first and obvious message is about the power of money, in which few of the specta-tors are likely to require any very intensive instruction. But it is important to understand that the money is *earned*. It has certainly been severed from traditional entrepreneurial activity; has nothing to do with those folk legends of young men in the early nineteenth century who walked into town with a shilling in their pocket and died as millionaires leaving a flourishing business. This new wealth may have all the excitement of the roulette wheel, but it has to be worked for. Thus it is that we hear of the TV star's 'tough schedule, filming in nine countries in as many months', roles that are 'physically and mentally exhausting' (*Celebrity* magazine); Joan Collins accuses her new husband of being 'a layabout, while she is up at dawn working on the set of *Dynasty*'. The pop group Status Quo take a 1,200 mile trek round Europe on a single day to play at three rock festivals: 12.30 a.m. Quo headline a top festival in Skanderborg, Denmark; 9.30 a.m. they fly to Heathrow and then travel by hired helicopters to the Knebworth Festival to support Queen. 4.30 p.m. they go on stage. Then helicopters whisk the band back to Luton airport for a flight to Switzerland. 11.30 p.m. they finish the day at Switzerland's Seepark Festival (the *Sun*). Tim Rice had to commute to Sweden to work in collaboration with Abba stars Bjorn and Benny; the England team are under the most rigorous training, 'no girls, no booze and in bed by ten' (the *Sun*), feats of discipline and endurance at which we can only wonder. Eddie Kidd, in order to win the star role in the new multi-million advertising campaign for Levi jeans, has been 'reshaped, remodelled and rebuilt. And he has come out at the other end like a sleek shiny racing machine' (the *Sun*). To do this he had to change that seventies look and rebuild his body: 'I began a rigorous training campaign. I cut out junk food and stopped drinking lager. I eat hardly anything during the day, but at night I have a good hunk of meat and plenty of fresh vegetables. Every morning I run about four miles. And I use a local pool three times a week to swim 25 lengths.' One of the most heroic feats recorded in 1986 was the 24-hour dash of a *Sun* reporter to New York to get copies of the new Bruce Springsteen album: he was bribing a cab-driver to carve up the rush hour traffic to get the flight home with the 100 albums he had acquired at record stores before they were available in Britain, so that the *Sun* could award them as prizes.

The second part of the lesson, too, brings few surprises. This is that money – despite its highly visible and undisputed benefits – doesn't bring happiness. And to reinforce this part of the teaching, there are the tragic deaths, the brilliant musician lying dead in the marble pool, the sirens of the ambulance carrying the inert figure to a nursing home after an overdose while the weeping crowds can only watch and pray; the children in permanent transit on their way to and from private schools in Switzerland, where they have created a scandal just to get themselves noticed by a busy parent; the search for drugs in the immaculate mews cottage, with the marks where police axes have broken down the door; the try-again fourth marriage, and the acrimony behind the fabulous record alimony settlement; the cops being called to the neo-Palladian villa where a naked model has been found dead in the grounds. The whole performance at once feeds our fantasies, yet makes us glad to be who we are, even though our lives may be dreary and empty, our own gestures to a life of leisure and romance constrained by poverty and an absence of such glittering talent. It is significant that it isn't the relentless work that destroys them, it is what happens to them in that public spectacle still sometimes quaintly referred to as their 'private life'; in other words, during their scanty and insufficient leisure. Indeed, these people demonstrate that there can be nothing more unwelcome than a surfeit of leisure, for that means a falling out of the public eye – that unblinking monocular glare – and hence into oblivion, where vigilant strangers come up to you and ask you if you were once the famous singer or the well-known TV personality. Nothing could be worse than becoming yesterday's news, last year's fashion, the flavour of last month; like Margaux Hemingway, for instance, whose life, according to *Celebrity* magazine, a few years ago could not have been brighter. She had a lucrative modelling contract, had married a millionaire and had just signed a $250,000 deal to advertise perfume – at the time the biggest single advertising contract landed by a woman. Now she is, according to a friend, 'reduced to being a vague celebrity who doesn't do anything except be seen and photographed at movies and parties' (*Celebrity* magazine).

The second act doesn't end there. The evidence of all those newly rich pop stars and famous people showing themselves up in an ugly night-club brawl, shocking their fans by saying something mean and cruel, their bad manners and unwholesome life style ('Bill Wyman boasts of sleeping with a thousand women; Boy George's heroin habit cost him a million-dollar contract; Alex Higgins head-butted a tournament boss in a row over a drugs test' (the *Sun*), etc.), the rumours about drying out in secret hideaways and receiving the latest therapy for their addiction – it all proves to us that at a deeper level, they (and by implication we ourselves for they are our sort) really don't know how to handle money. Those whom we can so easily identify with, well, it may be after all that we are not born to it. Look at how many of them finish up bankrupt, or drinking themselves into an early grave in that pub they bought with their earnings, or desperately seeking to make a pathetic comeback when they've been out of circulation for at least three years. It proves that we are not really fitted for riches, not worthy of them. It is almost as though it wasn't *meant*.

And this leads to the third part of the lesson. Sickened and wearied by this shameful public spectacle, we thank God that there is a higher social sphere to which we can raise our eyes, and which will reveal its more elevated, more spiritual significance. Above us, and above those who have got rich quickly, is a more exalted stratum of people who have always been wealthy, whose taste and breeding never falter and who offer an ideal, an unattainable model of perfection – those splendid creatures who are, after all, the guarantors of stability and continuity in our national life. Perhaps, after all, they *have* been set above us. While the parvenu stars strut and fume and play out their vulgar extravagances for all the world to see, those whose wealth is less volatile, attached as it so frequently is to more enduring things like the land, its forests and meadows and watercourses, go about their tranquil business. In fact, of course, theirs is the most lofty labour of all, for who would want *their* job (always on show, shaking all those hands, and helping to market our heritage for the tourist trade, that major modern industry?), serene and untouched by the squalors and scandals of those who are only a step or two above us, at least in origin if not in their way of living. And although that dizzying rise into a world of public display could always happen to us, this still leaves us remote from the real owners of wealth who occupy a far and shining region, too dazzling for our contemplation.

Yet even that remoteness is ambiguous. At times of heightened emotion – weddings and funerals and national crises – it is the 'ordinariness' of the royals that all the interviews insist upon, their 'closeness' to the people. At the time of the wedding of the Duke and Duchess of York, they were shown to be a hard-working yet fun couple, with whom everyone could identify. They are figures suitable for idealized projections of ourselves, as opposed to the reality of the selfish and tormented fantasies that the new rich act out on our behalf. The reports and the images of the event itself are immensely distancing – 'ceremony', 'pageantry', 'solemnity'. The social events leading up to the 'nuptials' (ordinary people, it seems, get married, the rich 'wed', only the most privileged have 'nuptials') were all stunning, glittering, breathtaking. On the wedding day, the bride entered Westminster Abbey with 'flowers crowning her glorious Titian hair girlishly hanging loose in pre-Raphaelite curls'; she left with a sparkling tiara having replaced her floral head-dress, dramatically symbolizing her metamorphosis from commoner to Her Royal Highness. This mystery occurred at the moment when the ring was placed upon her finger; indeed, the whole event took on the aspect of an ascension. Much was made of the dress: there would never be another to match it; it was a vision in ivory duchesse satin. The focus softens and the outlines blur: Sarah shimmered as she stepped out of the fairytale glass coach, the light reflecting hundreds upon hundreds of sequins. It was a dream come true; a magical ride to the Abbey; there were symbols of love sewn into a sea of satin; a renaissance silhouette; and she looked 'every inch a princess'; the dress that dreams are made of glittered; her radiance made the crowds forget their fatigue and the bad weather. These other-wordly descriptions sat side by side with the evocation of a working couple, intent on their 'careers'; and their ordinariness is adroitly combined with the supreme elevation of their station. Nothing could offer a more perfect example of how the leisure class has survived, and evolved into a guise more in keeping with the shifting demands placed upon it, while not surrendering anything of its traditional role, whereby 'all canons of reputability and decency are traced back by insensible gradations to the usages and habits of thought of the highest social and pecuniary class – the wealthy leisure class.'

Indeed the relationship between the new rich and the traditionally rich creates a self-reinforcing symmetry. The contrasts and interplay between them, the possibility of an easy passage of determined and talented individuals into the lower of these two castes, keep alive an agreeable sense of dynamic change, kindled hope and ambition in the more active and spirited sections of the population, and offer a possibility of vicarious consumption to the rest. They serve, not only as social models for the rest of us, but as psychological projections also: ego and superego, as it were, given corporeal and social shape: greed and self-control, gratification and self-denial. It is said, for instance, that when the Queen attends all those banquets to which duty summons her, she eats very sparingly. What a contrast with the new rich who, publicly and ostentatiously, cannot contain themselves, are like children at a party, incontinently reaching destructively into the pyramids of good things on the table. We, like they, would be quite unequal to the sublime abstinences and austerities of Her Majesty; we can only marvel, and be humbled. Perhaps this is why people say of royalty 'You must have someone to look up to', 'They're a figurehead', 'They set an example', 'They're above it all.'

In this way, the manifest function of both old and contemporary rich is easily distinguishable, even though both work unstintingly; where the former have onerous national duties, the latter are devoted to their career, their art, their performance, their high calling, their vocation, perfecting their talents, cultivating their skills, giving expression to their God-given abilities. But they also have a latent function, which is a byproduct of their more obvious purpose. The spectacular wealth, and the supreme achievements which provide it, have the effect of diminishing and belittling the faith of the majority of people in their own no less real talents and powers. This is not to deny that many of the celebrities and performers have substantial talent. It is simply that continuous and insistent glorification of them, the adulation and sycophancy which their money engenders, serve to repress our confidence in our own capacity for creativity and invention. For it is above all the stars and entertainers who point us firmly in the direction of a particular kind of leisure society: one that depends on marketed time, commoditized enjoyment, purchased pleasures. In other words, despite their often chaotic and disordered personal lives, these people find themselves pressed into the unlikely function of being powerful agents of discipline and social control.

Now, no longer objects of resentment, the rich have been able to command once more that veneration which, for a brief and levelling moment in the first half of the twentieth century, they looked as if they might have been in danger of forfeiting. Their rehabilitation has been accompanied by the ubiquitous display of their vital and irreplaceable social purpose. That this should have been, to a considerable extent, at the expense of real workers has been an insufficiently remarked phenomenon. If true, it has important consequences, not least for those political parties that claim to be – indeed, always have been – the representatives of labour; for the rich are, in the main, no friends of the working class, except in so far as the working class manifests itself in the modern world in its more benign form of fans, supporters, enthusiasts, consumers of the products and experiences which the rich create. This process may well help to account for the exhaustion of the Labour Party in Britain, its declining appeal, its growing estrangement from those it claims to defend and whose interests it exists to promote. A party devoted to the celebration of labour in a society which increasingly exalts leisure, and in which the privileged have taken upon themselves the work that appears (to the general agreement) to matter, must expect to see itself debilitated and, to a certain extent, rejected.

It cannot be said too clearly that this vast and eccentric project has been possible only as a result of the decay of much productive labour in Britain. When large numbers of people move out of work that is demonstrably both useful and necessary, the whole structure of employment lurches closer to fantasy. Service and leisure industries have the effect of opening up spaces for illusion (even delusion) about the purposes of work, which would never have been possible when the majority of people were engaged in the production of shoes or cloth or ships or chairs or cooking pots. This is not, of course, to harbour ideas of a past golden age of labour – it was as harsh as iron to those who worked in those industries – but to suggest that our version of a leisure society, in a world where so many people want basic necessities, is a cruel and bizarre enterprise; for it is only by means of the continued (and in some places intensified) enslavement of the poor of the earth that our 'liberation' into leisure (or fantasy) can occur. The distant enabling agents of whatever forms our leisure takes are the workers of South Africa and Chile, Brazil and South Korea. For though it is tempting for politicians to speak as though national economies were self-contained entities and susceptible to their control, this point has long been passed. Edward Zimmermann, writing of ancient Greece, said

'Societies, like men, cannot live in compartments. They cannot hope to achieve greatness by making amends in their use of leisure for the lives they have brutalized in acquiring it.'* And so it is with us.

James Robertson, in his otherwise visionary book, *The Sane Alternative*, looks briefly and incredulously at what is actually happening, and then dismisses it as preposterous.

> The hyper-expansionist scenario for the future claims to offer a solution to the problem of work: as super-technology and almost universal automation make more and more existing work unnecessary, most people's leisure will increase; the working day, the working week, the working year and the working life will all be reduced; most people will find their main satisfactions not in work, but in leisure; the work ethic will more or less disappear. But this solution has a fatal flaw. The work ethic would not disappear for Daniel Bell's pre-eminent professional and technical class who would be responsible for the high technology and sophisticated theoretic knowledge upon which that kind of post-industrial society would depend. Their work would be of vital importance. So that kind of society would suffer from a deep schizophrenia about work. The hoi polloi would have to be persuaded that work is unimportant, unsatisfying, unfulfilling, unnecessary; while the elites and their potential recruits would have to be continually impressed with the value of work and the high status which it confers. It just doesn't add up.†

But it does. For this is precisely what is appearing, as the privileged appropriate and enclose work in much the same way as they once enclosed land, dispossessing the peasantry of subsistence. It is true, as Robertson observes, that there are many and growing currents of resistance to the present ordering of post-industrial society. But these remain scattered and diffuse. They do not seriously impede (and therefore challenge) the dynamic process which drives the economic and social machine to which our lives are tethered, and to whose rhythms we must accommodate ourselves. It is sometimes easier to foretell the future (and always easier to create myths about the past) than to look closely at what is happening in the present, that awkward and always moving space in which lives are lived.

If the lesser labours of the contemporary working class have been devalued by the piratical incursions of the privileged, there is another

---

* Quoted in Murray Bookchin, *Post-scarcity Anarchism* (Wildwood House, 1974).
† James Robertson, *The Sane Alternative* (Ironbridge, Shropshire, 1983).

group whose plight has been aggravated – that of the poor, especially the unemployed, the supreme representatives of limitless leisure in the present-day context. 'Poverty', it used to be asserted by poor and working class alike, 'is not a crime'. Today, in the rich societies of the West, it is certainly no virtue; indeed, the abasement of the poor has been part consequence, part just another aspect of the remoralizing of the rich. Since one of the basic needs of the economy is to signal its eager desire to shower all the people with the benefits of its prodigious productive power, those who fail to avail themselves of the abundance that is everywhere on such conspicuous display are bound to incur a social stigma. Such a stigma is absent in a society where people are more generally poor, and where, however hard they try, and no matter what hours they labour, people are unable to provide enough for themselves and their families.

In the post-war period it was believed for a long time that poverty was simply a residual problem. It appeared – particularly during the period of full employment – no longer a danger to which most wage-earners were exposed, but the affliction of a dwindling minority whose misfortune it was to have been (temporarily) left behind. As Michael Harrington says of the United States' experience, 'The old poverty – the pace of social and economic time is accelerated and I am talking about the ancient days of twenty and thirty years ago – seemed to be an exception to the basic trends of the society. Everyone was progressing steadily; a minority had been left behind. Therefore it would be rather a simple matter to deduct some few billions as they poured out of our industrial cornucopia and use them to abolish the "pockets" of poverty.'*

It has taken the recent experience of mass unemployment and poverty to demonstrate that earlier assumptions about the elimination of poverty involved over-sanguine judgements about the capacity of capitalist society to change its nature and its purposes. In 1986, 16 million people in Britain were living at a level lower than 40 per cent above that set by the DHSS for supplementary benefit. The government's poverty line in 1986 was an income of £29.40 for a single person, and £44.80 for a couple. This far from generous assessment yields an official count of 8.8 million poor.

It can now be seen that the 'disappearing poor' of the fifties and sixties was an illusion, and that poverty remains a structural necessity in capitalist societies. That the poor should survive even the wealth that we have seen has been one of the most earnest endeavours of our time, and for this reason, that they are the living embodiment, the flesh-and-blood demonstration, that we are still far, far from achieving sufficiency for all. Their carefully engineered privations can be invoked as a justification for that

* Michael Harrington, *The New American Poverty* (Firethorn Press, 1985).

continuing growth and development that is the reason for existence of the capitalist economy; even though it ought to be plain to even the most casual observer that those forms of growth are increasingly disarticulated from the basic needs that they are, at least in some versions of progress, supposed to answer. In this way, even when we were in the depths of the worst recession for 50 years (the word 'recession' is an interesting euphemism, its faintly religious associations casting a spiritual and slightly uplifting glow over what used to be referred to more baldly as depression or slump), the markets were none the less crowded with products which might at first appear to be symptoms of the deranged fantasies of medieval despots. While famine and disease still haunt the earth, and so many people waste away in desolating idleness, we are invited to feed our cats with preparations of salmon and turkey in aspic, drink a cocktail of 12 tropical fruits, buy electric woks and hand-made Shanghai lacquer and blackwood furniture, send our friends kissograms, feast on strawberries from Ecuador in January, anoint our bodies with kiwi fruit lip-balm and strawberry body-salve, orchid oil cleansing milk, glycerine and oat facial lather, neck gel with cocoa butter, peppermint foot lotion, white grape skin tonic and wash in goat's milk with honey soap – activities redolent of embalming the dead rather than the daily cultural practice of the living. Here, we are at the heart of capitalism's leisure society, with its disabling enrichment which Ivan Illich describes: 'An addiction to paralyzing affluence, once it becomes engrained in a culture, generates "modernized poverty". This is a form of disvalue associated with the proliferation of commodities ... the decline in the individual–personal ability to do or to make is the price of every additional degree of commodity affluence.' It shows itself in the mass-marketing of aristocratic-derived notions of self-pampering, invitations to indulge the most random caprice as though this were absolute necessity, the urge to spoil ourselves, the prompting to let ourselves go, give ourselves treats and rewards, to take as much as we think we deserve. One consequence of this process is that, as belief in and dependency upon money grow, the individual's faith in her or his own powers decays. This, in turn leads to a sense of impotence, of inability to act even in the presence of the most baleful social evils that are thrown up by our version of plenty and leisure – the addictions and the crime, the secret suffering as well as the public violence – until all we are capable of is the helpless shrug of resignation, the turning away, 'What can you do about it?' One of the reasons why shopping is the most important cultural activity in Western society is because shops are the site of arrival of all the new products that will dispossess us of some areas of ingenuity or competence in which we previously had confidence. Shops and stores, halls of merchandise are the locus where we discover the extent of our plundered capacity for doing. This is the other side of that exchange, whereby we have surrendered to the rich and powerful the significant functions of the division of labour in society. It is a transaction which has left the poor more than ever excluded, stranded and conspicuous once more. It also explains why poverty remains so brutal and degrading, in spite of survival rations being more or less assured to all. Poverty, in this context, becomes more intractable, and far less an object of the charitable regard of the rich. The poor, subject to the same sense of de-powering as everyone else, are then left with only the most feeble purchasing power, and this is the sole means whereby we can reclaim at least something of the expropriated human substance.

Those who have sought to discover the reasons for the much-discussed waning of class consciousness in Britain, a generalized lure of most people towards a self-definition as middle class, might well find some clue in the ideological inversion of the relative importance of work, whereby the well-to-do have fraudulently laid hold of the important functions, traditional forms of labour have been stigmatized as archaic survivals obstructing the way to the realization of the leisure society, and the poor have been doubly excluded – a reserve army of labour almost completely demobilized. The leisure society, from this perspective, takes on lineaments that are far from the appealing visions of those people who insist that we forget the Protestant work ethic, set aside a superseded puritanism and prepare ourselves to enter what is capitalism's realm of freedom.

The busy self-advertisement of the essential work which the rich perform has yet another purpose. The urgency of their labours, the high salience of their endeavours, despite which a harsh poverty equally conspicuously remains, reinforces the illusion that nothing has changed despite their heroic efforts: this is all merely the living demonstration that we still live in a society of scarcity (they are always invoking 'scarce resources': what they don't say is that the scarcest have become the diminished human ones), and that the only possible road towards sufficiency lies in perpetuating the existing arrangements and, indeed, rendering them more efficient. Their elevated and mysterious avocations only conceal the truth of Veblen's observation that 'the need for conspicuous waste ... stands ready to absorb any increase in the community's industrial efficiency or output of goods, after the most elementary physical wants have been provided for ... As increased industrial efficiency makes it possible to procure the means of livelihood with less labor, the energies of the industrious members of the community are bent to the compassing of a higher result in conspicuous expenditure, rather than slackened to a more comfortable pace.'

If the people of Britain are, as Martin Wiener asserts, predisposed 'by a century of psychological and intellectual de-industrialisation' to the loss of work, there is no sign of this in the public performance of the privileged.* As the major consumers of the world's treasures, the primary users up of the earth, the major despoilers of its beauty, the most lofty task of the rich is to show the way that the rest of humankind must follow, not merely to those excluded unfortunates in the rich world, but to their delegates and representatives who are the elites of the Third World, and who can, no doubt, be trusted to impresss the same welcome lesson upon their own people. And this means, on the global scale, according to Wiener, 'fundamentally, the replacement of widespread, unquestioned competence at subsistence activities by the use and consumption of commodities; the monopoly of wage labor over all other kinds of work; redefinition of needs in terms of goods and services mass-produced according to export design; finally, the rearrangement of the environment in such a fashion that space, time, materials and design favor production and consumption while they degrade or paralyze use-value oriented activities that satisfy needs directly. And all such worldwide homogeneous changes and processes are valued as inevitable and good.'

From the earliest years of industrial society, its apologists foresaw that whatever the disruption and loss it brought to people, it promised, eventually, an end to poverty, the release of human beings from the ancient tyranny of work and want. And yet it hasn't happened, indeed, cannot happen, for these things are the very fuel that drives the engines of industrial society. It may be that productive labour can be transported to different parts of the world, may desert Lancashire and Pittsburgh and Lille and reappear in Taipei, Colombo or Sao Paulo. It is clear that insufficiency is the fate of the ill-rewarded workers of Santiago, Calcutta and Nairobi, while the poor of the rich world are left as dependants on decaying welfare systems; but any leisure society that evolves for a majority of the people in the West as a result of these movements does so only in so far as it is underpinned by exploitation, hunger and disease that are passed on to others elsewhere.

The distorted and one-sided version of leisure that we are being offered actually occupies the space where other real options might exist; 'an economy of cherished things' in Murray Bookchin's words, where work would not be abolished for some and intensified for others, where the measurement of wealth would not exclude the vast non-monetized realm of 'women's work', of those labours that we perform daily for each other and without which life would not be worth living; where leisure would not

* Martin J. Wiener, *English Culture and the Decline of the Industrial Spirit, 1850–1980* (Penguin, 1985).

mean the service of commodities – both visible and invisible – but the rediscovery of all the things we could do for each other, all the satisfactions and services we could furnish for one another beyond the money economy; Illich's 'convivial austerity', a development which would not be at the expense of but, on the contrary, in harmony with that of the poor of the earth. It is for the sake of concealment of these more modest and liberating formulations that the showy and spectacular forms of leisure society which we can see foreshadowed in the West exist; the epic charade of the rich recycling the work ethic for their own purposes is only one of its more dramatic and audacious manifestations.

As early as the 1950s, J. K. Galbraith said 'The greatest prospect that we face – indeed what must now be counted one of the central economic goals of our society – is to eliminate toil as a required institution. This is not a utopian vision. We are already on our way. Only an extraordinarily elaborate exercise in social camouflage has kept us from seeing what has been happening.' A generation later, André Gorz said much the same: 'What is happening is that industrial society is doing its best to hide the fact that the amount of socially necessary labour is declining rapidly and that everyone could benefit from this.' Gorz insists that the possibilities of transcending industrial (both capitalist and socialist) ideology already exist. It is only the religion of work and productivist logic that prevent us from seeing through the masquerade. Similarly, Rudolf Bahro, describing the same phenomenon, talks of 'illusion'. 'The technocratic and scientist faith that the progress of industry, science and technique will solve humanity's social problems virtually automatically is one of the illusions of the present age most hostile to life.'* Camouflage, illusion, masquerade – all of these are acknowledged. Most of the prophets of the post-industrial era have clear and powerful visions of the world they anticipate will appear, once all the illusions have been dispelled. James Robertson speaks of 'decolonisation' and 'liberation' in realms where these are seldom felt to be necessary:

> If managing the breakdown of overdeveloped institutions can be seen as decolonisation, developing one's own and other people's self-reliance can be seen as liberation. In health, in education, at work, in housing, in food, in transport, in energy, in politics, in religion, and in other economic and social aspects of our lives, many of us need to liberate ourselves and others from excessive dependence – on money and jobs; on big organisations, big technology and professionalised services; on men if we are women, and on women if we are men; on cities; on the industrialised countries if we live in the third

* Rudolf Bahro, *Socialism and Survival* (Heretic Books, 1982).

world; and on logic and intellect, if our intuitions and emotions have been stunted and underdeveloped.

André Gorz looks forward to a time of 'autonomous activity': 'For me, the only real autonomous activity is one that is neither an obligation imposed in the name of moral, religious or political principles, nor as a necessity for survival. But if it isn't to be either of these, subsistence must be taken care of by an advanced system of social production which provides all we need to live and demands only a small fraction of our time.'

The most constant feature in all the proposals of those who would deliver us from the exigencies and the oppressions of industrial society, a society in which the goods have long since ceased being delivered to the people, and the people are increasingly being delivered to the goods, is that it involves a leap of faith, a 'paradigm shift', a different 'mind-set'. The prescriptions are something 'we' must do, decisions 'our society' must make, paths 'our culture' or 'civilization' must follow. Liberation, transformation: Bahro indicates most clearly the nature of the changes that must occur: 'The crisis is insoluble ... without a movement of *conversion* that brings togther the most diverse alternative attempts in thinking and living, a movement that attains a degree of cohesion and agreement such as was reached in the past only through the claims of religion.'

The language of religious conversion makes the problem of transcending industrial society appear a relatively easy trajectory: an act of faith, a dispelling of illusion, a change of heart on a mass scale. The element that is suppressed in these projections is the way in which the needs and values of industrial society work through our lives, as a profound and organic structure of belief, purpose and meaning; and these cannot be disturbed without incalculable, perhaps even catastrophic, consequences. We are not dealing with something external, 'a system', but with the way this works through living flesh and blood, leaves its impress on the very tissue and substance of our humanity, imposes itself upon the imagination and the emotions, traces itself into the lineaments of the heart and spirit. For most people in the world, the capitalist/existing socialist conflict is the given universe, and a more or less satisfactory account of human possibilities. That we might be on the verge of the dissolution of this Manichean monolith is very exciting. The trouble is that this awareness remains the (open) secret of a new elite of visionaries and prophets, a priestly caste without, on the whole, votaries or congregation. What it does not offer is the motor whereby such epochal shifts as are required can be realized: an alternative structure of popular belief that will displace that faith in continued growth and expansion of industrial society. For it is this faith which operates, not as abstraction, but as a living power through humanity, shaping the ambitions and dreams of individuals, determining our hopes, our whole sense of ourselves and our purposes through time. The power of the existing structures of industrial society lies in its having legitimized, definitively it seems, the *appetitus divitiarum infinitus*, the unbounded appetite for riches, having transformed it from being the most deadly obstacle to our salvation into the only means of ensuring it.

Twenty years ago, Murray Bookchin seriously underestimated the powers of recuperation of a capitalist society that seemed on the edge of collapse, precisely because the problem of material scarcity had been resolved, and the apparatus of maintaining the illusion that it hadn't appeared increasingly cumbersome, oppressive and life-denying:

> The revolutionary struggle within the advanced capitalist countries has shifted to a historically new terrain: it has become a struggle between a generation of youth that has known no chronic economic crisis and the culture, values and institutions of an older conservative generation whose perspective on life has been shaped by scarcity, guilt, renunciation, the work ethic and the pursuit of material security. Our enemies are not only the visibly entrenched bourgeoisie and the state apparatus but also an outlook which finds its support among liberals, social democrats, the minions of a corrupt mass media, the 'revolutionary' parties of the past, and, painful as it may be to the acolytes of Marxism, the worker dominated by the factory hierarchy, by the industrial routine, and by the work ethic.

The recession of the eighties, together with the reappearance of mass poverty and unemployment, have reinvested the old illusion with new plausibility. A new generation has been persuaded that its best hope lies in the unchanging falsehood that growth and capitalist versions of development can relieve those very evils which it creates by its own activity in the world.

The capacity for survival of industrial society (and particularly of its capitalist incarnation) is prodigious. The promise that work can be, if not abolished, at least reduced to a peripheral and subordinate role in the lives of the people, while at the same time the exalted labour of the most privileged is haloed as heroic and self-sacrificing, is an awesome reversal of the earlier insistence upon both the indispensability and virtue of universal ceaseless toil. Indeed, it seems that the rich of the West have learnt a great deal from their socialist antagonists, having taken to themselves paeans of praise to toil that sound almost like earlier versions of socialist propaganda: not only is toil ennobling, but those who work are the only useful individuals in society; they are endowed with superior qualities which alone make them capable of judging what is good in industry, art, social organization.

It is impossible not to admire the mobility, the energy and adaptability of a system thus to turn itself upside down, to transfer all its old certitudes and imperatives in the interests of survival. It is, as Marx and Engels wrote in 1848, that 'all fixed fast-frozen relations, with their train of ancient and venerable prejudices and opinions, are swept away, all new-formed ones become antiquated before they can ossify. All that is solid melts into air, all that is holy is profaned....'* Given the mutability and fluidity of capital, it should scarcely surprise us that the version of a leisure society that we are bidden to welcome will depend on continuing capitalist expansion, and will exist in a world where the rich are the only ones engaged upon significant labour, while the rest of us are being prepared for forms of idleness and inutility that vary from permanent unemployment to forms of work servicing commodities that will be casual, intermittent, disabling, demeaning and futile.

André Gorz expresses it succinctly: 'The abolition of work alone is not liberation. Liberty, by its very essence, cannot come from technological change: it cannot be the effect of which technology is the cause. Technology can only create new material conditions. Those created by automation will encourage or jeopardise our personal development according to the social and political project underpinning their implementation.'

While other visions of a leisure society or of emancipatory movements are being conceived, actual existing leisure remains a vast and expanding source of profit. In the process, what Veblen's leisure class treasured as the most distinctive and exclusive marks of caste have become the commonplace possessions of millions of people in the rich societies of the West: what these thereby signal to the poor of the earth is very much what Veblen's leisured signalled to those who laboured so far beneath them at the end of the nineteenth century.

* Karl Marx and Friedrich Engels, *The Communist Manifesto* (Foreign Languages Publishing House, 1975).

3

From manufacture to service

Those who would represent leisure as liberation do so in the context of a
Britain in which place was virtually synonymous with function; where
most manufacturing towns and cities were sited where they are simply
because they contributed to a national division of labour. This gave a sense
of coherence and apparent stability (a period identified by E. Hobsbawm
as extending from about the 1870s to the time of the Second World War),
when the redbrick streets around mine, mill and factory took on the aspect
of permanent communities. For a time, it seemed that most goods in daily
use in the household could be identified with the place of their manufacture. When I was a child in the forties, I thought of most of the material
things in our house in terms of place: the cutlery was always from
Sheffield, the lino on the floor from Lancashire, the soap from Port
Sunlight, the woollens from the West Riding; even the lavatory pan was
stamped Burslem or Hanley; and the best tea-cups in the glass-fronted
cabinet were also from Stoke. Our boots and shoes could have been
nothing but a piece of locally tanned leather. We knew where the coal
came from, and the bricks on the building sites were marked Marston
Valley. Bloaters came in boxes from the east coast, linen from Belfast,
slates from Welsh quarries; most of the fresh produce was grown locally,
so that our diet followed the predictable growth of vegetables and fruits;
even the beer was brewed by the Northampton Brewery Company, with
the emblem of its red neon star fizzing over the gables of the pubs. This
created a world that was easily intelligible, even if the origin of certain
luxuries was more obscure – the nutmeg on the rice pudding for instance,
the rice itself, the cloves in the apple tart which were also used against
toothache, the tinned pineapple, the bedtime cocoa, tea and tobacco, and
the snuff that Uncle Harry spilled down his jacket – all the consolations of
the poor were deeply built into a colonial exploitation of which we at the
time knew little. The intensification of this process in our time makes us
less innocent, but also more dependent upon an intensified abuse of the
poor of the earth. No talk of a leisure society can omit this essential

dimension. It seems that even to talk of a leisure society in the presence of the suffering to which it is so closely allied is an affront to those who have no choice but to defray the expense of those amenities which we feel we not only deserve, but must have.

In our town, the boot and shoe industry remained a scattered and semi-domestic occupation for many workers until late into the nineteenth century. Large-scale factories were built only just outside the reach of living memory; and, because in the last generation the industry has decayed rapidly, the town offers an example of a staple trade which, although ancient, was industrialized late and vanished early. It is easy to follow, within the consciousness of people still living, memories of the rural origins of the craft, the brief time of apparent stability around the turn of the century, and the rapid decline of the industry, and its replacement by Barclaycard, Avon cosmetics, service industries.

The factories themselves still stand, many given over now to other purposes. Some still have whitewash on the windows, to mitigate the sun's flare, and perhaps to prevent any distraction of the operatives from their machines. In these buildings, there is a mouldering climate from long ago, in the earth-smelling dampness of the unused building; the tang of rotten wood and airless humidity where the machines stood in rows, with the lines of workers beside them. It evokes imperious forewomen in bleached aprons, and the shutting of the gate as the church clock with its tarnished gold figures and verdigris face chimed the half hour at 7.30. One old man who worked here knows that shoemakers of his name existed in Northampton at least as far back as 1805; as though his existence were simply a role in time that had to be filled by someone whose name he shared: a 180-year-old function occupied by the same person, replicated through time. As the old operatives talk, they speak of the sprawling families and the high rate of child mortality, as though it scarcely mattered which individuals survived, it sufficed that enough should live to take their places in the factories. They knew they were born to work (and to want and woe, as they sometimes add, although neither of these was the concern of their employers). Their poverty looks poignant to them now; while they lived it, they knew nothing else: the charity boots that chafed the ankles and had been perforated by the benevolent donors so that they couldn't be pawned or sold; the mothers with their bundles of second-hand clothing that they picked, washed, turned inside out and stitched up again to serve as new skirts and trousers. Only at Easter did they have new clothes, material $3\frac{3}{4}$d a yard, and that was the only time when the father went out with them because he was not ashamed of their shabbiness which was a reproach to his inadequate wages. They grew in the slightly shaming knowledge that Northampton prospered at times of war when there was a demand for military boots; and they consoled themselves with the stories of soldiers being saved by the Bible in their breast pocket, which a bullet had penetrated no further than the Book of Corinthians, halted in its murderous trajectory by the quality of Northampton leather binding.

Although they struggled against the conditions and inadequate rewards, they never doubted their function; those who dreamed (and acted) for a more just society never saw the removal of work itself as a feasible or desirable goal. They might have imagined it humanized, less ardous, better paid; but they didn't despise the skills, any more than they were contemptuous of the ingenuity women showed in their domestic labour. 'We got up of a Sunday morning, and we were to sing in the church choir at 11.0. We had no boots to wear; but between getting up at eight and time to go to church, we'd have new boots. Our mother would cut the upper, and father would close them, nail them with rivets.' They speak of the men who died, of consumption or in the war, leaving a woman with four children under the age of six: 'She went scrubbing and cleaning, and when she'd finished she'd go round the market at 11 o'clock on Saturday night when things were being sold off cheap, to get our supper. We never did eat before midnight.' They went begging leather chips at the factory to heat the copper for Sunday's wash; took a pillow-case to buy stale bread from the bakery before they went to school. Many of the old people themselves started work at 11 or 12, earning half a crown a week polishing silver at the vicarage or knot-tying in the factories. More often than not, it was the nearest factory they went to, or one where relatives worked, people who could be trusted to keep an eye on you, so that family and industrial discipline often merged into the same thing. Ten shillings a week; a shilling for yourself, the rest to your mother. 'It wasn't your money, you didn't feel it belonged to you.' 'I used to earn a bit extra by cleaning the glass roof of the factory. I was only a little lad. I had to clean the dust and mud and bird-muck off the glass. I fell through once. The timbers were rotten. I laid under a rainstorm of glass on the factory floor, covered in cuts. I got an extra half-crown.'

'You were set on without ceremony. Girls had to have an apron or pinafore, a pair of scissors and hammer, provide them yourself. I've still got mine.' She shows an iron-headed cylinder, which has worn thin where it has been held for 50 years in the same position. The factory loomed over their childhood with the force of a predestiny. 'The foreman called all the women Mary. "Oi there Mary, what you doing?", while Hannah or Irene shivered in their shoes and responded. They went home and told their mother "He calls me Mary." "Oh does he, well the fashion's changed, when I worked there he called everybody Jane." If you arrived late, he would wither you with sarcasm. "Is there any spare ground near where you live?"

"I don't know, why?" "Well, if we brought the factory to you perhaps you could get there on time." We worked from 7.30 to 12.15, and if you started to untie your pinafore 12.15, a bony hand would come and thump you in the back and a voice would say "Buzzer's not gone yet."'

Your time was not your own, it belonged to your employer, and you were not allowed to forget it. 'When my mother first started in the factory, you weren't allowed to take a flask of tea, nothing to eat or drink. You weren't allowed to sing or whistle or talk. "A whistling woman and a crowing hen is good for neither God nor men" the foreman used to say, he was a lay preacher, sententious old bugger.' 'But you did squeeze a few minutes out of the boss's time, and it had a sweetness no other time had' – a joke, a whispered piece of gossip, dancing the veleta between the oily machines when the forewoman dozed off. If you wore a touch of lipstick: 'Don't come into my factory wearing that bloody tup-reddle.' 'But the sleep you slept then, you were sometimes so tired after the factory that you were too exhausted to chew what was on your plate, and you woke up to find yourself with your head on the table'; such a different sleep from the chemical-induced unconsciousness that so many women need today to make their life more bearable. 'When you came home, your mother'd undo the laces of your boots, and you sank onto the cord sofa under the window, and she shushed the younger children; and they whispered and the clock ticked and you dreamed of escape, of a better future, a day at the seaside, or the smile of the boy on the other side of the factory to whom you had never spoken a word, but who you knew liked you, because he always managed to be wheeling his bike past when you came out.'

The vast division of labour in the boot factories created about 350 operations from start to finish in the making of a welted shoe. The first thing you want is the last, as they always said; a tired old joke then, but unfamiliar now. Then it went into the pattern room, the clicking room, the closing room and the making room. In the closing room alone there were 95 operations. 'People don't know what these jobs are now'; but the old can cite lists of archaic and forgotten occupations that people once recognized as their function: insole-channelling, heel-trimming, edge-trimming, edge-setting, inking, padding, brushing, bottom-scouring, heel-scouring, brushing off, knot-tying, stamping, skiving, feeding, under-trimming, cap-feeding, cap-beading, perforating.

'I started work latexing; a gummy substance in a jar, solution for the beaders. It smelt horrible and made me feel ill. I used to go home and cry and my mother used to say "Never mind my duck, you keep at it." It's like the stuff kids sniff, glue. I expect we were addicted to it. It probably affected my brain, that's why I'm so daft.' But she isn't and she knows it, with her keen intelligence and her eyes glistening as she remembers how hard they had to work. 'You had to work like mad, because each operation merged into the next, and you couldn't keep anybody waiting in the chain of operations or they wouldn't make their money up.'

'I started as a staining-boy. The strips at the back of the shoes had to be stained with ink. You had a pile of them and a mop at the end of a stick and dipped it into the liquid and spread it all round the edge of the shoe. You had nails that were permanently black.'

'You were just put on a job and supposed to pick it up as you went along from the other workers. It makes you laugh when you see all this training youngsters have to go through – they're not doing anything common sense couldn't teach you.'

'I had this jar of latex, turned upside down like a whisky bottle in a pub; you opened it with this little stopper and it ran into a trench and onto these rollers that solutioned the leather ready for the beaders. One night, I was sitting in the pictures, and it suddenly flashed through my mind, "Oh my goodness, I've not shut that jar up properly." I spent a sleepless night. When I got there next morning, this latex was all over the place, it had flooded the work bench and the floor. I sat and sobbed my heart out. I don't know why I never got the sack. I expect somebody covered up for me.'

The work pursued them outside; not only the feral smell on their clothes that associated them with the hides they worked, but also the repeated actions haunted their dreams. Even now, they sometimes wake up sweating, old men and women, dreaming they have to finish a given quantity of work before they can go home. There was the threat of bovine tuberculosis, chest diseases, the dust, the sun glaring through the whitewashed skylights. 'You had to be perfectionists; you couldn't afford the shoes for yourself, but you got some satisfaction, knowing it was a good piece of work; others might have got a bit of added joy from the knowledge that their handsome glacé dancing pumps had enabled the Prince of Wales to dance till dawn, or you knew they'd withstood the wet of the trenches, and perhaps saved a soldier's life, at least till he was blown to bits next day.'

'I was on a job called searing. Round the edges of the shoe, the skivers left a narrow edge that had to be seared. The searing machine was run by gas: a little blue light; and you had to run the shoe round and burn the edge off. It looked almost like beading, only it wasn't so good, it was an inferior process. They found out that sitting over this flame was bad for your health, so we had a pint of milk a day.'

'When you went in our shop at the top door, it was a sea of faces, hundreds of people, as far as you could see.'

'They played tricks on you when you started; it could be humiliating if you were a sensitive soul. They sent you for a sky hook, a long weight, a rubber hammer to knock in some glass tacks, a bucket of electricity; if you took it in good part, you were all right; you could fit in.'

To raise the question now of what they would have liked to do, now that they are old, is to touch an old hurt that still gives pain. 'My father wanted me to be a school teacher, but of course that was impossible then.' 'I wanted to be a carpenter. I had the letter in my hand, to go and be apprenticed to one of the big building firms, but the family needed the money'; and some of the ambitions are sadly modest, they didn't soar into fantasy. 'I could have been a professional cricketer. I played for years for the factory, but it was one of those dreams.' 'For me, it wasn't a matter of what are you going to do, it was which shoe factory you were going in, if you could get in.' 'I wanted to join the navy . . . but my Dad wouldn't hear of it.' 'You had the consolation of knowing that everybody shared the same fate. There was the excitement of going to work with your father or sister.'

'I don't think I thought of anything except going to work. That was the big transition in your life. As a matter of fact, I went into an office. I didn't like it because it was like still being at school. You all sat at desks, under the eye of the chief clerk all the time. My friends were all in the shoe factory, and I felt I was the odd one out. So I changed over; my Gran got me on at the place where she was.'

Because many of the boot and shoe firms had started in a small way, their family histories were known to the workers; sometimes they were resented as Gradgrinds, sometimes recalled with affection for individual acts of kindness to the work people. Everybody knew the scandal of the rich sons who squandered the money and finished up in worse case than their parents when they began. Many of the wives of factory owners had themselves started off as operatives, and had lived in streets where the workers came from, yet who gave themselves airs and graces and snubbed those they had been at school with, and yet often finished up in the asylum bloated with drink; there were even those who denied their own parents, who paid them to keep out of the way while they entertained their wealthy friends. Many of them, in the highly moral cautionary stories, finished up bankrupt because of their extravagance, or else they lived so meanly that they dined off a penny bloater behind velvet and lace curtains.

In the late 1930s, there were almost 20,000 members of the Boot and Shoe Union; even in 1946, there were still 16,000; and this concealed considerable numbers of homeworkers and small craftsmen; many of the homeworkers were women, machining leather helmets, boots, riding gear, handbags, with the result that there were few families unconnected with the shoe trade: over half the people working were employed, directly or indirectly, in the leather industry.

The rural hinterland of the industry, the country origin of tanning and leather, helped to preserve something peasant-like in the people, a stubbornness and parsimony. They had a superstitious and uncooperative nature, were parochial, but tenacious and persistent. There was a clearly defined regional sensibility, something quite distinct from that of people in the big cities. They were always slow to express feelings; they were moved by a compulsion to disagree with everything, a refusal to believe anything they were told, a persistent dissent from what were sometimes obvious truths and a failure to go with the grain. The shoe people were puritanical, sceptical, unimpressed by money or station, sour, self-righteous and deeply pessimistic. Alf Sharmn, 80: 'My wants are few, for the simple reason that no bugger's ever offered me anything. I'm never asked nobody for nothing all my life long. I can look any b. in the face, even me Maker – if I'm got one – and tell 'em I'm never owed nobody a penny-piece. I wouldn't be beholden to my best friend. I couldn't, because I ain't got one.'

The most obvious political expression of this sensibility occurred a hundred years ago, with the return to Parliament of Bradlaugh three times, twice after he had refused to take the oath. There is no doubt that he was supported by many members of the Nonconformist chapels as much as by 'atheistic shoemakers', of whom there were certainly not enough to elect him by themselves. He appealed to something perverse and awkward, a resistance to the power of the strong and privileged. They wanted him returned to Parliament on principle; not necessarily the principle he stood for, but on principles of their own.

By the time I was born, if the tradition had already been eroded, the war more or less froze everything. Certainly I had no inkling that it wouldn't last. It is always easy to mistake the moment of childhood for a timeless stability. But even the physical fabric of the town appeared then ancient and enduring, even though the old people talked of a time, comparatively recent, when streets and estates had been orchards and fields. Somehow, a sense of continuity in the long family memories, the laboriously acquired skills, that certainty of continuing poverty, easily overrode the change of setting that had substituted terraced streets for country yards and cottages; and, anyway, the country was easily accessible, visible through the funnel of the streets, within walking distance from every part of town.

The world in which we grew up seemed as if it would go on for ever. What my contemporaries and I didn't know was that the way of life which we found so oppressive and changeless was already at the edge of extinction. Time seemed so heavily structured in the streets, which formed a tight mesh in which human lives were snared; and within them, the more subtle webs of neighbourhood held them fast; the obligations of a net of kin kept them even closer. Ever since we could remember, there had been the sound of boots on the pavement at 7.30; the homegoing phalanx of bicycles at the factory gates at midday; the smell of leather they left behind when they returned to work at 1 o'clock. The pattern of the week was predictable, from the stoic and resigned return to work each Monday morning, the endurance of each day, with its slight variation, until the pulse of pleasure and relaxation on Friday and Saturday nights, swiftly halted on Sunday, with its sense of exhaustion and the jarring intimacies of family life; and the unbearable melancholy of Sunday evenings, with its sound of cracked church bells and the reminder of the week to come. It seemed closed to all innovation and change.

And yet we had a premature awareness that we would escape from it. We felt we would, heroically, repudiate the life of the previous generation of shoeworkers. We didn't quite know how. It was soon revealed to us that it was connected with our superior intelligence. The truth was that we were not required to follow them anyway: the structure of employment was already disintegrating. Slight mutations in the economic structure were occurring, but we were encouraged to view our deliverance as an act of personal merit.

The shoeworkers seemed to us as indestructible as the leather they worked; tough and ageless men in their shirts without collars, their slow, lugubrious humour, as sparing of words as of money. Their lives seemed to us no lives at all, but austere sketches of living: the exactions of work, the frugality of their unadorned houses, wooden chairs and cold lino, enamel bowls in fireclay sinks, laconic wives rattling their zinc pails and spreading arcs of cleanliness over the flags with their coarse scrubbing brushes. Their lives seemed an endless penance, and even their pleasures – drinking bitter beer and growing sour apples and rhubarb on their allotments, playing darts and talking dour philosophy – seemed astringent and without joy.

What we wanted to escape from was already in decay. What we sought to avoid was precisely that sense of place that has by now been almost effaced, the distinctive voice of the town where we were born, the dying music of its dialect and popular beliefs, the wasting fabric of its social and political tradition. The part of our identity that is shaped by a place, a town, a region, was already being eroded; and we with our flight, our epic of personal escape, our haste to be elsewhere, were in the forefront of this damaging process. Oh, those rough, sceptical, suspicious, pig-headed, parsimonious, disputatious, dissenting shoepeople! You were also just and fair and resolute and persistent and unimpressible; you would never yield to the mean orthodoxies and the shabby proprieties of your betters, always ready to quarrel with the easy opinions and ignoble decencies of the times. There is something of great worth in the tradition of that plain, undistinguished town, in what that humble and vanished population has to say to us, however hard it is to follow, however faint its echo down the years.

In our absence, a new generation has been shaped to a quite different structure: the service sector. Ian and Derek are the children of migrants from the Caribbean; Tim and Michelle from parents who have always lived in Northampton. They too dream of escape: Derek and Tim live for their music, Michelle would like to be a journalist; but in the meantime, they fill those work vacancies which the service economy offers in such casual and ill-paid profusion. 'I've been a jack of all trades, mostly aimless jobs. Meat-packing. It's a loathsome place. They told me I was an intelligent lad, and shouldn't be employed on the factory floor doing a run-of-the-mill job. My heart lifted. It transpired that the destiny they had in mind for me was chopping up cheese in a fridge. I had to wear a space-suit costume for hygiene and to keep the product fresh. It didn't matter about me: the cheese had to be chilled, therefore so did I. I could see the prospect of a life's career. What could I say at the end of it, in my lifetime, if the cheese I had chopped were laid end to end, it would go three times to the moon.'

'I was working at a hairdresser's, getting £25 a week as a junior,' says Tim. 'Then I became a perming technician; they have these elaborate names for quite simple operations – it creates hierarchies and statuses in what is basically child's play. I was a perming technician for two years. Perming people's hair all day, and they would look at themselves in the mirror as if you weren't there, £45 a week. You wanted to say to them, "Why bother, it isn't worth it, you're quite a nice old dear, don't waste your money." I'm still doing it now to supplement the dole, moonlighting. I mean, the cost of a hair-do is about £8; it might take 45 minutes. I'd get £1 of that and the rest goes into the employer's pocket. I'm not going to be ripped off like that.'

Derek 'dossed around for a few months' when he left school. 'I wanted to go to catering college, but I was offered painting and decorating. A lot of my mates are now chefs. Mind you, what they tell you about the posh restaurants. My mate cut his finger and it bled into the soup; so the people were drinking blood-flavoured soup. It could turn them into vampires if they got a taste for it. Then I saw a job advertised in a department store. It was supposed to be art display for the windows. Very nice. Self-expression, you know, dead twigs and coloured leaves to tell people it's autumn, a bit of tinsel for Christmas, polystyrene dolls with sunglasses for summer, real artistic. Anyway, when I got there, I was thrown at the back of the building which was where all the lorries unloaded. I had to count the boxes of merchandise coming in, do the dockets. Then I was promoted. I became a security person. Power. I had to check the handbags of all the workers as they came in and went out, make sure they hadn't nicked anything, because apparently the big stores lose as much from staff pilfering as they do from shoplifters crazed for merchandise. You can't blame them, they pay the workers such awful wages, people think nicking is part of the perks ...Anyway, that makes you feel very self-important. You got respect from people that way. Certain bags you didn't check; as a matter of fact, I never checked any of them. I never saw anything that had been nicked. It was hardly art-work, which was what I'd been paid to do. At the end of the day, I had the privilege of cleaning up, emptying the dustbins from the café. That's really fulfilling, half-eaten chips and cream cakes, lots of gunge. Then you had first choice of all the foodstuffs after the eat-by date had expired; a bit of food poisoning, but you don't die of it.

'Then I left and worked in a sweat-shop. I liked that, I liked the people I worked with. They were nearly all women there. A lot of them had two jobs, they needed them to make a living wage, one in the morning, one at night. They came in exhausted. You could tell they were killing themselves, sweat-shop by day, cleaning by night, they might earn £85 for the two if they were lucky; then they had to pay somebody to look after their kids when they came home, it was cruel. The boss was a slave-driver. I used to have to answer the phones to people who were demanding money, threatening to bring the police in. But it was a good experience. It actually teaches you that when you go into the shops to buy clothes, lovely dress, smart trousers, you know who's made them and what they've been paid, and what the profit is – you never look at them with the same eyes again. This is what the leisure society depends on – people working their heart out behind the scenes, so everybody else can put themselves into a good image and have a good time.

'It was strange working with women. I was the only bloke there. I felt a bit funny at first, but I've got a sewing machine at home, I knew what to do straightaway. The women thought it was a bit weird, a man doing what was seen as a woman's job.'

Michelle says: 'I've been working, because I'm studying at the moment. They take on students in the meat factory because they can get them cheap. I'm packing sandwiches in boxes. We have to work in refrigerated conditions so it doesn't get contaminated. You have to have a medical before you're allowed to handle food. They should do laboratory tests on the food, the rubbish that goes into it. You have to take samples of just about everything before you can work there, they check your hands, your skin, your ears, make sure you're not going to drip anything nasty into their tasty fillings. The irony is, you go in healthy, but you come out with all kinds of coughs and colds because of the change in temperature. You can be allergic to all the preservatives that go into it, bring you out in rashes.'

And Ian: 'People in general think you have no right to throw a job away when there's so many millions out of work. You ought to be grateful. It's an insult actually. The view of the service economy from underneath looks very different. All these people who own the companies have big houses, couple of cars, how do they know what it's like for the people who go scavenging round the dustbins at the back for what they've thrown away? I've got a job in a garage. I'm supposed to be on the dole. That's using my initiative, right? I'd disguise myself, but there's no need, if the bloke from the dole office sees me, he'll never know, to him all blacks are the same.'

Everything about the hamburger restaurant on the High Street suggests innocent enjoyment. A pure white light shines out from the windows onto a murky dusk, and an illuminated panel displays the tempting food – 99p for a quarter pounder, 34p french fries, 53p for a triple-thick milk shake. Inside, there are hanging baskets, wall paintings, a garden of winter cherry and ivy in a buff ceramic trough. A bright blend of colours in the decor – orange, lemon, olive – in the tiles; a red lid swings over the waste disposal chute.

Marie worked here for two years, behind the stainless silver-coloured counter, in a livery that evokes nostalgia for high-quality, old-fashioned butcher's shops: striped overalls and straw hats. For eight months, she kept the tables clean, wiping endlessly; she has an over-developed muscle in her right arm to prove it.

There are two peaks in the evening's business: just after school, the younger children are brought in by their parents. 'There was one women and she came in every single night. She said her little boy wouldn't eat anything else.' Later in the evening, the young adults take over; going there to be seen in their immaculate clothes, as though completing a tableau of perfection, with their energy and youth and innocence.

The hamburger has rapidly become staple fare for a whole generation. Its unvarying texture and taste, assured by stabilizers and preservatives, mean that kids get easily hooked. McDonalds is the world's largest fast-food chain, with global sales of over £11 billion a year. The target number of outlets in Britain is 1,000.

But beneath the aura of shining purity and cleanliness, there is another story. The political implications of the hamburger go wide and deep. For one thing, the production of beef on the scale required accelerates the consumption of grain by cattle, grain that could be fed to hungry human beings. It is well known that the production of one calorie of beef requires ten calories of grain; the animals themselves are a kind of inefficient food-processing machine.

The rising demand for beef for this characteristically American food (which in fact has its origins in the steak tartar of medieval Russia) means that great concentrations of beef-ranching are required. Much of this occupies land in central America which formerly supported subsistence farmers. Ranching contributes to the money economy of many poor countries, but provides nothing in the way of food for local consumption. Furthermore, the individual throwaway packaging, the cardboard, papier mâché and paper not only diminishes the jobs available, but intensifies pressure on the world's vanishing forests. The discarded containers are a further charge on public authorities who have to clean the streets, although Marie's branch did employ youngsters on 'clearance patrol' in the immediate vicinity of the branch.

It has been argued that fast-food chains are areas of job growth. This is true; but they employ young people at low wages, often part-time, with few long-term prospects. Few can expect to become graduates of Hamburger University, 20 miles from O'Hare airport in Chicago, where they might learn the vital lesson that hamburgers are not sold, but served. In this way, the wider implications are easily camouflaged. Market demand takes precedence over everything, and the damage that might be involved is easily conjured out of sight. The hamburger is a paradigm of much in the leisure society, where a large proportion of the real cost doesn't appear in the cover price, but is paid elsewhere, by the powerless and dispossessed, in distant places and at other times than at the brief and easily forgotten moment of consumption – by the low-paid, non-union labour, by displaced subsistence farmers and, in so far as grain is diverted from human consumption, the very starving of the earth. In such a context, the candour and innocence of the fast-food chains take on a more sinister aspect; and the choices and freedoms afforded by the leisure society are transformed.

'Freedom of choice' sounds like a rallying cry, one of the sure trumpet-calls in an uncertain world. But if our choices are made in a vacuum, then the absolute quality claimed for such freedom is seriously impaired. To be more precise: if we do not know who has suffered in the production of the most trivial commodities (and the decay of manufacturing industry in Britain can only make the dissociation easier) – fashions from the sweat-shops of Asia or from ill-paid homeworkers in South London, a tasty dish of scampi in our favourite restaurant made from prawns caught by factory ships that have pauperized half a million fishing families in Kerala or exotic fruits and vegetables from irrigated enclaves in the parched regions of sub-Saharan Africa – how can we judge what our choices mean?

Who or what permits us to detach each purchase from its significance for the destiny of others? What does the fabulous jojoba nut that enriches our shampoo mean to the economy of Brazil? Who will go hungry for the sake of the pyramids of petfood in the supermarket? For how long will a country like Kenya have to import the maize in which it was recently self-sufficient, in order to go on exporting flowers and *Asparagus plumosus* to Europe for those easy Interflora sprays that bring such delight to absent loved ones?

The practical unconcern about who else really pays for what we buy, in what coin, under what circumstances of life, and on whose terms, actually invalidates the cherished notion of adults freely choosing. It is more like the sheltered world of certain versions of childhood, in which the knowledge of sin or death may not enter. And nowhere is this relationship more apparent than in the food industry.

Because cooking has always been part of the traditional drudgery of women, it is often said in defence of convenience foods that they release women from pointless and repetitive labour for which they are not paid. Women, especially, it is argued, have been delivered of this chore, and given the chance to lead their own lives. But, of course, there is no reason why women should continue to be the main preparers of food. And in any case, that freedom depends upon so many suppressed connections, not least the relationship with those (themselves more often than not women) who labour in, for instance, the pineapple plantations in the Philippines for that easy can of fruit or on the tea estates of Sri Lanka for the sake of that restoring cuppa that makes you feel human again. Indeed, the ironies go even further. The hamburger and fast-food chains which supply such appetizing meals for kids have also become one of the main 'pioneers' in the recruitment of new forms of cheap young labour. 'It's 150,000 kids busting their tails out there that makes us tick', a director of McDonalds has been quoted as saying. Fast food, as Maria says, means slow money; and one person's leisure means the oppression, even the enslavement, of another.

Frank and Sharon are in their mid-twenties. Sharon has two children from a previous marriage, Toni and Michelle. Their own child is six months old. Michelle, who is two, has never seen electric light in her own home. All she knows is the single butane flare which lights one corner of the living room, and the candles which light them to bed and to the lavatory in the yard. Bedtime for the three children is a time of shadows: the flickering candle-light dancing in the draughts up the echoing staircase. Nightmares and bedwetting only add to the substantial burden of being poor.

Frank hasn't worked for four years. Today, he is preparing for Karen's christening. The poor have always clung to ceremony and celebration to mark the important events in their lives, which have scant recognition from outside. This is perhaps even more true now, when so many of the poor are without paid occupation, in the formless and meandering flow of time. Perhaps this is why you always see the first Christmas trees on the poor estates from about mid-November; the big limousines and the massed flowers forming Mam or Dad on the funeral cortège.

Frank is putting the finishing touches to the party. He has been baking: cheese shapes, rock cakes with icing, all laid out on the rickety melamine table, with some clingfilm to keep it fresh; fishpaste sandwiches, cheese on cocktail sticks, a dish of tomatoes; a little pile of plates. Frank is taping a piece of pasteboard over the living room door, one of the panels of which is missing, and re-hanging a portrait of Elvis. The threadbare brindled carpet is clean; two green velvet covers have been made for the seats of the plastic chairs with a remnant bought on the market two days before. The three-piece, which dates from the 1930s, has been pushed against the wall to make more space in the room.

The older girls appear in their new outfits: green check skirts with pinafore tops and blouses; all made out of an old dress of Sharon's by Frank. Sharon is wearing a plain turquoise dress she got at a jumble sale. She was anxious about the christening. 'I was on, and the blood was clotting. I thought I'd have to go into hospital, but fortunately it stopped yesterday. My Mum and Dad wanted me to postpone it till they could get here from Norfolk, but we'd booked the church.' Frank says 'My Mum has made us a cake'; a blue and white square cake with white loops and rosettes, and the name of the baby – Karen Christina – in pink. 'She charged me £3 for the ingredients. She said she might look in later. I don't expect she will.'

It is a wet afternoon. The rain is bouncing great silver darts in the gutter; the sky uniform inky grey. Chrissie and her husband are coming in their car – an F-registration Anglia – to take Sharon and the little ones to the church. The rest of us will walk; only ten minutes, but far enough to get drenched. Frank has a waistcoat and jacket of a striped brown suit, brown trousers that almost match and a brown, knitted tie. Sharon changes Karen into her christening clothes: a long dress with a lacy, scalloped bottom and ruched top; an elongated white christening cap that makes her look like an elf.

We walked through the deserted streets of the town centre; the houses, some boarded up, the factories on the street corners with 'to let' signs, the car park with broken beer bottles and dented soft drink cans strewn over the surface; the fire station, the new office building in its skeleton of scaffolding. Into the churchyard, bright green in the wet afternoon. Some builders' rubble, a pile of grey stone from the restoration of the building. In the porch, we sit on the stone benches facing each other, and wait for those who have come by car. Frank rolls a cigarette. The rain cascades down the shiny bitumen path.

There are no other children to be christened this afternoon. The chairs are set in a circle within the round of the thick Norman pillars, with their serrated stone decoration. The water is dripping through the church roof where the lead has been stripped, and it splashes onto the dull red and gold fleur-de-lis paving. Chrissie's husband drops off his wife, Sharon, the baby and the other children. He was to have been the other godparent, but he doesn't like going into churches. They make him feel uncomfortable. Chrissie says he wouldn't even go to his mother's funeral. It gives him the creeps. He says he will pick them up in about three-quarters of an hour.

The children, awed for a few minutes by the dim, cavernous church, shuffle awkwardly. But they soon get used to it and start chasing each other round the chairs. They have never had to sit still in the presence of anything so solemn; and they don't like it. There are four children present as well as the baby, the godparents and the children's mother and father. There is a delay, as we wait for Toni's schoolteacher who has promised to come. She arrives with her husband, just in time; a warm, kindly woman in her fifties. Her umbrella drips onto the dusty floor, making clean patches. The vicar gives out cards, with the order of service. The ceremony is very brief: it is all over within 12 minutes; the voices are lost in the oppressive atmosphere. The church is chill and dark. The baby is very good; she has been given a few drops of what Sharon calls 'cordial' to keep her calm. The water is splashed onto the child's head. She doesn't cry. The vicar apologizes for the weather.

Then it is all over. The teacher and her husband are invited back to the house for a sherry and a sandwich. We don't want to intrude. You won't be intruding. There's nobody else expected. The teacher takes Frank and the children back to the house. The rest of us – Sharon, Chrissie and I – wait for Chrissie's husband. He said three-quarters of an hour. That was only 20 minutes ago. We stand under the porch in the teeming rain. Something is not quite complete. 'I thought there'd be others.' 'Short and sweet wasn't it.' 'Being the Bank Holiday weekend, I expect.' The water swirls down the path; our feet are wet. 'We can't start walking, we don't know which way the car will come.' 'I've never been a godmother before', says Chrissie. 'What do you have to do?' 'Keep them on the straight and narrow.' Sharon says 'Well Tina's godmother hasn't done that for Tina; she's gone off it herself. And Michelle, her godparents won't have anything to do with us, because they didn't approve of me marrying Frank.' 'I think that's horrible. It's the kids they stand for, not the parents.' 'And the other one, she doesn't seem interested. I don't think I've seen her since the christening.'

Chrissie says she was a Methodist; she preferred the way it was done in chapel. She has six children, the eldest 18. He hasn't worked since he left school. They're having a birthday party for him. Her husband doesn't work, officially; a bit on the quiet for a catering firm. Instead of paying him, the firm is giving him £150-worth of buffet for the birthday. Michelle wants to wee. 'There's nobody about, go in the churchyard.' She won't, because of the gravestones. Sharon takes her into the gutter, where the water soon washes it away. By the time the car comes, almost an hour has passed. Everyone is wet and cold. We go back to the house. The children fall to on the good things. The single bottle of sherry is soon used up. There is a bottle of Pomagne. The cake is cut; everybody takes a piece and toasts the new baby. Frank and Sharon are pleased that the whole event cost less than £10; and they are surprised at how many things they were able to provide for themselves.

The strange death of Labour Britain   In the old-fashioned barber's shop on the edge of the vast enclosure of the British Rail Engineering Works in Swindon, the talk is now of the past: 150 years after the founding of the Great Western Railway, the works which once employed 14,000 people are now closed; only a few hundred are still employed in the spring shop and brass foundry.

Barbers' shops have always been places of all-male candour, where even the reticent skilled workers could let themselves go a little. They recall now the complex feelings of pride and humiliation in working for GWR ('God's Wonderful Railway'). The hairdresser himself tells how his grandfather's family came to Swindon after the Irish potato famine and found him work at the age of 12 in the trimming-shop; later, as foreman, when he took his family on the works' annual trip, he would permit them to ride only in the carriage that he and his gang had made. The older men remember the boys emloyed to call up the engine drivers at 2 or 3 o'clock in the morning, the foremen in their bowler hats who had the power to hire and fire, the military-style discipline in the sheds. 'You weren't allowed to have tea in the foundry. The men used to boil up in a tin can. The foreman would come by, and he'd stand there and watch it boil. Nobody dared move. He'd wait till the water boiled dry and the bottom fell out of the tin. Then he'd walk on.' They evoke forgotten skills – the boilermakers who always carried a sledgehammer and ate raw onions, deaf by the age of 30 from the sound of rivetting inside the boilers. 'The men who operated the steam-hammers, 15 tons of pressure, they could place a watch beneath the hammer, manipulate the lever so it came crashing down and stopped within a fraction of an inch from the watch.' They tell the story of the engine driver who went to India in the Second World War and raised the status of a princess by marrying her; they laugh at the apprentices who were sent for a bucket of steam on their first day, the initiation-rite into that tough male society where the skills acquired assured a Swindon-trained man a job on the railways anywhere in the world.

From the dingy, cramped office of the Works Defence Committee, with its battered chairs and tables, filing cabinets full of dusty minutes of distant union meetings, you can look out over the sheds with their heavy cranes, pounding presses, their half-assembled locomotives in high, glass-roofed halls cold as neglected cathedrals. The Works Defence Committee, in spite of all the energies that went into the (unsuccessful) campaign to preserve the skills which made Swindon prosperous, still found time to distribute the Christmas charity money that the unions collect each year: £200 to two old people's homes, £50 to a charity for the terminally ill, money for spastics, to Age Concern, for spina bifida and the hydrotherapy pool. The NUR tote will pay £9 to every retired worker this Christmas. There is a bereavement scheme which pays £300 to the family of any worker who dies. They have run a St John's Ambulance branch that covered every sporting event in town. This aspect of trade union work – and the members of the Works Defence Committee helped individuals with matrimonial, housing and welfare advice – has been a resource that served the whole community, one seldom perceived by outsiders and uncelebrated by those who are at such pains to represent the unions as wreckers. 'This is where you see the humanity and decency of the organized working class,' says Derek Rees, 'it's one of the few resistances to Thatcher's vision of Britain – a museum protected by missiles and fed by MacDonalds. What a future.'

And Swindon does illuminate the abrupt transition from manufacture to service with a starkness seen in few other places in Britain. The BREL works, the perfectly reserved model village built by the GWR in the 1840s of Bath and Costwold stone, each neat terrace ending in an imposing three-story foreman's house, the rambling Mechanics' Institute which once had a library of 40,000 books, the Medical Centre (4d a week for comprehensive medical care: one of the models to inspire Aneurin Bevan when he set up the National Health Service), the church with its ornate tombstones to diligent servants of the company – all this is reflected in the tinted glass cubes and bright metal of the new structures which house the oil and insurance companies, the retailing and distribution centres that have made Swindon one of the fastest-growing towns in Europe.

Dennis Keen, now 60, sits in the Works Committee Room, reading *The Times*; a big man with a strong local accent that shows his country origins. He started work as an apprentice boilermaker at 14. He remembers how his father used to cycle the seven miles to the works each day; and he had to eke out his wages by helping the farmer at haytime and harvest – a shilling a day and weak beer. 'I can see our mother at the window of our cottage, waiting for the light from his carbide lamp as he turned into the lane; she could never settle till he got home of an evening. We had to fetch every drop of water from the well; and he had to empty the family midden every week. He worked for years with asbestos, lining the boilers. He died of lung disease before anybody dreamed there was any connection; I can picture him now, breathing his last in an oxygen tent . . . The GWR used to have a purge twice a year. Father'd come home and say "So-and-so's got the sack"; but he knew he could feel a bit more secure till the next time came round.'

The GWR was both paternalistic and highly disciplined. Those who see the Japanese corporations as embodying practices alien to Britain might reflect on the GWR which, in the 1840s, literally enfolded its workers within a 16ft high wall, and overwhelmed them with a mixture of work and welfare; moulded the country people of Wiltshire to the new and unfamiliar rhythms of industrial production. There has been little tradition of militancy in Swindon; indeed, even during the years of decline, the workers have cooperated with all the plans for rationalization and re-organization, with the promise that this would guarantee continued operations. Now, after six generations of continuous production, the finest railway engineering in the world, it is not surprising that so many people are shocked and upset by the closure. For them, it is as if the identity of the town were being erased.

The works were a place apart; so much so, that the expression in Swindon was 'Are you inside?' 'If you didn't work inside, you didn't work.' The members of the Works Defence Committee insist that their fight hasn't been about nostalgia. 'Once these skills have been wiped out, they're gone for ever. Apart from the case for railways in the West, the Third World needs our expertise. A proper railway service in Sudan and Ethiopia would have saved millions from famine. Then, look at the new companies coming into the town. They offer no apprenticeships, they're not teaching our young people anything. Ours is the same argument as the miners: our people were at school together, they went through the war together, they worked together for a lifetime and comforted each other's families in death. What is the purpose of the economy – to serve us or to drive us?'

The pain behind these questions is palpable, yet so is the humour that weaves in and out of their speech. One man recalls the annual GWR flower show. 'I always used to win. I'd go down to the greengrocer's on the morning of the show and buy a couple of pounds of best carrots. There was one chap, used to feed his marrows on sugared water, it blew them up like balloons.' Then the mood changes again. 'There's some of the men, I've known them all my life; never knew their names, because you called them "brother"; and you meant it.' 'After 40 years here you leave with a gold watch and a double hernia; that was their gift to the workers.'

The works were extraordinarily self-sufficient. There was a laundry;

they made their own soap. There were apprenticeships in wood-carving, even in book-binding – for the great leather ledgers in which every misdemeanour, every late arrival, was entered in copperplate handwriting. The company had its own musical adviser for the bands and the annual eisteddfod; it operated a building society with loans at 5 per cent. The GWR owned its own forests in Oregon for the sleepers. And the works could produce anything. 'If you could draw it, we could make it.' 'The only thing they needed from outside was horse shit. They used that for casting the bells – the casting had to cool at a certain rate, and the most effective thing was horse shit. They do it with sophisticated glues now.'

As you walk through the depleted sheds, one of the most conspicuous features of each shop is the war memorial: a wooden tablet with an inscription 'To those who answered their country's call', and the names of those who died. There is bitterness when the men talk of their patriotism, and how different their love of England is from Tory jingoism. 'We're the true patriots, the people who create the wealth, those who use their skills to make things that are beautiful and useful; not those who can't wait to get their money out of the country where they can make even more with it. They don't owe their allegiance to Britain, they owe it to money, the dollar or the yen; that's the only patriotism they know.'

Bill Sargeant is now 81. He joined the GWR at 16, and was paid £45 a year. 'At 18, you went to sit an exam and be interviewed at Paddington. The only question they asked me was how many stations there were between Swindon and Paddington, and I could reel them off. I started in an office with 60 people, at Dickensian desks, on high stools. Only the overseer had padding on his stool. Clerical workers were taught to regard the workers as a breed beneath them. If you earned 46 shillings a week, your son had the right to be apprenticed to the same job as you – fitter, turner; if you earned 44 shillings your son could only take a lower apprenticeship – painter, trimmer, plumber; if you earned less than 44 shillings he'd get taken on, but only as a general labourer.'

'Of course the GWR never made great profits towards the end; the only way they could pay $2\frac{1}{2}$ per cent dividend was by closing the works for three weeks every summer, save on wages. The foremen were tyrants – you had to bribe them with vegetables from your allotment or eggs from your own fowls. If a new foreman or chief clerk was appointed, people would even change their religion to be seen by him at chapel or church … The company provided free whitewash to its employees, to clean out their lavatories, keep us free of fever. They had their own hearse for funerals; there was a swimming-bath with water heated from the boilers in the central power station in the works. They even had their own water supply – it tasted different from the water outside. But they worked you! A

fireman working on the Cornish Express, Paddington to Penzance would
shovel 4½ tons of coal on that journey. There was scarcely a railway in the
world that didn't have a representative of the GWR help in its construction. I once went to be interviewed for a job in Dar es Salaam. They
said "We understand you have rather liberal views." I said, "Yes, that is so."
"Well, let it be clearly understood that liberal views are not applicable. The
only way to get niggers to work is to kick their arses." I declined the job.'

At midday in the ornate Great Western Hotel, two men of 30, who have
known each other all their lives, meet for a drink. Dave Rees has worked
with BREL since he left school. He speaks with passion of the value of
work as a result of which there is a product that is clearly useful. His
friend, Steve, does not disagree. Steve is part of the new Swindon: he has
worked in catering and retailing, often on temporary contracts and on a
casual basis; was dismissed from one job and replaced by a school-leaver at
a lower rate of pay. He is now in an insurance company, handling the
general ledger, checking and validating computer print-outs. 'What's your
end product?' asks Dave. 'Profit. But not for me – I'm on £90 a week.'

Here you can actually feel the painful process of the workforce being
reshaped following the needs of a changed international division of labour;
it is a harsh, even violent, experience; much the same as that which transformed the agricultural labourers into servants of the GWR. Dave says 'If
anybody thinks we're doing the next generation a favour by knocking the
skills out of their hands, they couldn't be more wrong.'

At Paddington station there is a booth set up by British Rail, selling
objects to commemorate the 150 years of GWR: hand-painted pottery,
maps and pictures, prints and models of engines – an emblem of a Britain
that will soon be able to visit its manufacturing past only through relics,
reproduction and museums.

. . . and its reappearance in fantasy   In the community centre where the
railway club meets, the Christmas decorations are still in place, although it
is well into January. A few members have agreed to meet me to talk of their
passion for railways: all have different and specialized interests. 'I'm called
a kettle because I'm only interested in steam.' Ken is interested primarily
in making models of the engines; John is devoted to the Tal-y-llyn Railway;
Trevor prefers narrow-gauge railways. Everyone has a strong sense of his
own expertise: a feeling of control over a field of knowledge which distin-
guishes him, sets him apart: this gives their interest a strong *sectarian* feel.

'The Great Western Railway that everybody goes on about, it leaves me
cold. It was a cock-up from the start.'

'No it wasn't. The GWR engines were always looked after, clean,
polished up. The Midland used rusty old engines, there is no comparison.'

'As a boy I collected numbers. A steam-engine is a machine that breathes. Diesel are different – you just press a button and go. Steam depends on the driver, it's human beings interacting with the machine.'

'The history of the railways is our industrial history. The magic of the Golden Arrow, the charisma of the trains that went across the Continent.'

'That's why I like the Welsh narrow-gauge. They're something to ride on, but at the same time, you're aware they did a job. They were made for carrying slate to the coast; all that slate that became the roofs of the houses in the industrial towns. It brings alive the way people lived . . . In the early days, men were taken to work in the quarries in coaches without doors or windows. Whenever I go to a railway, I say "What's that doing there? Why was it built?" All the feedings in North Wales lead to the works. It reminds you of the days when they blasted with dynamite – if a few navvies got killed, give sixpence to the widow if she was lucky. . . .'

'If you are interested in the railways of a particular place, you can build models with all the relevant scenery, every individual stone or brick build-ing. People create absolutely authentic reconstructions of particular places – maybe Bletchley stations and engine-sheds. Models can be cheap or expensive – you can buy a model engine for anything from about £7 to about £5,000; it depends upon the degree of sophistication you want and working detail. Model railways in Britain aren't as good as the continental stuff, not a patch on the German manufacturers; but then the Germans have the whole continental market.'

'People like me concentrate on a particular railway, Tal-y-llyn. It's been going for 25 years, has about 3,000 members, who do all the work for it. Tywyn is the station, near Barmouth, opened in the 1860s, closed in 1947. Its gauge is only 2ft 3in. It's 7¼ miles, runs from Easter till October. It has five steam locos, the oldest from 1864. The maximum speed is 15 mph. The society has relaid the whole line, rebuilding and extending it. You can help in the shops, signalling, track-laying – it depends on the volunteers. Most have just enough permanent staff to keep them going, then use volunteers in the peak season – there are about 170,000 passengers in the summer months. It has to be strictly run, with a timetable. The Severn Valley Railway is run to the BR rule-book. It's a very serious business. They have to be maintained to a high standard of engineering. They can't take money from passengers unless they have a licence from the DoE Railway Inspectorate.'

'Severn Valley don't own any engines: they're owned by individuals or societies, then they put the engines at the disposal of the railway lines.'

'Even the smallest preservation groups have to become limited com-panies in case of an accident.'

'The Tal-y-llyn Preservation Society owns the railway outright. When the railways were nationalized, Tal-y-llyn was left out, as if completely forgotten. Some enthusiasts talked to the owner about taking it over. He died, and his widow said she wouldn't know what to do with it, said Go away and do it.'

'The Society of Model Engineers build locos from scratch – a full-scale plan; model engineering is a real skill; they have to submit to boiler tests and steam tests.'

'Train spotters, well that's not adult really, although adults do it. They're like little boys, get special passes to go into the sheds to collect numbers, just write the numbers down. Kids have always done that. I know one bloke who goes to London and sits on the Underground all day to spot Underground trains.'

'For me, it's a way of clinging to Britain's heritage. Britain is becoming a museum society. You go through parts of this country, the docks, the factories, you see it from the railways, it's all closed down, the industries that built Britain. Only sign of life is the working museum.'

'It should still be there.'

'You can recreate it all in model form. It is like trying to recapture something. I do industrial models. If the old industrial lines still existed from the factories, we'd still have the jobs, wouldn't we? I was speaking to an old boy in the crossing keeper's hut, he followed his Dad's job. People were secure. They might not have been all that well-paid, but they knew what they were going to do.'

'In Germany, the Deutsche Bahne, if a factory is within five miles of a station, the DB lets the factory owner lay in a piece of track, then buy himself an engine so it can take his goods to the interchange siding. Small private railways are commonplace.'

'Modelling, you can buy ready-made stuff, or self-assembly or you can scratch-build. That needs patience. Model railways are bought mainly by adults today. Kids would rather have other things – they're into computers, whizzing and flashing games. It is harking back to your own childhood . . . It reflects the time you were brought up, in the heyday of the railways. Kids now would rather push a button. You can tell from the shops and the exhibitions – they are geared to adults.'

'It is an escape from reality, up to a point. You model the world the way you'd like it to be . . . Looking back, you remember the good things, and you want to recapture them. Years ago, things seemed easier, everything was in its place, you could get jobs.'

'There are two or three publishers who do nothing but railway books. Then there are records of train journeys: get a good stereo, a recording of a steam-journey, you can judge from the sound the terrain it's passing through.'

'I buy reference books, guide books, pictorial records. Some people are fascinated by time-tables. I do collect tickets as well.'

'You mustn't think there's anything simple-minded in it; it's a very detailed and complex subject. Among those here, there's an accountant, a door-to-door salesman, Trevor works in a freight-forwarding office, I'm out of work at the moment. We also contribute to the community centre here, we raise money for cancer, for the hard of hearing unit. People who love railways are, on the whole, peaceful people. It's a way of relaxing; not being bored. We go on the odd journey a year. It's industrial history, people go to places and understand why they're there. You go on learning; it attracts all kinds of people – university lecturers, academics, industrialists.'

4

The leisured poor

Time, as Illich observed, has become money; and not only as a figure of speech, but almost a synonym for it. One spends time, gives time, gives up one's time; one saves or keeps time, beats it, serves it, uses it fruitfully, squanders it, spares it. One loses time, makes it, makes it up, wastes it. Time runs out, it is consumed, it can be frittered away; and in the end there is none left. Money is the most powerful absorber of time; and this suggests that those with the least of it will be the rich; and those with plenty of time are those whose activities have been crippled by an absence of the enabling substance – that is, the poorest. If it is true that the rich are the busiest in our society, it would follow that the poor will have most leisure, especially those without work; although the word 'leisure' is perhaps not the best description of those eventless hours, which are nevertheless so charged with anxiety about survival. Nowhere is this unwelcome inactivity more shocking than in those appalled and devastated places whose entire reason for existence was the labour they were called into being to perform.

Wednesday is giro day for most people on Bramble Farm Estate in Middlesbrough, and this turns the midweek evening into a substitute weekend, the time for a drink and meeting with friends without the worry of whether you'll be able to buy your round. Not that people are ungenerous: it's just that you have to keep your pride, even through the worst rigours of unemployment. On Monday and Tuesday nights, that's when those who've got something left over, or those who get their giro earlier in the week, offer a sub to neighbours and friends. Rab and Eddy don't even mention money: if he wants to borrow a fiver, Rab rubs his nose with a crooked forefinger; if Eddy can lend him one, he returns the sign – a sort of freemasonry of poverty; if he can't, he just shakes his head. On giro day itself, there might be seven or eight people sitting round the table. Time to pay back: the fiver comes out and circulates – sometimes it can no longer be decided whose it was in the first place, so it goes into the kitty for a round of drinks. They joke 'I've found a fiver.' 'It's mine.' 'How do you know it's yours?' 'It's blue and it's got the Queen's head on it.'

On Wednesdays there is a moment of expansion – pay off the week's debts, you don't need to avoid the neighbours, go round the back way. The pubs – gabled and conspicuous buildings surrounded by a lot of asphalt on corners of the wide streets – are full; places of comfort and escape. Hit songs of yesterday on the music centre: Frankie Laine's 'Ghost Riders in the Sky', Rosemary Clooney, 'This Old House', Vic Damone. Steve has just come back from the Falklands. In his late twenties, he is a muscular man with copper-coloured hair. He had gone out on a contract, originally for 12 months, as a labourer and docker at Port Stanley, unloading materials and goods for the construction companies at work building the airport. The contract was for £10,000 a year; he came back after three months because he couldn't stand it any longer. He had to pay his own fare home because he had broken the contract. 'It's a village on a rock. You wonder what all the fuss was about, let alone fight a fucking war over it. I was keen on it at the time; I really thought it was the greatest thing this country had done in my lifetime while the war was on. But when you get to see it, Jesus.' He shows round his photographs: the stores, Tumbledown Mountain, Bluff Cove, the Hotel; places invested with the glamour and romance of war for a generation which has never experienced the cruelty of it. 'The buildings are just shacks. The sunsets are beautiful and the wild life is great, but so they are on Teeside. The novelty wears off after about a week, then there's nothing. That's when depression sets in. There's nothing but work, sleep and drink. You get pissed out of your head every night. Then people do stupid things. There were six deaths while I was there in the space of three months. Two lads killed themselves, one cut his throat and the other hanged himself. Four died: one tried to jump between two ships when he was pissed and he got drowned, another got speared by a forklift truck which somebody was driving drunk. They say even fucking the sheep is overrated.'

They were sleeping in camps; it was cold and windy. Steve would never have gone if he hadn't spent two years unemployed in Middlesbrough. 'I'd been in Germany before. That was bad enough, but at least you can go out in the cities and enjoy yourself. The terrifying thing about being in the Falklands is that it throws you back on yourself, your own resources; something you're not used to. Even if you've got the money, there's nothing to spend it on. There was one lad, his mother and father were killed in a car crash, and it took 13 days before he could come home. The only way to get sent home was to be repatriated for misconduct. So on the day before the plane was due in, the blokes used to have fights, stage them, you know, set up a scrap, so they'd get sent to England in disgrace. There'd be about 16 people fighting on a night – and you had to do it seriously, so it looked bad enough to get reprimanded and repatriated; you had to draw blood, break something. If you went back any other way, you had to pay your own fare. There were some articles in the *Sun* and the *Mirror*; they said we were having orgies and taking drugs; were we hell. I had to ring my girlfriend, she said "What the heck's going on out there?" It was all a load of lies they were telling about us. It was boring. There was danger – they haven't found all the mines the Argies laid, and some of them are still being found the hard way. And the Argies keep on probing – you hear the jets take off in the night to warn them off. I'm going to Algeria next week on a contract; at least it's a bit nearer home. I wouldn't choose to leave Middlesbrough. I was born and brought up here; but when you've no choice, you have to take the work wherever you can find it.'

Towards the weekend, the money is running out; and by Tuesday the pubs are almost empty. By soon after 10.30, even on a warm night, the streets are deserted, even though the light lingers until after eleven: a few people in shirt sleeves, the dog taken onto the green for a shit; Tuesday night supper is a few chips and a couple of sausages; there is no sauce left; the sugar ran out several days ago; salt is the only condiment in the house. The furniture is wearing thin – you can't stop the baby from playing, and that makes things deteriorate fast; they're reduced to eating off tin plates. You can feel the house getting shabbier, and you know you won't be able to replace anything. Television is a necessity; not that you watch it all the time, but it's on, even in the afternoon. That is when the programmers show their contempt for women, who are believed to be the main audience – nothing challenging or serious, just a form of tranquillizer to help you get through time. Eileen says 'I got an interview for a job. It made my week; only then I found out they were interviewing everybody, then there was to be a second interview, and only the finalists would go on to a third. It was like bloody Miss World, and it was only an office job.'

People resent Middlesbrough being portrayed as a no-hope place, full of derelicts and deadbeats. 'They talk about us as if we're all sat on our arses waiting for sommat to turn up, living between the next hand-out and whatever falls off the back of a lorry. They did a programme about us on *Panorama*. What a load of cobblers. This lad, he lives near me, he went on screen and said "We all burgle off each other, everybody's ripping everybody else off." Next morning he had the cops on his doorstep, wanting names and addresses. His Mam and Dad said "He's been misquoted"; but he said it in his own words, so I don't know how they could misquote him.'

'The trouble is, people have been told for so long that they're useless that they begin to believe it. It damages people's faith in themselves.'

It is easy enough to represent Middlesbrough as a sad, even despairing, place; and it would be wrong to underestimate the effects of poverty and idleness; but people's lives are not the sum of the weekly income; nor do most make little effort to find work. Indeed, some of the attempts have been heroic. 'You can so easily feel it as a personal failing, even when you know it's a fault in the system. If they can get you to accept it's your fault, then you're finished.' Brian was apprenticed at Smith's Dock, a shipyard due to close at the end of 1986. 'I was apprenticed as a lad for five years. I'm a boilermaker. I enjoyed my time at work; oh yes, enjoyed it. I felt I was doing something worth while. I'm not a carpenter or a decorator, I'm a boilermaker. That five years learning was my security, that was to have been a trade in my fingers for life. I can sit in the flat where I live and watch the place being run down, fall into ruin. I remember my first day there, I was sent for a bucket of steam, like all apprentices; I learnt all I knew from the blokes there; you grow close to them, it's relationships and feelings.' He was made redundant in 1980. 'I got on my bike, I went to Wakefield where my father was living; and had a job there in an engineering company for two years till that went bust as well. While I was there, the Ripper murder investigation was going on. I was picked up by the police; they quizzed me for hours, because he was supposed to have had a Geordie accent. I said "I'm not a Geordie, I'm from Middlesbrough." That was too subtle for them. I said "I've come here to work, not to attack women, because the fucking work packed up in Middlesbrough." In the end, you don't know if you're telling the truth or not.' Brian came back to Middlesbrough and lived with his mother in her flat; only there was still no work and they began to get on each other's nerves. He now has a single person's flat in a reconditioned block of 1960s dwellings that have been gutted and rebuilt. At the entrance to the flats there is an intercom and a close circuit TV camera, so that people can see from their TV screen who is knocking at the door, 'whether it's somebody come to knife you or the man with a cheque from the Pools.' Brian visits his mother every day, runs her messages for her. 'Then I come down here in the middle of the day, have a pint, make it last. I wake up at five in the morning, by the time I've been to see Mam and the Bramble opens, half my day's over. I sit here till three, have a bite to eat, get my head down in the afternoon, wake up at six, have a wash, look at the paper, come back here half past seven, make another pint last till ten. Then I go to bed at eleven, only I'm not tired, so I'm awake again at five.'

Brian doubts that he will work again; from the day he was born, he says, he knew it was his destiny to work. He is not yet 50, but looks older, balding, with short grey hair, slightly stooped. People who were formed for labour in shipyards and steelworks, whose physical strength was the only attribute the market required of them, are now being told in mid-life to train for leisure. They see it, not as an opportunity, but as an insult. 'Your character is formed when you're a kid. We didn't need to be told we were born to work, it was in the air you breathed like the smoke from the bloody chimneys.'

A sense of waste hangs over these places, where there is no longer any getting up in the early morning; the curtains remain closed till ten or eleven, and the lights burn sometimes until dawn in the summer mornings. People talk of disorientation with time, nightmares, disrupted bodyrhythms. But the sense of waste doesn't stop there: even when people were working, the work for many involved not the cultivation of their intelligence and abilities but the most rigorous repression of these things. Survival has always meant the sacrifice of developing your tastes or your understanding or your mind.

But the mind and the understanding of people get developed just the same: the wisdom, the humour and the resilience of people are some of the joys and consolations of these poor working-class communities. This is not in any way to say that poverty and unemployment are in any way good things: it is simply that both work and the lack of it deny and limit people in different ways.

Rab came to Middlesbrough in 1974; this town that was called by Gladstone 'the infant Hercules', as a Victorian boom-town built on iron ore, with its docks, and its proximity to Northern Europe still visible in the German church and the Danish Vice-Consulate and the Swedish seamen's mission. The remaining redbrick Victorian warehouses and tall, narrow factories, eaten by ancient acid and grime, now to let, and in flower with willowherb and hawkweed growing out of the stones, make it hard to believe that it was still a place of migration and hope to those who came from more derelict areas in the 1960s and 1970s. Rab came from Paisley. He jokes 'I was going to Musselbrough, but I fell asleep on the train and woke up in Middlesbrough.' He worked in the shipyard, then at the British Steel rolling mill, then at Smith's Dock, then continuous casting at British Steel. 'I finished up with a job at a firm of industrial cleaners at £1.70 an hour. That was after the rot had set in. I'm 49 now, my chest has gone, I've chronic bronchitis. I've got a free bus pass, like a senior citizen. At 49, I've 16 years of work left in me, but I doubt I'll do them.' He is a smart man, sports coat and tie, grey trousers, receding hair, gingery moustache. 'I could run the Social Security offices for a start, with more efficiency and compassion. I uprooted myself from Paisley. Do you think that was a pleasure? I left behind my wife and three children because there was nowhere down here for them to live. You can't keep up a marriage by remote-control – it broke up. I came here for the money, not the fresh air;

that's what the world turns on. We're all capitalists at heart. You must have a top dog. If there were no bosses, somebody would pretty soon become one. There's no society, Aztecs, Eskimos, tribal societies, that doesn't have a head; and they're always the richest. In the same way that there's always a bellwether in a flock of sheep; if one cow gets up and moves, the rest will follow.' 'But we're not animals.' 'You can argue about that. Look at what human beings have done to each other in the twentieth century.'

'My old man voted Labour, that's how I got interested in politics. I'm a working man' – and then with sudden melancholy – 'perhaps I should say I *was* a working man. The Tories have never done anything for me; I didn't enjoy their work or their leisure. Though it was Wilson who said we needed half a million unemployed. I volunteered, and regretted it. I was apprenticed as a green sand moulder in an iron foundry, but I left after 15 months. I made the classic blunder – I left a job as an apprentice with minuscule wages to go to a higher-paid but dead-end job. I was 16 or 17, I saw my wage go up from £2 to £5, 150 per cent pay rise. I went labouring on a building site for 3/8d an hour.

'You remember your first wages. You remember how any amount of money seems a lot when you've never earned before; and how little it really is when you have to start living off it. That's the basic truth that government schemes have been built on. You can persuade kids to price themselves into jobs when they're living at home, subsidized by their parents. It's only when they come to start a family, look for somewhere to live that they realize they've been conned. The big baby boom of the sixties is just reaching that stage. There's gonna be a lot of angry young people. That's why Maggie Thatcher has been giving the police the weapons of death; she knows what's coming.

'That's how I finished up unskilled. Unskilled labourer, though I'm far from stupid. I've been in bed all day today. Lying in bed reading. I'm lucky: I can occupy myself. I got up this evening at half past seven. Mind you, I was out last night till three, with a woman friend. Tomorrow I shall be up at five. There's no rhythm in your life. They say we have to be flexible for the new jobs that are coming; well, what could be more flexible than getting up and going to bed at the same time on two consecutive days.

'There's a Russian proverb which says a pessimist says things are bad, will stay bad and may get worse; an optimist says things were bad in the past, bad in the present and can't get any worse.' Somebody counters with a quote from Oscar Wilde to the effect that an optimist says this is the best of all possible worlds, and a pessimist believes it.

Dave, much younger than Rab, also came down from Scotland. He says 'The first job I had was in Kilmarnock Bus Station. I had to sign the

Official Secrets Act. That was to promise you wouldn't tell anybody the times of the fucking buses.' Rab also had to sign the Official Secrets Act, 'When I was working in the shipyard subcontracting to Yarrow's on MOD work. The biggest official secret, you know what it is? It's that there's nothing we've got that they don't know.

'Teeside now, it's like Paisley was when I left it 12 years ago. There were so many things they used to make there, Robertson's jam, McRae and Drew, they did all the seating for the car industry; there was Coates Thread, the Anchor Thread Mill. You can still buy the products, but they're not made where they were. All these companies that close down in Britain, they're still alive and kicking in the world. The thread company went to Elizabeth in New Jersey; a lot of people from Paisley went with it. And the shipyard built the best dredgers in the world. Well, I uprooted myself then; I can't do it all over again.'

What emerges from these working-class towns is not the official story of British stability and continuity, the history of a peaceable island race: the memories are of migrations and upheavals, people parted by the ship to New Zealand, the voyage of hope to North America, the move down South, the walk to London in the thirties; and the echoes of this are still there, in the young people returning from London after they have spent six weeks living rough, going on the streets in despair; in the postcards from Riyadh, the temporary contracts, the endless displacement and reluctant mobility. 'There's nothing civilized about it; it's primitive and it's barbaric. I can remember the day I came to Middlesbrough. It was a Saturday afternoon, Scotland beat England, 2–0. I got off the train. First bloke I saw, "Where can I get a job straight away?" "There's ICI, British Steel." "Will I be able to start Monday?" "No, you'll have to fill forms in." That was no good to me, I had to start right away, I'd no money to take me beyond the weekend. I got a job on a Scotch derrick, a Montower crane. I'd only been here a couple of days, I bumped into Wally Reeves. He'd been here 15 years, and had grown up in Paisley round the corner from me. And he was with Jimmy Kendry, whose house I used to go into as a kid – he'd been here 30 years. I didn't know either of them was here.'

Rab is living in a bed-and-breakfast hotel: a functional kitchen with second-hand furniture, comfortless, £40 a week. Rab is on invalidity benefit, which leaves him £25 a week for everything else – 'meals and all those sort of luxuries the unemployed live on'. 'I put 50 pence on the horses. Occasionally I win. Once I got £120; more often than not if I win, it's a couple of pints of beer. What I'd do really well is lead the Tory Party. The skill I've got in losing money, I could get the jobless figures down to 1½ million in a month, I'd lose 2 million easily. They've changed the way they count them ten times, but they still can't get them below 3½ million.'

'They're advertising for strawberry pickers in the paper. They don't pay much, and it's back-breaking work. If you don't declare it, somebody'll bubble you to the DHSS.'

'Last September, they were picking potatoes, £8 a day. It was no privilege. The field was raided by DHSS officials – as if it was a vice-ring – to see who was there and claiming dole. You should've seen it. The whole field scattered, dropping potatoes in every direction; it emptied. I don't think anybody was daft enough to get caught. It was no pleasure, £8 a day; I had to sit in a bath two hours afterwards to ease my back ... Poor buggers, looking to get a few extras for the kiddies. Then the big tax-evaders get off scot-free. Is that fair? Is that England? We did live in a decent society. After the war, we had the beginnings of it. These lot, they've been undoing it all.'

'I've never been on the dole. I work for the British Beef Company; my two sons are working and my wife works in the Bingo Hall. I bought my house 15 years ago for two thousand pounds. But that hasn't turned me into a Tory.

'I know one lad, he was running a taxi service; he was on the dole. Somebody spragged on him to the Social. He gets a call one morning, "Could I have a cab at 7 o'clock?" He turns up; it's an official from the Social. "Hello Mr Grieves, shall we have a little discussion about the matter of your benefit?"'

'Being unemployed is the biggest test you can have of your marriage. You'll soon find out whether you made a mistake or not.'

'I always think of what George Orwell wrote in *Down and Out in London and Paris*. Whatever he went through, when he wanted to think of somebody worse off than himself, he always thought of the bloke unemployed in Middlesbrough. Is this the worst thing that can happen to you?'

'Yes there is. I went to a Special School for handicapped children because I always had a problem with my chest. It didn't stop me doing 35 years heavy labour. I always say that was my second handicap. My first was being born a Catholic in that part of Scotland. My name is spelt McLoughlin – that's a Catholic name. The minute I applied for a job and they said "fill in a form", I knew that was it, because on the form they always asked you what school you'd been to, and if it was St Something-or-other, you'd always know it was a Catholic school in the West of Scotland. I got so sick of it. In the end, I went to one place where they were advertising for workers. They said "Will you fill in a form?" I screwed the form up, threw it in the basket. I said "Forget it. I'm a Catholic." I got to the door. He called me back. "Wait a minute. This is a Catholic firm, you can start tomorrow." I said "No thanks. That makes you as bad as the other side. I wouldn't take it on principle."'

Even the jokes have a hard edge to them. 'What did the cannibal say when he saw a missionary on a bicycle?' 'Here comes meals on wheels.' 'Have you ever been abroad?' 'No, it's just the way I walk.' 'There's an interviewer talking to Frank Bruno, asking him what he thinks about other sportsmen in the World Cup. "Who do you admire in the Argentine team?" "Uh, Maradonna." "What about the West Germans?" He can't think of anyone, so the interviewer says, "have you heard o' Rumenigge?" He says "What rumour?"' There is a strong vein of racism, sexism, anti-gay sentiment: these offer uneasy points of definition to men in places where defining purposes have decayed: a sense that nothing remains but their maleness. There are a lot of jokes about the size of cocks, getting it up, as though the deep unease left by the rejected physical strength has nowhere else to go. The energy claimed by work cannot be so easily deflected into doing nothing. What has been done here is also a form of violence; inflicted by the changing needs of a capitalist system that has been diversified, globalized, so much of its labour transferred to other parts of the world or to increasingly sophisticated machinery. In the traditional working-class community, much male violence was domestic, inflicted upon wives and daughters; a transfer of the cruelties and rigours that industrial discipline imposed upon them. It is quite in keeping with the changes we have seen that male violence against women is increasingly directed against *strangers*. Where the agents of industrial violence were highly visible – the factory or millowner in his opulent villa in the same town – the new manipulators of wealth are invisible, in offices fortified by concrete and distance, in Houston or Osaka or Dusseldorf; so male violence now is directed outwards, randomly, arbitrarily. However generalized patriarchy may be, it always works through particular social forms and institutions: these things are not abstractions.

As people become distant from the decaying traditional industries, there can be heard the note of nostalgia that has been so prevalent in attitudes to the countryside from which they were evicted so long ago. 'This isn't the town we used to know' is a common theme. 'You could leave work at dinner time and start somewhere else in the afternoon for an extra penny an hour.' 'Your mates were more than friends, they were brothers. You used to see more of them than you did of your wife.' In July 1986, one of the great talking points in Middlesbrough was whether the Boro football team was going to be rescued from bankruptcy. 'Once your football side goes, it's a sure sign the town is on the skids.'

'I was sent for a job by the Jobcentre. It was a filthy job in a foundry, disgusting hole, something out of Dickens. I took one look at it, decided to make myself as obnoxious as I could, so I didn't get it. They offered it me. I went to the DHSS for a grant for boots and jeans to start, I'd no working clothes. There was an entitlement at that time to, I think, £7 for boots and jeans. They refused me. "You had one a year ago." That was Tuf boots, guaranteed only six months, working in hot metal they had been ruined. Nothing. So I went to the library, and read up all the Social Security Acts, all the Amendments. I pored over them. In the afternoon I went back, this time for a redecoration grant, clothing for the wife and kids, clothing for myself. "Oh, you won't get that." "It's not your job to tell me what I'm entitled to." They sent somebody down. "Weren't you here this morning?" "This is a different matter." I showed him my claim, quoted the Act, the Section, the Amendment. A few minutes later, he said "There'll be a giro in the post tomorrow." I said, "It would've been cheaper to let me have my £7." The giro was for £94.'

John retired three years ago. His brother is in New Zealand, and John has just returned from a visit. He got someone to paint a picture of the view from the room where he stayed: a painting of mountains, grass, rocks, water. 'He'd never come back now. It was a big wrench, but he wouldn't change it now ... We were brought up in a rough part of town. Down there, if you locked your door you were considered a snob, or you were doing something you shouldn't. There used to be these back-arch book-makers. If the coppers came, they'd dash through the houses; they would be four or five streets away in no time. It was nothing to see somebody running through your kitchen. I can remember all the names of the people in the street when I was a kid, what their job was, what their family circumstances were. At the time of the Means Test, if lads lived at home and were working, their father and mother were expected to take money from them. As soon as the Means Test man set foot in the street, the lads'd take the tent and go off camping for a day or two. Nobody ever did what they do now – write letters anonymously to the Social, grass on their neighbours. When I was 14 I left school, and went to work in a foundry. I went to work with my dad eventually. He was a straightener of rails, and I was a gagger. When they cast the rails, they weren't straight, they had to be evened out by hand. Leisure society. Don't know what it means. I've never been bored. We used to stand outside the window of the first house in the street that had the wireless. We were kept too busy to be bored. When I started, it was slave labour. I was overawed. It was filthy in the foundry, noisy, there were no toilets, you had to go out on the riverbank. I was small, so they put me cleaning locos. I had to get inside the boilers to clean them. I enjoyed it. I'd come home filthy. I never expected anything else. If you get fair pay, you feel you've given your best. I've done all kinds of things, dipping components in paint at one time, the fumes were overpowering, you got addicted to them; then to wash it off, you used kerosene, you were a walking fire hazard, danger of fire, explosion, damage to the lungs and eyes. It didn't bother you. I do voluntary work for the church now I'm retired. I've got a little three-wheeler car, I go out over the moors. It's the best countryside in the world. I love it here. This is my home. Middlesbrough I say, and that tells me who I am. It's not distinguished, you wouldn't stay here for health reasons, but the people, the way they are, the way they talk.'

Bob is working for the Tenants' Association which is trying to bring work back onto the estate. They have an old building in which to start a community laundry, a printing shop, a do-it-yourself workshop, a skills exchange and services for the old – garden clearing, shopping, minor repairs. This is to be started with funding from the Manpower Services Commission. They hope it will bring other kinds of employment. 'You can do things without money. Being poor doesn't stop you socializing, being a good neighbour. People don't know each other on the estates; well, they know who each other are, but that isn't the same thing. There's a lot of skills in people, crafts, work with wood, metal, making things, furniture, toys. If you were to add up all the skills there are on this estate, you'd be amazed at what we can do. Just because nobody's prepared to pay wages, doesn't mean to say we're useless.

'I myself left school on Friday, started as a building labourer on the Saturday. Then I went into the forces for $19\frac{1}{2}$ years. I was in Borneo, Malaya, Cyprus, Northern Ireland.' He shows the tattoos along his arm, one from each place he has been. 'I was in Malaya when they were fighting for independence. But I was born and bred in Middlesbrough, I always come back here. Only I never thought I'd see it like it is today. People have taken a pasting. If you mention the word holiday, it's like swearing at them. Will my lads be given the chance to work for a living? Leisure, unemployment – what's the difference? Without money you can't do a thing.

'I worked on the YTS as a supervisor. I was expected to teach kids to use a grasscutter or a hammer – those things are second nature to people up here. That's no giving a kid skills. When they finish the govvy schemes, the employers don't want to know, the youngsters still don't have the knowledge. Apprenticeship is the only way to teach kids, show them the job. There's no substitute for learning through work, through practice. This is why all the training schemes are just window-dressing – the government itself has no idea where the jobs are coming from. The training isn't adequate, the pay isn't adequate. The young people are at risk, they use machines without guards, there are loads of accidents. My lad left school at 15 to go on a scheme in agriculture. He wants to work with animals. YTS. After two weeks he was expected to be able to reverse a tractor and trailer through some bollards. He started on 16 June. Two weeks later they told him he wasn't suitable. Finished. How about that for breaking a youngster's confidence?'

'My lad has just started with Wimpy's, the builders, as a brickie,' says Mr Collins. 'I said to him "Don't think of anything else. That's your backbone. Once you've got a trade. Prove you're worthy of the two years. Learn from the tradesmen."' He smiles. 'When I was born, God said "This is an ugly bugger, we'll give him a bit of common sense to make up for his looks." My father was a master pipe-fitter. I learnt from him. I've proved to myself, I can do most things. I'm not a mechanic, but I can replace a car wing so's you wouldn't know it had been done. These people who've got their cards saying they're brickies or fitters or whatever, don't you believe it. Bloke in club was moaning he didn't have a trade. I said "What do you want to be?" He said "I'm a brickie." "All right. Give us ten quid. I'll give it you back." He gave me ten quid. I went to a club out of town, and I said "Will you give me a brickie's card for ten quid?" I took the card back to him. "Now you're a qualified brickie." I took it back and got him his ten quid back. Oh, you can get anything. You can get an MOT certificate, a clean licence will cost you £25, with log-book and everything. At this club, you can get any qualification you want. It's only a piece of paper after all; expert artists, forge you anything. That's how people survive. Of course they'll play the system. It's bloody unfair, everybody knows that. Whatever you want, fitter, painter, welder, scaffolder, anything, if you can pay for it.'

'We don't set the rules; and the bastards who do don't live by them.'

'What about this girl, whatsername, Olivia Channon? Well, I'm sorry for her, don't get me wrong. Her and the son of Jonathan Guinness. What I'd like to say to their parents is "What right do you think you've got to tell working-class kids what to do, when you can't see the system is destroying your own?" They're supposed to be in charge, and look what a fuck-up they make of raising their own. What authority have they got to tell us what to do?'

'I hear Mrs Thatcher's having a street-party for the unemployed. She's hiring the M1.'

'When they gave me my baby's birth certificate to sign, they said I could put my previous occupation on it, which I did. I put slaughterman, to save the humiliation of putting unemployed. When I knew Eileen was pregnant, I thought "Oh, I'll have to get a job before the baby's born." You feel you have no right not to be working. The only good thing that's come out of unemployment is that the families are more together: men take more care of the kids, they know a bit more what it's like for a woman. But the first time I took the pram out, I felt awful. But then I looked round and saw that no end of men were doing it. I just hadn't noticed.'

'Don't talk to me about the good old days. I was in a lumber camp in

Suffolk owned by a match company in the 1930s. Four shillings a week.
Then I worked on the runways at Mildenhall air-base. So the Yanks could
come and occupy us. If I'd known what it was going to be used for, I'd've
put craters in the middle.'

'I went on the tramp. Round the farms. Knock on the door in August.
Kid comes to the door. "Dad, there's a tramp at the door." "That's not a
tramp, that's a worker come for the harvest." Go back a bit later in the
year. Same kid answers the door. "Dad, there's a workman at the door."
"That ain't a workman, it's a tramp."'

How the transition is going to occur between mass unemployment and
the leisure society is far from clear. Will those in work give up some of
their income to split jobs, spending the rest of their time in more satisfying
pursuits for less money, as Charles Handy and others suggest? It is
difficult to see how redistribution of work, as of income, is going to be
turned into an acceptable political programme. What is certain is that the
humanity and the humour and the solidarities on estates like these,
although stretched, remain strong. Whether and how the undoubted
generosity of the more privileged is going to be extended so that they will
share their good fortune with the increasingly impoverished and be-
leaguered minority is another question.

It is an easier time altogether on the poor estates on the edge of the city,
when being close to the countryside offers scope for relaxation that
doesn't cost anything. Red poppies grow on the grass verges, people linger
in their gardens until the light fades. Down by the reservoir, the men
crowd the trampled places between the reeds, flinging out their floats onto
the rippling water. Hawthorn and elder bushes in acrid flower provide
some screen from the noise and fumes of the busy motorway nearby.

This is where Mike comes in the evenings. He sits on what he regards as
his own little promontory of dry earth, watching the insects skim over the
water, and the gold stain of a smudged sun on the surface. His eight-year-
old daughter, Katie, is content to sit beside him, drawing shapes in the
well-trodden earth with a sharp stone. Suddenly, his rod jerks. Mike pulls
vigorously, and a tench of about 1½ pounds leaps from the water. Mike had
been distracted by talking, and the hook has gone deep into the fish's
gullet. With great care, he prises out the sharp metal, while the fish's
mouth gasps. It escapes his hold and falls, writhing for a moment in the dry
earth at his feet. Mike picks it up and throws it into the green nylon net
that concertinas in the shallows at the edge of the reservoir. 'Tench don't
get eaten by other fish. They're known as doctor-fish: if other fish get
injured, they rub themselves against the tench, and that is supposed to heal
the wound.'

Mike comes here to get away from the pressure of three years without work, four children, one of them desperately ill with cancer. He loves the serene open sky, the intense concentration, the silence. In the next clump of yellow water-iris sits a Pole who, calling on a skill acquired during his distant peasant childhood, can catch fish with his bare hands.

Not that Mike's long-term unemployment has been wasted time. He has organized a football team of young unemployed which has just been promoted to the Premier League. He works for charity, and is devoted to his sick daughter and spends many hours with her. Her hair has fallen out and she is wasted unrecognizably from the healthy girl she was this time last year. 'Fishing calms you. It's cheap once you have a rod. It's like everything else, you can buy all the fancy equipment, but I don't know that you get any more pleasure out of it for all that. Some of the animal liberation people tell you it's a cruel sport. I think they're wrong. You always throw back what you catch – a few poor buggers who've got nothing else might cook them and eat them, but they're very insipid. The only expense is the maggots – £1.20 a pint. Fishing is the biggest pastime in Britain. It relaxes people. If you take fishing away from the unemployed, you will have riots in the streets.'

The perimeter of the reservoir is little more than a mile. It has been 'environmentalized' by the local authority; a patch has been cut through the nettles and willowherb, and pink gravel strewn over it, to prevent it from being overgrown by 'weeds'. Uprooted trees lie on their sides, the devastated nests of finches scattered. On the north side, some new saplings have been planted, weeping willows. Boys on BMX bikes ride the new path, enjoying the sharp bumps and deep hollows. Gary stands in the middle of a small crowd of 18-year-olds, feet on the ground, yellow-and-black bike moving to and fro beneath him. He lifts his T-shirt off to display a scar from a wound he received two weeks ago: a cut, about three inches long, with a regular line of stitch-marks on either side. The blade had gone in just below the right nipple. Another inch or two, and the liver would have been pierced. Gary's mates are resolved on revenge. It began when the girl of Gary's best mate Picco, Shelley, had been called a slag by an 18-year-old. Shelley is 15½, still at school, and she has Picco's baby. Picco is devoted to the child, and intends marrying Shelley as soon as she is sixteen. Gary and Picco went to get Shelley's tormentor. When they found him, he was with four of his mates. 'All right. We'll take you on, we can match you.' Gary and Picco started into them; the four fell back. Gary and Picco turned round to go; as they did so, a girl sitting in a car owned by one of their adversaries gave her boyfriend a knife. Gary sees the knife in the boy's hand. He warns Picco, and throws himself in front of his friend to deflect the blow. The knife goes in, a quick downward stroke. Gary manages to land a couple of blows before he realizes how badly injured he is. He is bleeding profusely. The assailants have scattered and driven off. His T-shirt is soaked with blood. Picco runs to get a friend's car to take Gary to hospital.

At home, Gary's mother is getting anxious. It is 11.30 when the doorbell rings. Gary's younger brother answers the door. A policewoman is standing there. 'Is your father in?' 'No.' 'Does he always stay out this late of a Sunday night?' Gary's mother gets up. 'Who wants to know?' She is outraged because, she says, the policewoman is smelling of drink. 'I could smell it. Being a non-drinker myself, I always can. She said to me "Your son's been stabbed. He's in the hospital."' Gary was in intensive care. 'You can't judge how bad it is from the way they tell you. The way she put it, it sounded terrible. I can't think about it now without going hot and cold. "Your son." My boys are everything to me. I could have lost him. And she was so casual about it.'

The boys who did it are on the run. They haven't been arrested, even though a few days after the incident, they were seen at the estate's annual carnival. Gary's friends informed a policeman. Go and tell the desk sergeant. Nothing happened. When his mother went to the police station to remonstrate, she was told to go and make a citizen's arrest. 'He knifed my boy and I'm supposed to go and arrest him. You can only wonder what the job of the police is.'

Jim, Gary's uncle, says that on the poor estates you feel you're on your own. 'They leave the poor to fight it out among themselves.' It is easy to see how people become estranged from the police. Gary's mother phoned the superintendent, who visited the house and explained that there was a warrant out for the boy's arrest. But the family were left with the feeling that they had been neglected: not enough recognition had been given to what was for them a desperate experience. Jim had tried to intervene one night in a fight between some teenagers and two young Indians who were running a mobile fish and chip van that was parked outside the pub. The van had been overturned and set on fire, and when Jim went to help the owners, he had been attacked and beaten and kicked in the balls. The police response had been that if the Indians didn't want trouble, they should stay away from the estate.

Gary's friends are angry. In the huddle around the BMX bikes, they are planning elaborate campaigns of revenge. Gary has been in trouble once or twice. It appears to his mates that the police are waiting for them to take the law into their own hands, so that they can come down all the harder on Gary.

The estate was built in the 1950s. Many of the unemployed people spend a lot of time in their gardens: runner beans snaking up bamboo tripods, rows of potatoes, roses winding round a peeling trellis of birch-branches. Ken and Jackie live in a hard-to-let house which they have transformed. In the garden is a greenhouse made of polythene: in it a sturdy vine is growing, with the grapes already forming in hard green clusters. Ken is 38; corn-coloured hair, deep-set blue eyes; a tough but gentle Scot, who lost his job last year as a long-distance lorry driver. Several were sacked from the firm at the same time: all were drivers who refused to take risks by driving more than the permitted eight out of 11 hours registered on the tachograph, or by increasing the load on their vehicles to a tonnage greater than that allowed for the size of the vehicle. Since then he has not worked. Ken waves his HGV licence. 'This used to be a passport to a safe job.' Last week, he phoned in reply to an advertisement for long-distance drivers. 'They told me I was too old. At 38. You're too young to be employed in your teens and twenties and too old at 38. When will they employ you, for a fortnight around your 30th birthday?'

Ken's real job, which he gave up when his daughter started school four years ago, was animal trainer in a circus. He had always been brought up to travel because his father worked in a fair. Ken used to go to a different school every week, had been teased and bullied, called a didicoy and a gipsy. He didn't want his child to be treated like that. Ken started work at 14, picking up papers around the circus ground. Then he worked in the stables, sleeping close to the horses. From those, he 'graduated', as he says, to the elephants; and then, finally, to his great love – the big cats – pumas, leopards, lions; and what he doesn't know about them isn't worth knowing. 'The tiger is the only cat that can change its direction in mid-air in pursuit of its prey; that's why it is the most dangerous of them all.' There are mementoes of circus life all over the house: china elephants and tigers; photographs of his daughter, as a child of five, bottle-feeding a tiger-cub; pictures of her christening, which took place in the circus-ring: the minister was baptizing five children that day. There is a cutting from the local paper where they were performing. 'That tiger-cub used to sleep in the caravan with us.'

Ken misses the circus. 'We had our own language; some of it comes from the Italian and French. "Munjari", that is food. "Josser", that's anybody from outside, someone who is not a circus person.' Ken would go back to that life tomorrow if he could; but Jackie, although she enjoyed the friendships and camaraderie, is happy to be settled in her home town. She works in a Bingo Hall, relishes the banter with the old people. Ken insists that the circus is not cruel, although most of them have now given up their animals, or have settled with them in safari parks. 'I was only attacked once.' He rolls up his left sleeve: deep in the freckled flesh, white shiny scars of a clawmark. 'A young tiger cub. Before it was trained. If training animals was cruel, nobody who trained them would survive. They'd get you. You can't possibly keep an eye on them all the time. The minute your back was turned, that would be it. But they don't, because of the relationship they have with you.

'The friendliness of circus people is wonderful. You all helped to assemble the Big Top and dismantle it. Even the little kids learned to cooperate. Of course, they were very superstitious. You'd never go back into the Big Top after midnight. They believed that all the performers who'd been killed came back after midnight and relived their act all over again. I never went in. And it's true that at night, when it's empty, you can hear a lot of creaking and rustling – just as though there are people there. And they used to say that if you looked into a horse's left ear at night, you'd see the devil there. And then, of course, they would never have goats in a circus because the goat is the emblem of the devil.

'You get to know the animals. You have a real relationship with them. It isn't just sentiment.' Jackie agrees. 'Oh yes, they know you and they love you. Once, when I was leading the elephants out of the ring, I tripped and fell down just in front of them; and although it looks as if elephants are moving slowly, you have to run to keep pace with them. The spot where I fell was exactly where the elephant would have put her foot next. But she didn't – she stayed with it poised in the air. Well, if the animals resented you, they wouldn't treat you like that.'

Ken adds 'The whip is made of Spanish willow, and the thong is leather; but the crack is made by a little string tassel at the end. It's all show; it isn't meant to hurt the animals. You learn to anticipate their reactions and feelings; you sort of absorb it through your skin, an instinct.

'My mate was killed. We'd packed up, going from Bedford to Luton. It was a short journey, only just down the road. And I didn't go with him in the van we usually travelled in. I said to him "Oh well, I'll see you a bit later." He said "No, you won't." I didn't pay any attention; but a lot of circus people are gifted with second sight. As we were going down this hill into Luton, we saw a police car, flashing lights. We were turned back. We never knew who it was, and they didn't tell us till after the performance. How did he know? He wouldn't travel in the same van with me that day; it was like he knew it was his time, but not mine.

'I've been all over Europe with the circus. We used to have beautiful Andalusian horses. When you were training them, you had to work them 12 hours a day at the beginning, walking them one way round the ring, then the other way; what patience! Then you gently placed a cloth on their back, then a saddle, and then a weight; and eventually, a weight that was the equivalent of a human body, before anybody could think of mounting them. They were beautiful creatures. When you were learning, you had to groom them. You combed and groomed the horse onto a white cloth spread on the ground beneath, so that you could see the hair and the dust that had come off, prove to the ringmaster that you'd done it properly. And then, when you'd finished, he'd come and rub the horse's body with his hand wearing a white glove; and when he looked at the glove, if there was the faintest mark or speck of dust, you'd have to start all over again.'

Jackie is getting ready to go to work. She likes the Bingo Hall, but would prefer to work in an old people's home. Talk of work makes Ken uncomfortable. Jackie is lucky. She doesn't realize that the jobs that are going are part-time, mainly for women. Ken applied to an agency for occasional part-time HGV driving. The agency wanted 25 per cent of the earnings for any work they placed his way. 'They wanted drivers who don't mind risking the limit of the tonnage, and driving beyond the hours allowed. If you get caught, you're on your own. £1,000 fine. The agency plays the innocent, oh no, they knew nothing about it.'

During his time out of work, Ken has befriended Peter, a thin, timid man in his early thirties. He lives with his elderly mother in a cluttered, untidy house scented with the smell of the leggy geraniums that struggle for position in the back window. Peter was probably the first person from this estate to go to university, where he suffered from a severe depressive illness. Frightened by DHSS inquiries, he failed to claim benefit for two and a half years, and lived on his mother's pension. They got into hopeless arrears with rent before it was discovered that he had never claimed his entitlement. Peter is angry at the abuse of drugs in the treatment of psychiatric illness such as his. He is a creative and intelligent man, whose powers have been wasted by inappropriate medication over the years. He writes poetry, but prefers to write parody rather than more direct expression of his own feelings, which easily overwhelm his fragile recovery.

In the same road lives Joe, now 59, who finished work when the pit closed two years ago. He doesn't expect to work again. Rita, his wife, has a job cleaning in the school, and earning just enough to disqualify Joe from any benefit at all. When he stopped work, he learned how to cook. But the novelty has worn off, he has lost interest; indeed, his political radicalism is turning to bitterness. None of his three children has worked since leaving school. Joe no longer goes to the pub where he has been drinking all his working life. He knows that people would not hesitate to buy him a drink. 'That's not the point. I've bought people a drink when they've been down, but I couldn't go in there now, because I know I could never return it. I know it's wrong, but I can't bear not to be able to pay my way. When you've no money, you feel worthless. That's what they've done to us. They've made us feel we're just as good as the amount of money we've got in our pocket. Isn't that what they say about people, "What's he or she worth?" You know it's all wrong, but there it is. There's one bloke goes in the pub, he's crowing over us because he's still working. He says he hopes Thatcher gets in again. I said to him "Yes, I hope so an' all. She can't do anything else to me, I've lost everything already. It's only you buggers singing over we that can come down. And when you do, you won't find any sympathy here." ' Joe is losing interest in the things that sustained him all his life. His daughter Jane, who is 17, has a horse in the back garden, which opens out onto a field, and the bridge over the motorway: a place of rank buttercups and long grass. In the back garden there are also 25 rabbits, two cats and two dogs. Jane is grooming the horse. 'It isn't mine. I'm looking after it for a man who was being evicted from his small-holding. The council wanted the land. He said he didn't mind what they did to him, but he wasn't having his horse destroyed.' She grins. 'Council'd go mad if they knew we had a horse here.'

Outside the pub, a couple sit on the bench, rocking a baby in its pram. Both are wearing anoraks because the wind is chilly over the reservoir in the late evening. They are sharing a single half-pint, all they can afford. Other young people are sprawled in the long grass, where some warmth from the day lingers. They are telling jokes; an edge of cynicism. 'What's thin and white and gets you drunk?' 'A giro.' One girl says to her friend 'Whisky makes him frisky, brandy makes him randy, beer makes him queer.' Her boyfriend pulls her by the hair and she wriggles on the grass. 'Look at her, she's such a bag, when we travel on the train she has to go in the luggage compartment.' 'Ouch, the love-bites on me bum are turning septic.' 'How have you got love-bites on your bum?' 'He thought it was her face. Smells a bit sweeter.' She throws the dregs of her lager in her friend's face. 'Cheeky cow.'

Only Gracie is frightened of the long summer holidays just starting. She is alone with her three children. 'What am I going to do with them? I can't afford to take them anywhere.' She dreads the rain, because if they stay in they will wreck the house; and in the fine weather, she is constantly afraid that they will run away, get lost, be molested, get run over. 'They want money all the time. Where can I get it from? How can I tell them? All the other kids have spending money. I'm frightened to be alone with my kids. You'll think I'm a terrible mother to hear me talk like that. I shall be thankful when the summer's over. Last year, I nearly strangled my little girl. I just couldn't control myself. She'd been on and on about sommat she wanted. That's how it gets you. Don't misunderstand, I love my kids. But being alone with them, you get so lonely. Because they can't know what you're going through. You find yourself talking to them as if they were grown up, telling them how you feel. Then they start to cry, and you feel ashamed, you've taken advantage of them, they shouldn't be hearing all this at their age. That's what summer means to me. I'm frightened of it;

frightened the neighbours will hear me shouting and report me. I'll get called an unfit mother and they'll take them away from me. Their father'd love that; it'd prove that everything he says about me is right.'

The light fades over the reservoir. It is cold. The couple with the pram walk off down the road, his arm around her shoulder. Windows slam, dogs bark, milk bottles rattle on the doorstep. Only a few young couples are left in the grass around the water's edge, pressing against each other for warmth.

Jasvinder is 20. Drinking in an austere street-corner pub, waiting for his friends to finish their game of pool. He considers himself lucky: he works as a grinder, taking home £110 a week, even if the metal and dust do get into his lungs, so that he has to drink seven pints of lager every night. Archaic patterns of working-class leisure are replicated in the lives of many young black workers; so many of them, after all, occupy positions only recently evacuated by their white brothers. Of Jasvinder's friends in the pub, one is a motor mechanic, one studies law at the Technical College, the other three are unemployed. Jasvinder's future appears clear. His wife is expecting their first baby in a few months' time. He spends his evenings in the pub. His two sisters will eventually marry and leave the little terraced house in the Midland city, where he will remain with his wife and children and his parents. Jasvinder and his friends have learnt that there are certain no-go areas in the city. He stays away from the all-white council estates; he won't expose himself to the humiliation of being asked to leave the working men's club.

White racism confines many young Indians to those parts of the city that are safe and familiar. To move too far from the beaten path incurs risks of insult and injury; to move into all-white areas invites ostracism, petitions, bricks through the window or worse. There are many stories of families who had worked their way out being compelled to return to the ghetto; of councils having to rehouse people as the least disruptive way of dealing with an intractable racism which many local authorities shrink from confronting. It creates for many Asians a strange perspective on the freedoms that are supposed to be the proudest feature of our life.

One consequence of this curtailment of their liberty is to give great poignancy to conflicts between young people who were born in Britain and their parents, many of whom were migrants in the fifties and sixties. The young find themselves fighting with those they love for a measure of emancipation and autonomy; only to step then into a world bitterly circumscribed by hostility and resentment. This gives them a wry and disabused view of the official social and political rhetoric. Their time is quite differently structured.

Sundip is 21; a troubled young man, wearing an olive combat jacket, with a thin growth of beard and a gold ring in his left ear. He has spent a year in London. 'I was a trainee manager in a hotel.' His friend, Jag, laughs. 'You were working in the bakery.' Sundip protests. 'I was going to do management. They had me lined up for it.' His time in London is a source of great glamour and daring. 'But I had to come home, didn't I?' His parents had arranged the marriage. The wedding took place two days ago; already Sundip has taken his position with his friends in the pub. 'I had to give up everything,' he says vehemently, 'my job, my future, my girl; for someone I didn't even know.' He spent a year living in a flat with his girlfriend. He had to part from her to come home for the wedding. In protest, he jumped out of the car on the way to the ceremony. The car was travelling at about 50 miles an hour. His parents and the bride were sitting at the back. They assumed he was drunk. In any case, he was unhurt.

Jasvinder says that he didn't know his wife either when they married. But he liked her. Now, he feels, he is beginning to love her, and she loves him. How can it be wrong, when your parents do what's best for you? How could those who love you so much do anything against your interests? Sundip says 'There's nothing wrong with arranged marriages, as long as you're not involved with someone else.' His friends agree. 'What they don't understand is that here you mix, at school, at work, at college. You can't not meet girls, you can't stop yourself falling in love with them.' None of them objects to an arranged marriage on principle. You only have to look in the newspapers to see that people who presumably married for love don't have a particularly good record of successful marriages: they fight, torment, even kill each other. A third of marriages end in divorce; how can this possibly be better than traditional customs?

'If only they had given me two or three years longer,' Sundip says, 'I could have accepted it then. But at 21, to be cut off from all the life I had made for myself.' On the day before the wedding, Sundip cut his wrists with a kitchen knife. He was taken to hospital for stitches. He wears a soiled crêpe bandage on each wrist. Jag is less than sympathetic. 'You'll get used to it in a couple of years.' 'Look at my cousin,' Sundip says, 'He's been married for three years, and still they haven't had sexual intercourse. He can't consummate it, because he's a mummy's boy.' Sanjay asks 'What about your wife's feelings? It can't be much fun for her, to get all dressed up for her wedding, and to find you cutting your wrists. She must think there's something wrong with her. She must feel insulted. Does she know what's been happening, how you were living in London?' 'Of course not.' 'Well, she probably thinks you can't stand her.' 'I can't.' 'It must be hell for her.' Sundip is sobered; he hadn't thought of it like that.

When the pub closes, Jasvinder insists that we go back to his house. It is

about 11.30. The house is in darkness, everyone is sleeping. We sit on the
leather sofa, beneath a large portrait of Bhindranwale, and some loops of
electric blue tinsel against the pale wallpaper. Jasvinder goes into the
kitchen, fetches a bottle of Bacardi, a litre bottle of Coke and some apricot
brandy. He pours them into tumblers in reckless quantities. Sundip drinks
half a glass of Bacardi, then the same of apricot brandy. After the lager in
the pub, he is quite drunk. He is reluctant to go home. At long past midnight, he is still standing on the windy street-corner, trying to persuade his
friends to go home with him for another drink. 'For my wedding,' he
pleads. 'Please come. Please.' His eyes are full of tears; though perhaps not
because of his friends' reluctance to disturb the household so late at night.

Sita is the daughter of a Hindu family from Punjab. She lives with her
married sister at a corner shop in the heart of the inner-city area. She has
just celebrated her 21st birthday; all the cards are pinned to the chimney
breast. She wears a lilac sweater and jeans; her hair is in a thick single plait.
She is working on a Community Programme scheme, painting and
decorating. She has become a karate expert, having reached black belt
level. She says proudly 'I was the only Asian girl in the beginning. There
were other girls, but they dropped out. In the end, I was the only woman.'
Sita is individualistic and defiant. She doesn't care what people think of
her. She has never particularly thought of herself as a girl, and as a child
never showed the slightest interest in playing with dolls. She hates sex
stereotyping. 'It's my life, and I'll do what I want with it. Other people
don't bother me. If they do, they'll soon find out they've made a mistake. I
can defend myself. I walk home by myself late at night. I can't stand
women who shrink away and hide from the world. That's one thing I've
learned in Britain: you have to look after yourself, you can't depend on
anybody but yourself. I hope to have my own decorating business one day.
I'm the best worker they've got on the scheme. Racism? That's their
problem. I like this country, because you can be yourself. I've been to the
Punjab, I went back to my family's village. I could never live there. If I'd
never known anything else, maybe it would be different. But I couldn't
now.' Sita's grandmother brings in a plate of vegetable fritters. The old
woman listens to her grand-daughter, partly in admiration, partly in
bewilderment. When her grandmother is present, Sita's face softens. They
smile at each other, the two women divided, not only by the years, but by
languages in which neither can communicate with the other.

Sita's life sounds uncomplicated compared with that of Yasmin and
Rehana, articulate but very different Muslim sisters. Yasmin works in a
bank. The job bores her, although she is well aware that most of her friends
in this depressed area of the city see her as privileged. Rehana, passionate
and angry, works in a crèche. Both have had a long struggle with their

family to gain a degree of personal freedom. 'You have to fight, to beg, to threaten; and then, when you achieve what you wanted, you find it's the freedom to be treated as though you don't exist; the freedom to stand at a bus stop and hear white people talking about you as if you couldn't understand a word they say; and that of course gives them the right to say anything in front of you. I'm always butting into conversations and saying to people "Please don't treat me as if I were a piece of street furniture."'

Their father and mother have not been happy together. Yasmin says that they would have been better apart; their lives have been a mutual antagonism; but this has not altered their belief in traditional ways of doing things. Quite the reverse in fact. 'They haven't made each other happy, so you would think that they can't very well tell you to follow their example. But it doesn't work like that. It seems sometimes the more unhappy people are, the more they cling to irrational beliefs, the more they are devoted to the traditional obligations.'

Rehana says 'I was born here, but I don't feel I belong. I just can't get on with living my life, because my life is defined at every turn by white people. I never know if it's going to be disrupted; you never know what lies in wait for you. So many people are unemployed: they see black people as the cause of it. It makes you very sensitive, you monitor every slight response; the lifting of an eyebrow, the exchange of a glance; you learn to interpret everything. I was in a shop last week; I didn't buy anything, and as I went out of the door, I smiled at the assistant to let her know that I hadn't found what I wanted. As soon as I got outside, she came running after me. "Excuse me, I think you've taken something." I said "I smiled at you to show you that I hadn't." She said "Can I look in your bag?" Nothing. "Oh, I'm sorry." Then the moment I stepped outside again, I heard her speaking to the other people in the shop. "They're so touchy." Rehana went back in and said "It's bad enough to be accused of shoplifting, but it's even worse to hear yourself talked about as though you had no right to protest when you've been unjustly accused." "Oh, I never meant anything." Rehana says she wants to go up to people and say to them "What makes you think we're not the same as you, have the same feelings, the same conflicts with our parents, the same hopes and fears?" They'd think you were mad.'

Because Yasmin and Rehana are both capable and attractive, they have always been invited by white people to dissociate themselves from their background, detach themselves from the Muslim community. It is very seductive. Teachers at school would hold them up as examples to their less fluent and less able friends. 'And you'd then give them the right to lay into the poor kids who can't cope. "Yasmin can do it, why can't you?" I used to hate that. A lot of people will talk racist in front of you, and then say "Oh we don't mean you. It's the others."'

'I spent a lot of time when I was little wondering why I wasn't white, and wishing I could wake up one day and be white as snow.' Rehana is angry at the humiliations of Muslim women. 'I know one woman whose husband visited her only when he wanted her for sex. He lives with another woman. His wife has seven children, and she has to bring them up alone. Another woman we know had an arm and a leg broken by her husband; and then he wouldn't even let her go to hospital for treatment.'

Yasmin interrupts: 'The trouble is that as soon as you say anything critical about your own culture, the white people love it. "There you are," they say, "isn't it terrible?" What I would like to ask them is what is so wonderful about a culture that judges people by the amount of money they have?'

Some of the young people try to resolve the conflicts by over-conforming. 'My brother', says one of Yasmin's friends, 'only has white friends. He thinks of himself as white, and won't have anything to do with Indians.' Another boy said 'It makes you hard. That's what growing up in Britain has meant to me. It has taught us that nobody will defend us, so we'll have to do it ourselves.' Many are happy to remain in the shelter of family structures; others have recourse to drink, or live fantasies of an India where they have never lived. A few – like Rehana – are driven into political activity. She says 'The tragedy is that so much energy has to go into surviving, battles that should never have to be fought; such battles exhaust you, leave no time for the delights and ordinary pursuits that make other people's lives rich and rewarding. And that's before you even start to face unemployment, poverty and disappointed hopes.'

5

Ordinary passions

It is clear that if there is even an element of truth in the foregoing, the kind
of leisure society that we can expect to evolve will be bleak indeed.
Happily, when we look at how people actually spend their free time, the
theories and prophecies dissolve, for they are often contradicted by direct
experience. This is not to say that the invasive power of money does not
threaten even the most gentle and traditionally non-monetized activity. It
is equally true that a great deal of leisure time readily assumes those rather
disciplined and compulsive qualities associated with archaic patterns of
labour. There is a constant preoccupation with escape: being elsewhere,
assuming another identity, an absorption in another time and a different
place from where life must be lived. There is often a strong compensatory
element for dissatisfactions in work or other areas of daily life. On the
other hand, what people gain from their leisure occupations in terms of
expertise and specialized knowledge, the breadth and range of interests on
which the British engage in their free time are extraordinary. It is also
deeply reassuring to observe how much of even the most escapist and play-
acting activity serves charitable ends; sometimes, it seems, half the
country is dressing up in order to entertain the other half, with the
proceeds going to deserving causes. The links and bonds that are formed
between people in a common endeavour also form distinctive communities, communities that remain invisible to the outsider, for they are
governed, not by physical propinquity but by shared passions; and those
who lament the decay of traditional forms of community should consider
all these voluntary associations that have been constructed in their place.
These can be no less supporting, no less loving; for instance, in one local
fuchsia-growing society in a Midland town, one of the members had
cancer. She was visited and helped and borne up by the members of the
society as effectively as by her own neighbourhood and family, and she
quite readily acknowledged this.

It is essentially in leisure associations that many people build up their
resistances to the encroachments of a world that seems to them increas-

ingly bewildering and hostile. In becoming an expert in some esoteric field, a space is opened where meaning and significance can be created, where you can know all there is to know, where you become distinguished, special once more, in ways that mass markets and consumption patterns cannot provide. A subtle and delicate cluster of satisfactions – as well as contradictions – can be found in what is sometimes an extreme dedication to a project, an interest, an area of study, the cultivation of a skill. People are often shy of admitting their interest to strangers: 'You don't want to hear about that'; or they submit to the amused tolerance of family and friends who do not share the same commitment. 'She's off again', 'Don't get him talking about his garden or you'll be here all night', 'What she doesn't know about horses isn't worth knowing.' And they will hide the pages of notebooks containing the lists of numbers of railway engines, the words of pop songs, the tables of cricket performances, the daily weather reports; perhaps it is because these things suggest something immature, even infantile; may be seen as regressive and open to ridicule, and therefore open the individuals concerned to the possibility of being hurt. For it is in such activities that many of us show ourselves to be vulnerable in ways that do not occur in the main arenas of social intercourse. It is perhaps the sense of make-believe, of collusion, of obsessive devotion to one narrow aspect of experience which depends for its sustaining power on the suspension of disbelief of those who share the same concerns. These occupations often involve the setting up of a whole world in miniature, in which the individual is manipulator and controller, enjoys a total power which for more and more of us is absent in any degree in what is sometimes called, with decreasing conviction, 'the real world'; an attempt to reclaim a sense of order and coherence in opposition to a society which seems to have created such a widespread feeling of confusion and impotence in its people.

The examples of leisure cited in this section are arbitrary and represent the merest fraction of what are not even the most common leisure activities, although any view of all those areas of experience that have not been included would probably offer similar responses and patterns.

Charles Handy, in *The Future of Work*, says that the average adult (that statistical phantom beloved of market researchers) has 61 hours a week of free time (not spent in formal working or sleeping). He points out that this is much more than the average person spends at work in a job. Richard Rose has calculated that while we spend the biggest chunk of free time doing nothing or on pastimes like walking and talking that cost no money (21 hours a week), and some of it on leisure activities like travel and pubs that do cost money (17 hours a week), we spend even more of it on unpaid

housework and productive leisure (gardening or knitting, for example).*
This leaves vast areas of human experience outside the cash economy; and
it is only to be expected that these will be the object of some interest to
those intent on bringing more and more of our freely given time and cost-
free occupations into the incalculably civilizing realm of monetized
transactions. This comes through nearly all the accounts that people give
of their leisure.

Mr and Mrs Davies are in their fifties. They live on the edge of a Midland
town in a bungalow built in the 1950s. Mr Davies is a fork-lift truck driver,
working on a shift system, so that he works nights one week in three. This
seriously disturbs their lives; but he is glad to have a job, having spent
three years out of work. His principal leisure activity at that time became a
major preoccupation. It was, he insists, the saving of him.

Mrs Davies has no paid employment. She suffers from an eye defect that
she has had since childhood, and wears thick pebble glasses. She walks two
hours every day with their two dogs, one of which is now 16, barely able to
waddle. Mr and Mrs Davies have no children. Their bungalow is comfortable, with a huge mural pasted on to the end wall, a landscape of birch
trees, rhododendrons in flower and a calm lake, so that it appears that they
look out onto a permanent springtime. The other walls are covered with
the evidence of their shared passion for butterflies. There is a huge moth in
a case on its own – the largest known, spanning several inches; and a tray
of butterflies, the fabric of their wings a vivid blue silky texture. These
butterflies are from South America the wings are used for jewellery.

In the hall, where there is no direct sunlight, there is a tray of all 70
known species of butterfly in Britain. Many of these are now extinct, so it
becomes more and more rare to find a complete collection. In this display,
the Short-tailed Blue – long vanished from Britain – is damaged. Mr and
Mrs Davies are on the waiting list for a replacement. They were recently
offered £500 for their specimen of the Large Blue. Certain butterflies have
become restricted to only a few localities now: the Green Hairstreak is
found only in the High Wycombe area, the Chequered Skipper is limited to
parts of Scotland. Others are rare and unfamiliar – the Camberwell Beauty
and the Purple Emperor still look magnificent even under glass. Berger's
Clouded Yellow can still be seen occasionally; the Silver-studded Blue has
gone.

Collectors become very knowledgeable about their area of interest. Mrs
Davies says that the Large Blue became extinct when a cetain kind of ant
on which they depended died out. The ants used to drag the larva of the

---

* Quoted in Charles Handy, *The Future of Work* (Blackwell, 1984).

Large Blue into their ant-hills, attracted to them by the scent, and there the butterfly emerged from its chrysalis in the passage-ways of the ant-hills. The Black-veined White has been extinct in this country for almost 200 years. The Hedge Brown is known familiarly as 'the gatekeeper' because of its habitat; the Monarch hangs down like a weeping willow leaf; the Camberwell Beauty likes dark hollows in trees; the Marbled White is found in meadows and rough grass; the Fritillaries are seen in shady wooded places. The White Admiral was common when Mr and Mrs Davies were children in rural Buckinghamshire, but now it is rare. The Speckled Wood butterfly will fly on dull days, unlike most of the others which require warmth and sunshine.

Mr Davies collected butterflies as a child. It was common then to see a tray of moths and butterflies on the walls of front parlours. He returned to his interest during a prolonged period of unemployment. One day he saw a Clouded Yellow, and that started him off again. Mrs Davies says 'I took a piece of net curtain, dyed it black so that it shouldn't distract the butter-flies, made a net with a cane, and took a jamjar. It cost nothing. This is what people miss today – the beauty of the world that is all around them. We've since been to Sherborne, to Godden's World-wide Butterfly Farm – all the butterflies in the world are there. They feed on nectar, so they put sugared water on all the plants; you can buy eggs and chrysalises of most of the butterflies.'

Mr Davies breeds moths; he will keep the odd single specimen and then release the rest. In this way, he feels he is adding to the store of moths or butterflies, not wiping them out. 'People don't know what a pleasure it is. I found a poor battered moth that had laid its eggs in the curtain. We hatched them and watched them develop. You make up a full collection from existing collections that have been broken up. You learn such a lot. For instance, you can't keep two caterpillars of the Orange Tip together, they'll eat each other.' Mr Davies takes out drawers full of moths, all layered in cabinets he made himself. 'You have to keep mothballs in each drawer, because if you don't the bodies of the moths get eaten by mites.' Indeed, some of them have crumbled to minute specks of dust. The biggest moth in the case is the Atlas moth from Taiwan, or Formosa as it is labelled in the glass case.

'The Hawk-moths like potato plants, at least the Death's Head does. It has markings like a skull. The Garden Tiger-moth likes garden privet. You always know where to look for them – the Old Lady moth, so called because you always find them hiding behind the curtains; the Oleander Hawk-moth's caterpillars feed on oleanders and periwinkle. The Bee Hawk-moth has transparent wings; there is a Lime-hawk, the Pine-moth; the Puss-moth has caterpillars like a cat. Look at this one.' He takes from the tray a rare hawk-moth on a pin with a tiny label in smudged copper-plate, indicating that it was bred in August 1909.

'As you walk through the woods, you see certain day-moths flying, although of course most fly at night. The lighted windows of the factory where I work attract hundreds of different species. There are over 2,000 kinds of moth known in Britain; not all of them have been classified. Sometimes we go round the trading estate at night with our nets. If anyone saw us they'd think we were burglars.'

Mrs Davies says 'I started as a child. The fields were covered with wild flowers then, and you'd see, oh, blankets of butterflies; there was like a rippling fabric over the fields of butterflies' wings. I had a dream of a father, I used to go with him, and he knew so much about nature. I think the satisfaction comes from looking at something of beauty, and also learning about them, their habitat and their lifecycle. I'm not a professional, only a passionate amateur. I prefer nature on our walls rather than pictures.'

She takes the little glass-topped wooden cabinets from the wall: Morphs, Didus from Peru, Hecuba, Aega; the Morpho Blues are used in pictures. 'The largest butterfly in the world is the Owl-butterfly. It comes from Japan. When you look at the underside, the markings look like big eyes, just like an owl. I love the Emerald moth – it has a green fabric on the upper wing, with a silver bottom wing. I'm proud of that one because the colour green is very hard to preserve. That is why it's no use trying to keep dragonflies; the iridescence fades and they go grey.'

Mr Davies says 'Unemployment definitely gave me a fascination and an interest that saved me. We'd go off in the morning, take a flask of tea, the dogs, some sandwiches, into the countryside, the fresh air.' Mrs Davies says 'I've always been naturally inquisitive. When I was a little girl, I used to ask "What's an apple made of?" and I never did get a satisfactory answer.'

'I'm not an expert, you understand. It would be a full time job if you were.' He takes out the killing jar, a more sinister aspect of his love of butterflies: a little anaesthetic in a Kilner preserving jar. 'I use acetone, chloroform discolours, and it isn't legal, anyway. It takes about half an hour to make sure they're dead. Then you take the specimen and lay it on a damp sponge' – he uses a plastic butter dish and a piece of moist green foam. 'You leave it on the foam in a warm airing cupboard for 24 hours; then lay it out on a specially prepared board, pinning a piece of cellophane across the wings, after you've separated the upper from the lower pair. Then you leave them for two weeks before putting them in the drawers or the cabinet.'

'They've been trying to reintroduce certain species that have become extinct, importing them from Europe. The Large Blue, for instance, they've tried to bring back into Norfolk; the precise location is kept secret, because people will catch and sell them. It's against the law to collect, but not to breed, so that is the way to get round it. Caring for nature is the most wonderful thing. I wouldn't change what we've got for all the money in the world.'

Small terraced house with bay window in a quiet street. Although the evening is light, the curtains are already drawn, enclosing a rather sombre house, with heavy wooden furniture, a place from which the still summer evening with its prosaic sounds of children playing can be excluded in favour of Dusty and Jim's make-believe other life. They are devoted to the Wild West. Dusty is a tough handsome woman in her thirties, energetically committed to her role as Atlanta, a fast-shooting Western gal, while Jim, who has only one arm, in his incarnation of the American West of the 1860s is called, perhaps predictably, Bandit.

'You can always tell when a Western film is not authentic. I can spot any inconsistency. We know everything, down to the last detail, of the way the West really was. The horses they used came from Spain, Andalusian, mixed with mustangs, with long manes and long tails. They use Arabian horses in spaghetti Westerns. They used chubby horses for round-ups, with heavy hindquarters and strong shoulders for driving the cattle. Cattle-men valued their horses too highly to mistreat them; the Spanish bits were too severe, so they used more humane spurs and bits. If you used some of the Spanish spurs, they would make great holes in the poor creature's flank. Mexican spurs were lethal. In Texas, they used rounded, daisy-shaped spurs. They loved their horses. They were on the trail for months at a time, they valued their horses and their saddles. There was always competition between Texas and Mexico: if one adopted one fashion, the other would take the opposite. My saddle was made in Mexico.' She fetches the beautifully wrought leather saddle and places it on the floor. 'I also do trick riding, lying over the saddle with my hands in the stirrups, and making scissor-movements with my legs. I'm learning stunt-riding.

'In the West, they always had slack reins, because the bridles give a big leverage on the horses' mouths. Unlike English riding, which has always been more uptight and controlled, they used to keep the reins slack. The Western way was good for horses, it doesn't spoil them. Everything we have is an exact replica. These black leather chaps, for instance. You need them. At the rodeos, they would come down the chute and drop onto the back of the wild ponies and grab a handful of mane to stay on. I have done it, with wild Welsh ponies. I fell off, put my elbow out and hurt my head, but I didn't want to miss the finals, so I didn't have any medical attention. It was a good thing I didn't, because in the finals, I landed in exactly the same position and did it again. They use the mechanical bull now, they don't use the wild ponies.

'I belong to the Western Horseman's Association, and I teach Western riding. I go to a round-up three times a year. I have a diploma; you have to pass a test, do a quiz and ride horses. I'm not so keen on dressage because it's too obsessed with perfection. My horse is Arabian: they won't accept the discipline. They're like dogs, pets really. I had her six weeks before I caught her. I do lassoing, arm-wrestling, shooting, fast-draw. Lassoing, it looks easy, but there's a way of holding the loop, and a proper lasso should be weighted according to your own weight. I won the ladies' arm-wrestling, and I'm the champion ladies' fast-draw. They judge you by a light-bulb on a stand: as soon as it comes on you go for your gun as fast as you can; they do it electronically in some places. You have to bring your gun up level before you fire it. There's a balloon on a stick beside you, the side-blast bursts the balloon if the gun is in the right position; so if the balloon doesn't burst, you haven't done it properly and you're disqualified. If it's done electronically, there's no argument about it. The champion can draw in 0.3 seconds. I can do it in 0.5.

'My horse is called Blaze, and he took a Western saddle with no problem. The best saddles are silver-tooled and made in Texas. They are very expensive. You have to tie the girths beneath, because when you've got cows attached to the saddle, it will tip forward. The way they make horses buck is to tie bucking straps around its stomach; that will make them buck like mad. They're illegal in Britain. They used to do them up too tight and that damaged the horses, even killed them.

'Of course, Texas is Mecca to Western fans. We belong to a group; some are mountain-men, some Civil War soldiers, others cowboys. Our mountain-men friends dress in buckskins, blanket coats, furs for the women and they carry long rifles. My mate dresses as an Indian. We have to have the right clothes, whichever group we belong to. For instance, in the Civil War, women got their fashions later than those on the East Coast, so while the Yankee women had gone into straight dresses, the Southerners were still wearing crinolines. We use the same materials they used then, ballgowns of satin and velvet, no modern polyesters. Fashions in the 1860s in the United States came from France and Britain and took some years to spread across the whole country. All our colours have to be right, no zips or buttons, just hooks and eyes. We get our inspiration from pictures, books in the library. We were at a Civil War wedding last weekend.' And she takes out a picture of an English country church, with the guard of honour dressed in Southern Civil War uniform, grey and red, with swords raised. The bride is in crinolines, with garlands looped around the hem of her dress. 'After that, we have to come back to reality for a time.' 'What is reality though?' 'It makes life very dull. We live for the next meeting, the next show. We put on shows at carnivals, fêtes, parties, a different one each year. This year it's been Shoot-out at the OK Corral. There's a plot, it's like a play really, you learn the lines. We do a hanging, that's quite popular. The man to be hanged is tried and sentenced. He wears a parachute harness under his clothes, so that the rope couldn't hurt him, even if there was a mistake. He acts up the part, lets his tongue roll out. We take the scenery in a big furniture van, set it up on the site where we're going to perform. There's a whole street of furniture – school, general store, sheriff's office, Red Ace Saloon, school house, baths. We do a performance every weekend in summer – Birmingham, Southampton, Kent. In Kent there is a mock-up of Laredo, a whole Western town.

'The most expensive things are the guns and holsters. I use a Colt 45, 3 lb weight; there's a slightly lighter one for women. You can shoot thumb-busting or fanning back the lever with the left hand; I prefer fanning. You can tell on the films if they're authentic or not. You see a cowboy riding the same horse after he's supposed to have travelled hundreds of miles. They could never do that, they took at least three on long journeys, the *remuda* they called it, they could never ride one all the time, it'd kill it.' Dusty shows the medals she has won, The Longhorn Western Club, Peter-borough Convention 1985, Fast-Draw Fanning Championship. 'Only two women do fast-draw in this area, me and my mate Linda. We compete once a fortnight over a period of about six months, then add up the points. I came fourth this year. Jim came third. I was first among the women.

'If Country and Western singers want to get a good crowd, they'll have a fast-draw competition. We're going to the Isle of Wight for an eight-day event. You put on your Stetson and guns in the morning, live as cowboys for the duration. You never have to be yourself at all. We have Western films, Western pub, Western dance-hall. Everybody outdoes each other with the gear – trouble is, all the army are colonels and all the Indians chiefs; nobody wants the more ordinary parts. When we do a Civil War battle, the women can only be nurses on the battlefield, because no women fought then. I have to wear a dress in Western clubs. If her man dies, a girl could grab the gun and get a bit of the action, but it's not so exciting for women. You can be Belle Starr, but she wouldn't have been like she is in the movies. She wore rough old skirts. Calamity Jane too. We call each other by our Western names. We're known as the Wild Bunch – they were outlaws from Colorado, and we stick with that era. We started by doing shows in small clubs, wearing chaps and satin shirts. And while we were doing that we met up with the Wild Bunch, and we just knew that was what we wanted to be. Because, of course, guns are not acceptable in country music circles, they looked on us as "yahoo cowboys", the old cowboy image.

'We've made it our speciality now. We're learning all the time. The 10-gallon hats were for water, to give the horses a drink. Everything had a function; the bandanna was used as a bandage, or to cover the mouth in a dust storm, and the hat was laid over the cowboy's face in death. The cowboys wore gloves to show they were different from the ranch hands, whose hands were much rougher. Their boots were so uncomfortable they often couldn't walk in them. They wanted to look elegant, they were dandies. The cowboys really were the elite.

'We don't make any profit out of the shows. The money goes to charity. We just cover our expenses, and the rest we donate. It's for the love of the thing that we do it. We buy toys and presents for kids or old people in the hospitals at Christmas.' Dusty takes out a newspaper cutting: a picture of Jim and herself with an old lady of 90 in a geriatric ward holding their pistol and pointing it at them while they pretend to be frightened.

Jim started off in 1974. His brother-in-law was in a club and introduced him to it. 'You build up the gear gradually. I wear a double-holster, two guns with six shots each. You have to oil and clean the guns, get rid of the residue from the bullets, wash them in boiling water and then clean them with a black powder solvent. They're all blanks of course, but the bullets vary, and some give off an almighty crack. You can't practise at home because of the noise. You wouldn't want people in the street to think there was a shoot-out going on. I went into a bank one morning, and I was looking for my bank book in my bag, and I'd still got the gun there. I laid it on the counter. I saw the bank clerk looking, I said "It's all right, it's not real." We did a show in one of the pubs, a singer invited us along with all the gear, and during the performance a chap in the bar nicked my gun in the holster. We had to report it to the police because they were scared he might go and hold up one of the all-night garages.'

Dusty made her own waistcoat: a beautifully crafted piece of work which she made from a sheet of tanned leather from the local market. 'It didn't cost much, but it was a real labour of love.' It is lined with an old black shirt, has been oiled and rumpled so that it looks old. There are transfers of a rose, a mountain lion, a rodeo horse and a cowboy, while her name has been carved as a frieze along the base: ATLANTA. It is laced up with leather. 'You do the patterns with tracing paper, go over it with a sharp pencil when the leather is wet. That leaves an indentation in the leather. Then you go over it with the leather tools to make the outlines stand out more. To make it look old I creased it up, and hammered like mad; it's the real thing.'

Dusty works as a cleaner in a college library; Jim is a cleaner in a shoe factory. 'They call me Bandit', he says, 'because I've only one arm. In one of the shows I wear a false arm. An Indian chops it off. That always goes down well. People come up to you and say "Where"s your arm?" I say to them "Come and feel it, see if you can find it. If you don't find it, buy me a pint; if you do, I'll buy you one."

'We like to do things realistically. When somebody is shot in the show, you have to have real blood. You get a hen's egg, blow it, seal it at one end with wax, then fill it with theatrical blood; seal it at the other end. Then, when you're shot, you just squash it and wait for the blood to flow. It's very lifelike; strap it to the chest or wherever it is you're going to be shot. People think my missing arm is part of the show. They say "That was really good, how do you do it?" Then, when they catch on, they're very embarrassed. I don't mind, I enjoy it.

'We all have names we know each other by better than our own names. There's Vegas and Carolina, Palomino, Wishbone – he's a tall skinny bloke, he plays the part of the undertaker in the show; he always carries two wishbones in his hatband. There's Navaho, Cattle Annie, Little Breeches. At the wedding last weekend, his name was Blue, hers was Belle. They never found out each other's real names until they came to get married – David and Sue. We travel in convoy to wherever the show is, communicate with each other over CB. It makes life very exciting. The only trouble is, you have to come down to earth at the end of it.'

Louise Heron is a warm, energetic woman in her early fifties. She lives in a neat council flat in a tower block; a comfortable and ornate interior, with glass objects and coloured vases, little animals, fluffy carpets and floral fabrics. Louise is a woman not embittered by adversity and unhappiness. She comes from a country village in East Anglia, and there is the friendly burr of country accent in her voice. Her father kept a pub, was Jewish and reared goats, which she loved. 'Oh, they'd eat the washing off the line, you'd feel something nibbling behind you, and when you turned round, half your dress was gone.' She was the fourth of ten children, the fourth girl. 'As a result, they called me Paddy-the-next-best-thing (to a boy), which was a popular novel of the time. I was called Paddy as a child, and it's only now I've gone back to the name of Louise. My father gave me a French name because he was wounded on the Somme. He had been 6 ft 3 in as a young man, but with a bullet lodged in his spine, he shrank for the rest of his life, and finished up almost a foot smaller.'

Louise now lives alone. One of the consolations of being on her own is that she can ring in regularly to the local radio station, take part in all the competitions. It provides her with a lifeline, as she says. But the great pleasure of her life is writing poetry, poetry that celebrates the sadness and joy of her own life, which pours spontaneously from her feelings. It is the poetry of Country and Western songs, that people's art which proclaims the primacy of the feelings over everything else.

Louise was married at 19, and had three stillbirths before any of the three who lived was born. Her first husband died when Calvin, the eldest, was 11. 'He tried to take his father's place, tried to look after me, bless him. He's always been a bit special. But his brother feels that I preferred Calvin. I didn't. I love them both, but they're so different; and both Pisces too. I used to believe in astrology, but they're chalk and cheese. Their wives are both Taurus as well, and they too couldn't be more different.

'My eldest has a little shop, he is doing very well. The other is a lorry driver, he doesn't have a care in the world. My daughter is about to be married. I wanted her to have a church wedding, I'd set my heart on it, I like things to be done properly. She's been living with her bloke. You might say it's hypocritical, having a church wedding after you've lived together, but I've always dreamed of it. I'm very traditional, and very romantic. I'm all for the family; only you can't tell young people that. They don't want to know, and that makes me mad.

'I loved the big family I came from, my brothers and sisters. The youngest was a mongol. He's in a subnormality hospital now. But my mother always said she had more love from him than from the rest of us put together. He's a high-grade mongol, he can do some things for himself, he's lovely really. I had a brother killed on his motorbike when he was 19. I've written a poem about him too. I used to write poetry when I was a teenager. My mother wrote poetry to relieve her feelings. When I got married the first time, I threw it all away. I think I must've imagined I was going to get enough romance in real life without having to find it in poems. I couldn't have been more wrong.

'It's only since my second marriage broke up that I've taken up writing again. That's what brought me to Northampton. But he was violent. I stayed with him for 14 years. It was only two years ago that I had the courage to leave him. I always thought a woman on her own, well it isn't natural, she couldn't survive without a man. My mother died at the same time. I was in a women's refuge. I thought he would reform. He always used to say how sorry he was after he'd beaten me, and he'd never do it again. I believed him. That's why I stuck it so long. My father died five years ago. My mother married again within a year, the village postmaster.

'I've a lovely dog. She was a stray I got from the RSPCA. I didn't really want such a big dog, but as soon as I saw her, I fell in love with her. She takes up a lot of my time because I can't write at the moment because I've a swollen hand. They told me it was arthritis, then I left it for a year, and it turns out it's the tendons and guides. I just can't use it, and it does give me terrible pain. It's frustrating, not being able to write. My friend comes sometimes and writes the poems out for me.

'I've a lot of time on my hands. I get lonely. You can't really go out much socially, a woman on her own, especially round here, you'd soon get propositioned. Of course, I get lonely. But I manage to take the dog out once a day, do my bit of housework, listen to the radio; and I love my Country and Western – Kenny Rogers, Conway Twitty, Billy Jo Spiers, Tammy Wynette.

'The poetry I've been doing recently is more serious. I'm still romantic, I do Valentines and things like that, but I also write down my own feelings. Such a lot of people don't know what they feel. They're cut off even from themselves. At least that is one thing I can be pleased with. I'm on invalidity benefit because I had cancer of the cervix when I was 45. I had ten weeks' radium treatment; they couldn't operate because I'd already had one kidney removed. I recovered from the cancer, but I get bladder trouble and some days I'm very tired. They told me that if they cured the cancer, it would take five years. So on my 50th birthday, I had a disco, one helluva party. That was really something to celebrate. I don't complain – there's nobody going to listen if you do. I think I'm like my mother – she never told anyone her feelings, and that was why she used to write. I keep it all inside me, then when I'm alone, I write it all down.

'I had a wonderful childhood, the freedom of the village. In the war, all the Americans were there, near the base at Chelveston. My Dad used to do a bit of fiddling, then they'd bring some stuff in exchange for a drink – meat, sweets, things from the base that he could sell. It was a golden time. My brothers and sisters are all scattered now. I keep in touch with them. My sister went to America as a GI bride.'

My Sons

Oh isn't it strange how brothers can be
Two sons I have both dear to me
Entirely different in their life-style
One keeps his life in a clean tidy file
Goes around in a coat neat and white
Running his store and keeping things right.
Behind a counter selling bacon and meat
Serving his customers whatever the treat
A job of importance he worked hard to get
His feet on the ground so firmly set.
Medium build and hair of fair
Pale blue eyes seeing his future clear

The younger sees his world behind a bigwheel
Not knowing where or when he'll get his next meal.
A truck driver he chose to be
Travelling the country on the turn of the key.
The cab is his bed when long journeys he makes
Keen eye on the road and sure foot on the brakes
As big as a giant and dark is his hair
He looks at life without a care
Always covered in grease and dirt
In blue denim jeans and baggy T-shirt.
One works with his brain, his hands unsoiled
The other with hands which callouses spoiled
Although different patterns of life they weave
Both equal in my eyes and my love they receive.

My Father

A bowed head and a back bent in pain
Two sticks to help his legs take the strain
His steps so unsure and progress was slow
With eyes looking down where e'er he did go.
He once was a tall man, handsome and strong
And marched with others singing their song.
On dark dusty roads in faraway lands
In deep damp trenches and blood-soaked sands.
Just like a lion, such courage and pride
Standing erect with gun by his side.
It was for us he suffered, for his country he fought
But one day in France a bullet he caught.
He lived six foot tall, but died six foot none,
Fought for his life when all hope was gone.
Some of his pals never made it at all
They stood by his side and he saw them fall.
But he was left to tell us his story
To show us his medals for valour and glory.
As in war in peacetime he did his best
Till at least free from pain his body can rest.
I knew this man, he was the best pal I had
Remember him with love, cause he was my Dad.

In their late sixties, Mr and Mrs Leach live in a modest but comfortable
terraced house with a cramped but sunny back garden, covered with wild

cyclamen, fuchsias, camellias and pelargoniums. A cluttered front room, with a suite that is too big for the space it occupies, dolls in national costume from all over Europe; reproductions of Gerard Ter Borch and Canaletto; pictures of daughter and grand-daughter; vases of chrysanthemums and dahlias, red-pompom and pink semi-cactus dahlias.

Mr Leach has always loved flowers. As a child he lived in a poor part of the town where there was no garden, but his family always retained a deep love of the country from which they came. His father was in the First World War in the air flying corps, but was invalided out and became a newsvendor in the 1920s. Mr Leach was an only child; was fascinated by botany at school, and loved drawing and painting flowers. The school kept all his books, he admits shyly, so that his drawings could be shown to future pupils. His father always had an allotment. For many years he also had a piece of ground, now ploughed up with a new estate on it. When he recalls the produce that the allotments provided, he says 'People don't know what varieties of fruit and vegetables we've given up. Who has ever heard of Pitmaston Duchess pears now? The allotment I had, there were two great pear trees, the fruit used to turn yellow and the juice would spill down your chin when you ate into one. They were so big, if you were standing under the tree in October and you got one of them falling on your head, it could near knock you out. I used to get half a ton of pears off them. The trees were 60 ft high, 100 years old, they were like forest trees. You can't get them off a dwarf stock, that's why they don't grow them now, the fruit would be too heavy for the branches. The only fruit they want to grow now is the sort you can pick without ladders. I took an old boy's ground over when he retired. He'd been a school's gardener in the days when gardening was still a school subject; he had 20 pole of ground, ten of it fruit. He used to exhibit stuff – Peasgood Nonsuch apples, Lane's Prince Albert, James Grieves, Reverend Wilkins. You never see them now. The Prince Albert were huge, without a blemish, bright green; the Peasgood Nonsuch went yellowish, lovely flavour. But everything has been standardized; if they want to grow half a million trees, you'll get the easy varieties of apple, Granny Smith, Golden Delicious, all identical size, all without flavour, turnips and cotton wool. Don't you believe that we get freedom of choice – we get the apples they can mass-market the easiest.

'It's like tomatoes, Moneymaker, everybody grows them, but only because they're prolific, they're not the best.'

In their leisure, many people retain knowledge and skills that have decayed in work; a kind of knowledge that has not exactly been suppressed, but has been crowded out of consciousness by the clamour of the markets. Mr Leach goes on: 'Alicante tomatoes, you'll still find those among connoisseurs, but you don't get so many of them on each plant. But if you're growing your own, that's when you get freedom of choice. But, of course, it's hard work. People want the easiest. Of course, the allotments are disappearing, there's less and less ground given over to them now. My allotment is privately owned; and what happens, if one falls vacant, an old man dies, his widow hangs on to the bit of ground, hoping the price will go up, and in the meantime, the land goes to ruin. I've known a ten-pole piece of ground change hands for £500 if it's a prime piece of ground like mine is. My biggest problem up there is badgers, digging things up. I planted 2,000 gladioli this year, and I've stock worth two or three thousand on it. I plant hybrid gladioli, not the big ones; only the badgers are a ruddy nuisance, they scratch up anything for the sheer hell of it.

'I've got raspberries, they've been in 12 years, I think they're about finished. I've been used to getting 150 lb a year. This year we only got about 60 lb. I eat a few every day, then freeze some for the winter. They're the best fruit to freeze.' He fetches a Tupperware box full of frozen raspberries. 'Malling Admiral, not so acidy as some raspberries.'

'I have 25 pole of allotment now; that is 154 yd long, 20 ft wide. I don't grow brassicas – cauliflower, cabbage – only peas and beans. Just freeze them straight from the vine, none of this blanching nonsense, they're beautiful; a row of early potatoes and a row of lates. We don't have to buy any fruit or vegetables.

'I've been growing dahlias for 40 years. These in the vases are Vaguely Noble and Pink Shirley Albana. The president of our club, he raises new varieties of dahlias, he's one of the best growers in England. He doesn't do special crossings, but leaves it to nature; uses the best seed-carriers rather than any fertilizing agent. He can predict they'll be 80 per cent full of double flowers.

'I had a visit from the Office of Fair Trading here yesterday. A man had bought a polythene pack of dahlias from a garden centre. They'd been bought as poms and miniature decoratives. Well, a pom, a real pom is only 2 inches. He'd planted them, and what came up was rubbish, just two rows of petals and a single disc. He was disappointed, so he took them back to the garden centre. Of course, they buy in from Holland, or rather, they were packed in Britain by a company from Holland, so by the time they reached the garden centre they'd already gone through three different pairs of hands. Nobody was to blame; but, of course, it's easy to sell things to people who don't know anything about what they're buying. Not one in a hundred would complain. I go to these garden centres sometimes. You see people wheeling a trolley with £60 or £70 worth of plants, ericas, rhododendrons, conifers – they've no idea that they all require quite different circumstances. You want to tell them, "Don't bother, half the stuff you've got there can't flourish." But of course, you can't. You see people paying out for flowers in full bloom that won't last overnight, they want instant gardens; and most of the things could be got for nothing except a bit of patience.

'It's hard work, but you have to enjoy it. There's a lot of rivalry between those who go for different kinds of plants. Chrysanthemum growers will refer to dahlias as weeds. All I know is that I love nature and the beauty of flowers. I suppose I began during the war, in the Dig for Victory campaign; my father had an allotment up the park. I used to go up the allotment and watch my Dad. I remember one day going past a seed merchant 43 years ago, and I bought two dahlias. One was a Baron von Malk, the other Baron von Sittars; ball dahlias, one pink and the other orange with a brown tip. I stuck them in the garden and was thrilled to bits when they came up. It was a cracker. It was perfect. I thought no bugger's ever grown a better dahlia than that. I was in engineering in the war, and the foreman there knew a nurseryman, so he said "Go up and see him." Well, he had the most handsome display of dahlias you could ever imagine. I though "Oh this is a bit of all right." He said "Go and pick some flowers, one of all those you like, and I'll save you a tuber of every one." I thought "How can he possibly know all the names if I pick them." But he did.

'There are 12 or 13 different types of dahlias, poms, miniature, decorative, ball, small ball, cactus, small semi-cactus, large cactus, giant dec., giant cactus. The biggest is the giant dec. or cactus, they're 14 inches in diameter. Well, I thought it was fabulous. The nurseryman said "Come up in October and I'll have the tubers ready for you." Well, I pushed my daughter up there in her push-chair, and he had two sacks of the things. I paid 30 shillings for the lot, I pushed them back home in the pram, while the wife and the little girl had to go home on the bus. In fact, my wife said "Fancy paying all that money for a few tubers." But they were beautiful.

'The Dahlia Society was founded in Northampton in 1961, it'll be our silver jubilee next year. We have about 85 members, although because we do trading discounts of 20 or 30 per cent, some just pay their pound to join for the sake of what they can get out of it. But most participate, and there's a nucleus of real enthusiasts. We have a plant sale every May – auction off all the plants that are left over; we made £180 this year in an hour and a half. It keeps the society going. There's a newsletter four times a year. I don't do that, thank goodness. We have film shows and talks from top growers; slides and talks from fuchsia and chrysanthemum growers. I don't like fuchsias because finance has taken over. We have a dahlia show, but you don't win big prizes. You don't grow dahlias to get rich. The big dahlia shows, the problem is getting there with your flowers in perfect condition. I used to travel around with a bucket on the back of my push-bike; it always kept the flowers fresh.

'But showing is killing dahlias. Dahlia growing is being strangled by the National Dahlia Show at Westminster. They test the size of the blooms with a ring to make sure they are the correct size for each class. It has nothing to do with nature; if the dahlia is slightly over size – if the ring passes over it and touches the petals – they write n.a.s. on the card, not according to schedule. The pom dahlia, for instance, has to be exactly 2 in in diameter. People come from all over England to Westminster, and then when they get there, they see n.a.s. written on their card. This year brought it to a head. With the wet summer, they couldn't keep the size of the flower down to the rules. There was one man who came from Crewe, he'd 148 small cactus dahlias. As soon as you get there, they start judging, and the judging goes on right through the night. They have to put the ring over every bloom. They discarded about 50 per cent of the exhibits. It was down to the last 18, and by this time it was 3 a.m. And when the man from Crewe looked at his, they'd all got n.a.s. on the card. Since they'd been in water, they'd all come out that little bit more, so they wouldn't pass. I said to one of the judges "Has it ever occurred to you why fewer and fewer people are showing dahlias?" Compared to eight years ago there was only half the number there'd been. I said "People don't come all this way to be insulted."

'It's different in the chrysanth world; there's small reflexing, medium and large incurving. They don't have all this fuss about size. We've sent a resolution to the National Dahlia Conference, deploring the exhibition world. Only a tiny percentage of dahlia growers show. No nurseryman gets wealthy through exhibitions; their bread and butter is the back garden people.

'There's one thing about dahlias – you don't have to do what the books tell you. What you do between November and March is what counts. You have to remember that people who write books about it want to sell dahlias. You should ignore them. They tell you "Leave one foot of the stem on, turn upside down, wash them, dry in flowers of sulphur to stop mildew, bore a hole through the stem to let the air in." It's rubbish. I leave mine in the ground till December, cut down to the bare wood, so there's only half an inch of stem, trim all the surplus roots off, stick them in the cellar and leave them. They come up perfect.

'It's the same with the glads. They tell you to wait till the leaves die, then hang them upside down. That way you'll lose them all. It's all a load of nonsense. Experts. Don't trust them. They make a mystery over nothing. You see them on television, with all the equipment. It's a con-job, they're just advertising all the tackle, on a retainer I shouldn't wonder from the companies to promote their goods. You don't need all that. With glads, nine weeks after they flower, cut them off in the green, leave them to dry; peel them down to the corms, that is, the part that makes up the current year's leaf growth. With a corm, you can't see the embryonic flower, unlike a bulb, a tulip for instance. You have to pare them down because of the risk of soil-borne fungus, you can't see what's going on otherwise. Experts? Never listen to them. Look what experts said about the Titanic, and see what happened to that.

'I've grown a lot of hybrid glads from seed. Charles Unwin, the seedsman, when he was 80, he was going blind, so he gave all his seeds to the National Gladioli Society. I bought two manila envelopes full of seeds for 10 pence each. I sowed them, they came up like grass; took three years to bloom, miniatures, primulinas. I now grow 2,000. One florist in the town buys the lot. Cutting them is the biggest job, you have to cut them when the bottom floret is just showing colour. I deliver a load of them to the florist on my scooter, then go back to the allotment for more, by the time I get back, the first lot have been used in wreaths and sprays. I also grow Peruvian lilies from seed. You listen to the TV people, they'll tell you how difficult it is, oh it can't be done. That'll convince you you can't do anything. Well it's all nonsense.

'I plan my allotment out each year. I've got it all settled by the end of February, although nothing goes in till late March. Then I put in the dahlias at 9 ins depth, you won't get frosts penetrating that deep by then; and they'll appear mid-May.

'People tell you that growing Peruvian lillies is like climbing Everest – it can't be done, it's a miracle if you can do it. They do take three months to a year to germinate, you need patience. I got 4,000 seeds from mine; whereas if you buy them they'll cost £1 for 20 seeds. I soak them 36 hours. Last year I planted them on 4 March, tipped the rest in a peat-filled polythene bag, by the end of May I had 6 in plants as thick as mustard and cress. I planted them out in 16 trenches, had perfect tubers.

'I used to work at an engineering factory, aircraft parts. Then I was made redundant at 55, so I thought well, the daughter was grown up, I'll do what I want to do. I got a job on the council, working for the Parks Department. I was in charge of one of the parks; I dropped about £30 a week in salary, but I loved it. All the years I put up with a job I hated, just for the sake of the family. I always used to go up to the allotment after work, there I could breathe, get a sense of freedom and the beauty of natural things. When I worked in the park, I used to leave the house at 7.20 every day for a day in the park; and get paid for it. What a wonderful experience! In the factory I had a skilled job, I was an auto setter. It doesn't exist any more. The allotment was the only way I kept my sanity. As a kid, I'd always been roaming the countryside and always loved art. And one of the grandchildren has turned out to be an artist. The other is in the Navy. The youngest is still at school. Our daughter has had to bring them up on her own. She has had a struggle. She is wardrobe mistress at the local theatre. Her work is her pleasure too.'

Mr McMahon is 73. He and his wife have just celebrated their golden wedding: a plate hangs on the wall of their small town-centre council flat, commemorating their 50 years together. They had known each other as children, lived and played with each other in neighbouring streets. Mrs McMahon says her leisure is TV; she finds it difficult to get around. Her husband is bursting with vigour and energy, and devoted to coarse fishing, and his small angling club in particular. He takes his sport seriously. Ideas about amateurism are quite false. Any team, any club demands a high standard of both discipline and responsibility. 'There's scruffy anglers like there's scruffy people', he says sternly. 'You have to have discipline in a club. If a member breaks the rules, abuses the landowner or whatever, he'll have to appear before the committee. If you didn't do that, it would get out of hand. Of course, you can't patrol the waters seven days a week, but you have to be as sure as you can that people respect the rule, don't leave rubbish – polythene bags, tins, fag packets.

'When we have a match, you peg the match along the canal; and if there's any rubbish there, the bloke in that position has to clear it up, even if it's not his. You draw for each peg; there's maybe 30 take part in a match. You fish with the flow of the river. If the water is still, you have 10 yards either side – that is a peg of 20 yards per person, each one's swim, as we call it. Some clubs have their water permanently pegged. There's been all hell let loose in the fishing world this year, the way the British Waterways Board is relinquishing all the leases. They've had the marketing people in, letting the canals according to a new fixed rate. The Board was losing money on its fishing, so they now suggest a rate of £15 a year for national clubs, £10 for regional, £2.50 for local. Well, we lease our water, it's been leased privately since 1961, and we pay about £10 a mile. We rent a stretch from the council. When the canals were originally cut, some farms retained the fishing and gaming rights, others sold them. So the Board don't by any means own all the fishing rights. There is over 1,000 miles of canal belonging to them. In 1984, they took only £110,000 from anglers, whereas from the boats they took £2 million. So this is what it's all about. The Board is subsidized, and this government has given them the order to get their finger out and make some more money out of the anglers.

'Over the past ten or 15 years, the prize money has gone up in match fishing. The entrance fees have all gone up. For some people, it's big business now. I know one bloke who picked up over £1,000 in one match. It's one of the few things they won't put on TV – there's not enough action, so they won't ever do a snooker or a darts on it; all these ordinary people's pastimes that have become big money. Who'd watch those things on TV, if there wasn't a fortune for somebody at the end of it?

'There's no closed season for pike fishing; and you can count them in your catch in coarse fishing matches; a lot of what you'll get are what we call nits, the little fish. In a match you'll spend most of your time scratting for little bits and pieces – roach, gudgeon, skimmer, bream.

'This year me and my mate were on holiday in the Fens. We went for a fishing match on one of the drains – the irrigated canals. It was an open match. We thought we'd go from our digs to the venue, got tickets, but when we got there, it was all the tackle-trade wallahs, the maggot breeders. We drew up beside the drain; it was blowing a gale, there were waves on the canals. Only 30 people had turned up, so they said "Oh, we'd better up the entrance fee to a fiver." We pulled out. We were the only two individuals there, all the others were match professionals.

'Ours is a social club. We have a sweepstake each week and plough the money back to the members, that subsidizes the coaches when we go to matches. I joined my club when I was 17, it cost 5 shillings. Well, my wage was only a pound then. Years ago, maggots cost 6½d a pint, they used to breed them off the skins from the tanneries. Now, of course, they have maggot factories. They breed the flies off offal or fish; you get several blows off fish. They cost £1.20 a pint, £1.40 for casters – that's when they reach the stage just before they become flies. Caster-fishing is a phenomenon of the last 15 years. It's good groundbait, deadly.' Mr McMahon gets the maggots out of the fridge, a writhing mass of yellow and bronze. 'Since Smithy, the Birmingham angler, died of cancer there has been a lot of talk about banning the dye that colours the maggots, chrysadene. The casters are hard, shiny brown casings. He feeds a few to some enormous goldfish in a tank on the kitchen shelf. They gobble them up. He says 'Fish-food is one of the biggest rackets. 95 per cent of it is dog-biscuit dust.

'The greybottle produces the best maggots; then there are the pink maggots which turn into the almost transparent green flies. The breeders dye the maggots when feeding them. Anglers always have stories about leaving boxes of maggots in warm places so they hatch out overnight.' He laughs. 'We left some in the bathroom. "Come up here", she called. There were these flies everywhere, we were sucking them up with the vacuum cleaner, squashing them all over the wall.' (Another angler I spoke to told me how maggots had broken up his marriage. To get his own back after a quarrel with his wife, he'd left a tin of maggots on the radiator all night. When she got up in the morning, the house was swarming with blow-flies. She had left home and never gone back.)

'Fishing, like so many other things, is big business. You can see people with £1,000's worth of fishing gear in some of the big matches. They'll use poles that can cost anything from £300 to £800 apiece. I don't need it. They invest a lot in perfecting the materials. The continentals have swept the board in match angling. We used to use the old Tonkin cane, China bamboo which was heavy and thick; then the female bamboo which was lighter. Then came the Spanish reed, which was hollow and lighter still. But you don't see any of those made from natural materials today. It's all either fibreglass or carbon fibre or boron that's spun on mandrels, it's the lightest and most expensive. But this is what has happened to fishing – there's a lot of money to be made out of all the paraphernalia; in fact, that becomes more important than the fish to some people.

'I used to make rods, when purchase tax used to be 66 per cent. I made them out of female bamboo, got the supplies from Nottingham. I had a workshop at the back of the little terraced house where we lived. I used to make first-class lightweight rods for match fishing. But, of course, with these new synthetic materials, they'll make a rod up to 12 ft which weighs less than an ounce per foot; over that, well I think a 14 ft rod weighs 15 oz, but a 12 ft one is as little as 10 oz. I know one thing – they won't last like the ones I used to make. My mate is still using a rod I made in 1952 out of Spanish reed. The one I use is fibreglass. But you can pay £700 for a 30 ft pole; 90 per cent of those are carbon fibre; and the shafts of the landing-nets are made of fibreglass too.

'I used to work on the railway, and it was my delight to get out in the country for a few hours' fishing. I'd take the train, quarter-fare concessionary to Oundle; all I took was a few bread cubes and some hempseed; they banned hempseed because they thought you'd spoil the fish and wouldn't be able to catch them with anything else. It was a fallacy, like so many other bits of expert advice. They use hemp as groundbait now – that is what you throw in the water to get the fish all excited – so that proves it was a mistake. You need something to feed your swim, they go barmy over hempseed ... That used to get 'em going, Manchurian hempseed, 2d a pack, later Chilean; you can't get it now. If you don't use groundbait, you'll find you're striking fresh air all the time.

'Of course, a lot of water's been overfished; 1985 was a poor season. And the heavy rains wash more and more of the chemicals from the farms into the water. We've had fish dying in front of us, 3 or 4 lb bream. Like in the fens, when the peas have finished, they take up the vines and stack them; the rain comes, and as the vines rot, it all drains into the canals and it de-oxygenates the water. No wonder there isn't the fish there was.

'I was county champion in 1967.' He takes down a trophy: a silver urn, with a silver model of a fish on top; inscribed Twentieth Century Working Men's Club, Angling Section.

'In a match, you weigh up your catch at the end. You'll fish maybe four or five hours; anything from 15 to 20 lb of bream, 8 or 9 lb of roach. In the county championship the winner got 67 lb of bream this year, and the biggest fish weighed only 7 lb 2 oz. I think the record is 111 lb. People do eat it. As a kid, I used to take home gudgeon; my Mam used to cook them, just run her thumb through them, just twist the head off. People used to say it was the best fish there is. Sometimes they'd cook roach, but they were inspid. I don't like killing fish, and I don't believe in live-baiting either; although pike will kill them anyway. The fish you get in coarse angling – perch, chub, dace, bream, ruffer . . . I've fished all over England. In 1954 it was so wet, with all the rains, the water was flowing the wrong way, flowing backwards.

'It started when I was a kid. What else was there then? We used to go down the dairyfields; we started with a cane out of the garden – canes they used for the runner beans – and a bent pin. That didn't cost anything. Then gradually I got a bamboo pole with a goose quill and an elastic band, a hook and one shot. We used to lean over the brook catching sticklebacks with a worm or two worms tied in a granny knot. Then you advanced to a hook, pellets of paste hanging from a tree over the river.

'When you're fishing, there's two things happen. Your mind departs from all that is going on in the world; you sit by the side of the bank, and everything else simply melts away, you're in a world of your own choosing; and you know it's your wits against theirs in the water. Even if you don't catch a thing, it's no matter, the water, the play of the light, the sunshine. The Ouse is my favourite river, Olney, St Neots, the scenery, that's England to me, that's what I love and what is familiar.

'I was a founder member of the fishing section of our railway club. I was made redundant in 1970, my job finished after 34 years, thanks to Beeching. Before that I worked in a piano factory where they made the pedals. And all the years I was on the railway, after work I'd cycle from the station to the canal at Stoke Bruerne – 12 miles. In the days I was courting, I took her on the crossbar of my bike, didn't I, Doll? Sometimes she rode on the back. Only once ever fell off, didn't you love, that time we'd gathered a load of blackberries and she fell off with the whole lot of them.

'Fishing has been a great consolation to me. My father died when I was eight. He had consumption, like so many of the poor buggers in them days, especially in the leather industry, the dust in the factories, and the TB from the cattle, of course. All my life I've loved fishing, and I've done it on a shoestring. For bait, a few cubes of bread out of a steam loaf; for ground-bait, bread dried in the oven. I caught more fish then than you do now.

'At the Britannia Club we pay subs of £3.50 a year; we're a hundred strong; have a big do once a year. There's only two women members. We started in an old town centre pub in 1933; then when pub modernization came, the landlord chucked us out. We get a room at the working men's club for nothing.

'The British Waterways Board is trying to run its water now to make money. Sixty per cent of clubs will have to fold if that happens. After more than 80 years of tenancy, the various governing bodies of the waterways have given them one year's notice of termination of agreement. It's a shame; there are some places where you can't even fish at weekends because of the number of boats. And the Board hasn't touched our canal for 17 years, no edging. We've had to keep the waterway towpaths open ourselves. The clubs have done it voluntarily. If you leave the paths even for one year, they'd be so overgrown they'd be impassable. And now after 17 years they've ordered us not to do it. I was fishing one day, and these two officials came down and asked who'd done the edges. I didn't even turn round to look at them. I told them to get stuffed. "Will you move your umbrella?" I never even looked at them. They went away again.'

Colin Webb is in his late twenties. He used to be a policeman, but now works for the Post Office. He is Secretary of the Knights of the Rose. The society was formed in 1979; it is not a national organization, but there are medieval societies in most towns and cities. 'Some specialize in court and politics; our interest is medieval warfare. We provide entertainment for other people's banquets on an amateur basis – not like at Warwick Castle where they do it on a commercial basis. We do it for people who are celebrating and want something a bit different – a church fête, the sub-aqua club, an international scouting jamboree. Most of our work is in summer, it has to be out of doors. You can't stage fights in a confined space – from the safety point of view you need a sizeable arena.

'I like the period. I like the chivalry and its romantic ideals – something that's lacking in today's life. Mind you, life was brutal and basic then if you were a peasant. Most of the parts we play are nobles, knights: I suppose their present-day equivalent would be generals and field-marshals; they were the top echelon of the military order of the period. It's part of our constitution that newcomers have to join us as a man-at-arms or an archer. They have to make their necessary safety equipment before they can progress, and they have to stay a year to make sure they fit in. They act as a body-carrier, a peasant or a body-robber before they can become a knight. We teach the skills so people can become knights – more mobility than there was in the Middle Ages! Most of us can use a sword. People who watch TV films are likely to get it wrong – they use a sword as a fencing sword. You could never do that with our sword, the wrist movements would be impossible, it's too heavy. They used their swords at that time to strike blows at their opponent, and they used a whole arm movement. The idea was to hit as hard as you could, not to pierce the body. When you see old films, you realize how wrong they were. In recent years, they've perfected the period detail.'

He fetches his sword and lays it on the table of the small council flat where he lives with his elderly parents. 'This is a slashing and cutting sword. We make the gear ourselves.' The sword has a thick broad blade, much battered into rough serrations at the edges where it has struck the shields and mail-suits of his adversaries in battle. Colin has made his own link-mail head-cover: rows of tiny metal loops linked together in a dense mesh. The finished article is very heavy. 'You make it with 1 or 2mm of wire, high tensile wire, wound round and round a 6 in nail. It comes out like a spring, you cut it out in individual rings, then link them all together. It's a very tedious job, it took me several months to make the head-cover; to make a full suit would need 18 months or two years. They didn't use the word chain-mail; that's a Victorian invention. This is called a quaff – it covers the head and protects the back and front of the neck.' There are a few rows of brass links for decoration at the base. Great authenticity is necessary, and much ingenuity goes into making the equipment. 'During the probation period for newcomers, they have to make their own sword and an ackton – that's a padded jacket with mail sleeves, and a full shirt of mail armour.

'This is the helm.' It is a kind of inverted bucket, padded with felt and rivetted together, several plates of metal. There is a visor at the front. 'We've had one or two near misses during the fights, but nothing serious. Every fight we do is choreographed, there's no free-for-all. This is called a barrel-helm, five plates of 16-gauge steel rivetted together. We make everything, except a few ceremonial things, like the daggers. This, for instance; you may think this is a Nazi dagger; actually, the Nazis copied the Holbein dagger; they modelled their ceremonial things on the Middle Ages. I had mine – it's a classic basic medieval dagger – made by a knife-smith in London. I don't use it in combat, it's too dangerous. And this is the dress-sword: the handle is a piece of dowling stained brown. The knight would have carried this court-sword on ceremonial occasions, at banquets maybe. There is also a hand-axe, a horseman's axe with a studded handle. We don't use horses because they are too expensive, although some of the medieval societies specialize in horses. We charge only £30 for a 45-minute display. The most we've ever charged is £200, but that included £90 travelling expenses. There is a group called the Knights' Jousting Association, they charge far more, and they use professional stunt-men. We can't match that.

'I work in the Post Office; other members are in Avon Cosmetics, they work in garages, building societies, nursing, libraries. We are only the tip of the iceberg of the interest there is in these things. There are big companies being set up – Timescape Adventures, they own an island and big houses. You pay to stay with them for a week, and live out the life they would have lived in medieval times; or it may be outer space, science fiction, whatever your fantasy is.

'We work out each fight beforehand, down to the last detail. I play the figure of the Earl Marshal; that is, in modern terms, a sort of referee of the fight. I would have been second only to the King himself, a very powerful person. The tournaments would have been for sport or for practice for battle. Then, of course, there was the challenge of the duel to the death. The fights between the knights themselves were over land, for favours from the King, to get castles, land, peasants and retainers. People were chattels, slaves really.

'Our plays have a kind of scenario. There's one about King Richard. There are two sides engaged in battle, and on one side there is a monk who is always interfering; he is advising the fighters what to do. In the end, when they've won, he throws off his disguise and it's King Richard. Or there are shorter ones; one where two knights are fighting over a lady's hand. We have six or seven women in the group, of a core membership of around 30.

'We do our own research, and we've gradually acquired considerable knowledge about weaponry and armour. We keep strictly to the code of heraldry in the combinations of colours that would have been used then. For instance, black and red was not permitted. We are learning all the time. You get more and more deeply involved, the more you discover. We use local libraries, we go to Warwick Castle, the Tower of London; we've organized a trip to see the reserve collection of armour at the Tower, we'll visit their workshops. They only allow that to specialist groups. This year was the 500th anniversary of the Battle of Bosworth; that was the turning point in the Wars of the Roses, so we went there with societies from all over England. We find that people are very ignorant. They imagine they know. But we are there to inform them. We have displays of weaponry at the local show in the park, we have people actually making mail-armour, talking to visitors. At fêtes, we set up a have-a-go stall with archery. It takes up a lot of time. Being the secretary, I have to get things organized. We have an annual banquet, and we sell tickets to anybody who wants to come. We serve up the kind of food they would have eaten then – syllabub and chicken in honey, vegetable broth, boar's head, which our caterer decorates – we don't actually eat it, apart from some small bits, we actually eat belly of pork. A musician plays the Boar's Head Carol, on the keyboard actually, as he walks round the room.

'My full title is Sir Arthur de Neville, Lord High Sheriff of Bedford, Earl-Marshal of All England. We never use real titles, especially if they still exist. If we wanted to do that, we would have to approach the present bearers of the title first. But we do use proper medieval-type names.

'It opens up a new world of history. I can't say school did anything to kindle my historical imagination. Quite the opposite. I did O-level British Political History. Since I've been involved in this, I've developed skills I didn't know I had. We go every year to Belvoir Castle to do a display of archery. Of course, target archery, with the round target, was the medieval sport. Field archery has been developed in America. It began during the closed season for hunting; it's a bit like golf – you have a series of targets around a course. The Swedes are very good at it. The European field-archery championship was held at Woburn Abbey this year.

'There's a big range of equipment and shooting styles. A beginner's bow is £50; a Yamaha would cost £500 for the basic bow, all the associated equipment would add £300 – stabilizers, sights, top-class arrows, made of aluminium alloy, high-tensile aluminium cost £5 each; for carbon fibre/aluminium alloy mix they're £220 for ten. Archery is a growing sport.

'Where I work, it doesn't involve deep thought. You could say it is a humdrum job. So this is something to escape into and to look forward to. My work is coding: we have automatic sorting machines and do the sorting for the whole country. The letter comes up in front of you automatically, I tap the code on a machine, numbers appear as phosphorescent dots, there's a box at the end, and they get sorted into the right town. You can only sit two hours at a time at the coding machine. There's piped radio to each desk, but it is very tedious.

'There are a lot of people interested in these various historical moments. There's the Odin's Guard people, the Ermine Street Guard, the Roman Imperial Army. Partly it's escape, partly it's educational. We make a medieval pilgrimage every year, wearing the costume, sleeping rough. We raise money for local hospitals. We've been to Canterbury, Salisbury to Wells, that's 90 miles in three and a half days, Chepstow to Gloucester, York to Durham. We wear hose, stout boots, smock-shirts, hat and shoulder-bag for blankets and food. We wear an ankle-boot with a low heel. They used to wear leather armour because they couldn't afford metal; we wear metal because we can't afford leather. They used the shoulder-hide for greaves (shin-pads) and pobleyns (knee-pads), a mail shirt called a quaff, a padded coat; they carried a wooden shield covered with leather. My colours are a red and white surcoat. They used linen, and their padding was horse-hair; I use felt. Our aim is to recreate their medieval way of life fully, to an orderly code of conduct. We insist that people abide by the rules and regulations, keep it as authentic as possible.

Of course, real life was cheap then, especially if you were a peasant. We concentrate on the good bits. When we do a show, we play up the crowd, we want to get their participation, we insult them, get them to shout back. We have music and songs from the medieval period; we have a fire-eater who breathes fireballs into the air, he uses paraffin or lighter oil – he's better than some professionals. We have an electronic keyboard, which simulates a reed-organ, pipes, bombard, which is a loud bagpipe, recorders.

'We go in for parody and send-up. We do St George and the Dragon; the story is that the dragon loses its puff, so we bring on a case of Heineken. We do a St George – This is Your Life, complete with big red book. We have King Arthur and the Holy Grail; the holy grail, everybody is searching high and low for it, and it turns out to be the cup that God keeps his false teeth in.'

Colin takes out a catalogue of bows: the compound bow – PSE laser 2 – is an American bow with no British equivalent. 'English bows are the field-hunting bows, you can get a traditional English longbow made to individual order, a cheap one would cost £100, but you can pay three times as much. The wood is yew, hickory or rosewood; lemonwood from the West Indies is excellent.'

Dave and Maggie, in their late thirties, live in a new house on an estate on the edge of town: a warm, comfortable interior, oatmeal three-piece suite, floral carpet, drawings and paintings of German Shepherd dogs on the walls; a picture of Trigga, as a puppy, now ten and sleeping under the stairs: the picture has been executed on laminated plastic to simulate wood. Both Dave and Maggie have been married before. This time they have decided not to marry, but have been together for 12 years. One of their consuming interests – which brought them together in the first place – is their affection for German Shepherd dogs. Maggie, slim and small, chain smokes; Dave is somewhat slower, with dark-brown eyes that kindle with great enthusiasm when he talks of dogs. His knowledge and understanding of them are extraordinary. He has a living and passionate relationship with the great Alsatians that live in a concreted pen in the garden. When he goes out to them, they rear up with their heavy paws on the wire fencing, their tongues lolling; beautiful creatures, far from the vicious Alsatian of popular lore.

Maggie met Dave at the Pathfinders' Display Team, with whom he puts on shows at fêtes and celebrations. He had his old dog, King, at that time who died in February this year at the age of 16. This dog was mated with a friend's dog, and they kept another dog from the litter, and then two more. 'My daughter took one of them when she went to live with her boyfriend; when they split up, the boyfriend threw the dog back, "Keep your dog and your daughter sort of thing."' They now have four dogs. Trigga is old, and ought to be put down for his own dignity, but he has been a very good performing dog, and Dave is reluctant to say goodbye to him, even though he is lame in one of his back legs.

Dave has worked for 25 years in the brewery as drayman. He is fit and wiry, with dark hair. He smiles as he says 'German Shepherds have a bad name. People tend to be terrified of them.' Maggie says people cross the street if they see her coming with the dogs. She took Trigga to be photographed at a studio in town because they wanted a permanent memory of him. The woman at the studio was German: she was terrified of him because she had been in a concentration camp and the guard dogs had been German Shepherds or Alsatians, as they became known during the War because of the negative associations of all things German. But, contrary to what most people think, they are the same thing. 'If a German Shepherd dog bites somebody, it's all over the front page of the paper. Any other dog, you never hear anything about it. The breed has improved over the years. It's a better-natured dog now, more docile. Dogs are bred for the characteristics that are wanted. The dogs that are bred for show are high-strung and temperamental. It's what Maggie calls the back-street breeding that has improved them. I don't breed for looks or show or money. Dogs for temperament, not for appearance, is the aim of the back-street breeder, the ordinary person who is interested in dogs for obedience or display-training. Real breeders would deny it, of course. The three dogs out there, they are as soft as anything. But there is big money in it – you can pay anything up to £250 for a German Shepherd pup at eight weeks. There might be eight pups in a litter, and that can mean twice a year, so you can see the possibilities of making money out of it. To get that money, you have to have its pedigree, enter it in shows so it gets the reputation, and then people will want to get some of its offspring.'

Maggie shows me the pedigree of Trigga. It goes back five generations, to the great-great-grandparents, both dam and sire. The family tree is all written out in fine copperplate handwriting, with the names of the champions in red. Three of Trigga's great-grandparents were champions, from the Greenveldt breeders. 'My friend, her dog's father was registered, but not the mother; she was a good working dog, but that is nothing to the Kennel Club; that's where you have to register all pedigree dogs.

'I suppose the original German working sheep-dog went back to an original set of dogs. I think now they've gone over to Rottweilers: they were the first cross between two pedigree breeds, German Shepherd and Labrador. They breed them and create new breeds according to what they want from dogs. Guide dogs are a mixture of Retriever and Labrador, to get the right temperament.

'I love other dogs too. I'd love a Cocker Spaniel. My friend has a Dachsie, and whenever she comes here, the little Dachshund gets washed from head to foot by the Shepherds. Mind you, the cat rules the roost here. When the dogs are pups, she stands her ground to them, nips them on the nose. They know who's boss. The youngest dog is scared of her. Trigga is the son of Greenveldt Indian Hawk; he has a lot of dogs from Spain and Germany in his pedigree – they breed all over Europe. Trigga retired from demonstration team work two years ago; the nerves in his spine crumbled. I'd have him put down – time's time, for his own sake, it's time to go. But you get very attached. I chose Trigga. We went to see a friend's litter, and he had a distinctive white tip on his tail. Dave said no; he was a scrawny little thing, running across the grass. But I said "This is the one I want." Your feelings get all mixed and muddled up with the dog, it's your selfishness against their dignity when it's time for them to go. You have to have respect for animals. A dog will sense it, just like a kid. Dogs, like kids, sense an atmosphere, tensions. It has to be a partnership with them, a mutual relationship. Shepherds are pack dogs, there's always a leader of the pack that will dominate. You've got to become that leader. You must dominate them altogether. Some people ruin their dogs, then their lives are ruled by them. Their dogs can't be left, they'll rip up the house if you go out and leave them. My daughter's dog, if he was left, he'd go and rip the bed-clothes from the bed and tear them up. She had to get dog-sitters whenever she went out. It was just that they'd never been left, and they can't get used to not having the company. You have to start with them as you mean to go on. If you've been carrying a dog around 24 hours a day, and then you start leaving it, the dog will retaliate. Treat dogs as you'd treat kids – teach them right from wrong, then they'll know if they've done something wrong. They *know*. If you catch them, smack them there and then, not two hours later. They can be very frustrating. For some reason, that one likes chewing wood up. We've tried sprays, everything. That's just his little way. You don't have to leave him in the drawing-room with chairs and tables, else you'll come back and find your furniture's got no legs on . . . You have to train them from the minute you have them, toilet training. It varies. Of my four, one took a year, one six weeks, one was clean from the word go – and all from the same parents.

'Trigga was bred outside. He hated it when he first came indoors. He cried and cried at first. When we brought him home, he sat at the door, it was pouring with rain; the minute we opened the door, out he jumped. He took a year to train. An average litter will be about eight pups; they can go up to 13 or as low as one. Any over eight will generally be put down, because the dog has only eight nipples, and you've got to bottle-feed them, which is a big chore. They have to be inoculated against hardpad, distemper, parvo – that's diarrhoea and sickness, it dehydrates them, that's an airborne virus. They have to be done every year. When you get epidemics, people tend to neglect the ordinary inoculations – kennel cough for instance. It's just like whooping cough. People will go for the one that threatens immediate danger. It can be expensive to have them all done properly.

'Dave is lucky. His demonstration team is sponsored by Omega Petfoods. Training for obedience is one thing, but Pathfinders is another. We do displays in Scotland, Wales, from April to September there are bookings all over the British Isles. There are 12 dogs and handlers in the team. That's how I met Dave, watching a display, agility work. We had one of our dogs on *That's Life*, where she carries an egg in her mouth, goes through hoops of fire. They climb an 18 ft tower, go through a ring of fire. We train them to walk the tight-rope – two ropes actually; it used to be 12 ft long, now it's been increased to 18.

'A versatile working dog, you can train them to do anything; he'll do anything to please you. Trigga used to do the crossed swords: Dave crouched down, crossed a pair of swords from the Sealed Knot above his head, and Trigga would jump between them. We did a guard of honour of the Demo Team at a friend's wedding.

'German Shepherds chase criminals. They'll bring a bloke down. When fully grown, they weigh about eight stone. Alan finishes off the display by carrying Trigga on his back. I'm more obedience-minded than display. Trigga does the magic-box trick: a child in the audience shows the dog a flag of one of five colours, then the dog goes into the box and comes out with a flag of the right colour. Nine times out of ten he does it right. Then the dog fetches a dumb-bell on fire and carries it through flaming hoops. You can see on the video how they enjoy it. There's no way you'd get dogs to do that if they were unhappy. That was how Trigga first became disabled. He was jumping through the swords, and at that moment a dog barked, the sound broke his concentration: he caught the swords, they fell and cut Dave's eye. We didn't think Trigga was hurt. He limped for a couple of days, although there was no cut. But he must have done something more than that. Dave has had a few bites, when the dogs get excited.

'If a dog is ill-treated when small, you can tell. It stays with him. King had been attacked by a Golden Labrador as a young dog. If he saw a Labrador, he'd go for it first. Trigga copied King, and as a result he hated Labs too. I take the dogs out first thing in the morning, again lunchtime, at teatime and last thing at night. My two girls are now 18 and 20, they both like dogs. They've grown up with them. Kids and dogs get very jealous of each other, if you're not careful. If you give too much attention to one or the other, you soon hear about it. If Dave and I stand too close together at the window and the dogs see us, they soon start barking. If you're walking too close, the dogs will come between you, separate you. Sue was sitting on her boyfriend's lap the other day, I said "You'll have to get up, you're really winding that dog up." They think they own you, they really do. You can soon tell if your own dog is not up to the mark, if he's off; you get a sixth sense. Like with the girls, if something is wrong, you know it's there, even though you may not know what it is. The only thing is, you've got to work a bit harder with a dog than a kiddie, because a dog can't tell you.

'Of course, they have a bad reputation because of the POW camps and the concentrations camps. They can be trained to rip people to bits. Police use them for man-work, although they've now gone over to Rottweilers. You want a Labrador for scent, a Shepherd dog for tracking. The army use Labs and Shepherds for sniffing out drugs or bombs.'

We open the french windows into the garden. Immediately the dogs leap up and down, run the length of their pen, barking excitedly. Maggie says 'Khan will dance for you. Khan and Anchor are almost indistinguishable; Bear, the third dog is darker in colour and more nervous.'

Dave says 'After the show, we have to leave the dogs 20 minutes to unwind because all the kids want to hug them and make a fuss of them; you have to let them settle down before anybody touches them. There's one dog in our display team that my mate picked up off the side of the road. He'd been thrown out of a car. So many people think a dog is a pet; it'll obey them, be a performing animal instantly, without any training. It takes a lot of time and trouble. One of our dogs was an ex-police dog that they threw out because it didn't have the courage to do its work. We can now get it to retrieve the burning dumb-bells and jump through the blazing hoop with them. They threw him out too soon. It needs a lot of patience. Generally the wives do the puppy-walking.' 'And then,' says Maggie, 'the men take over. They get to do all the best parts.' 'I take over at 8–12 months. No dog should jump before it is 15–18 months old because its bones aren't set. It could be deformed.

'Our dogs all have different personalities. At $4\frac{1}{2}$, Khan is always eager to go, he can't wait . . . When we're performing, normally you run alongside your dog; but Khan is always racing me. With Bear, he is on the same side as me, he comes back to heel after each jump, but not Khan. They're four and in their prime, but you have to talk to each one differently. Anchor requires more firmness, I have to change my voice. If I speak lightly, he pays no notice, you have to be more gruff to get him to respond. Each dog requires a different kind of training. Trigga, it was a case of once shown, never forgotten, whereas with Khan – who is Trigga's son – he was mad-headed, a show-off, always in a rush, as if to say "Of course I can do it." He thinks he doesn't need telling, then of course he can't do it. Bear needs showing only twice. Trigga was trained to police standard; chase and attack. Bear also. When they've finished performing, you put a different collar on. I use a leather collar when they're performing, then an ordinary check chain.

'We run a training club for dogs. You very quickly get the feel of a dog, you can soon see what the owners have done wrong. You've got an aggressive dog and a shy dog: the aggressive one is always easier to train. A shy dog is embarrassed, he'll cower. You have to *show* people how to train their particular dog, it's no good just telling them. Some people are scared of their own dogs. It has to be an interaction between individual people and individual dogs.' Maggie says 'There's a dog-owner, a dog-handler and a dog-lover. If he falls over the dog, the dog gets in his way, the dog-owner will say "Sorry, but you shouldn't have been there." The dog-lover will fall on its neck and say how sorry he is and apologize and hope he hasn't hurt him; the dog-handler will belt it and say "Get out the bloody way"; not cruelly, not kick it, but with firmness.'

Mr Grosskurth is 92; he lives in a warden-controlled old person's maisonette, set apart from a busy main road: the houses are arranged in gardens with benches under flowering cherry trees; phlox and cabbage-roses in flower. Mr Grosskurth retired 20 years ago. Since then he as taught himself to paint, mostly copies of masterpieces in the National Gallery and Louvre: the Mona Lisa, Rembrandt, Rubens, the Impressionists, Goya; all of them meticulously executed. Particularly good are the renderings of faces and their expressions. Mr Grosskurth was an embroiderer in the East End, working on contracts to the big fashion houses. Some of the motifs he designed himself, operating a machine, guiding the needle over the pattern as though it were a pen. He had no idea that he possessed any artistic talent until he was well into his forties. One day, he idly copied a line-drawing from the newspaper, and discovered he could reproduce it almost exactly. He did his first painting when he was almost 60.

He has produced a number of paintings that are not copies: an Hasidic wedding; a picture of himself sitting morosely by a stylized candle, cold electric fire and with a blanket round his knees, called 'Power Cut'; a self-portrait from his image in the mirror; a painting of the fort at Masada, with the fires already burning, and the last ten men drawing lots to see who shall be the last to remain with, in the background, the tents of the Romans pitched on the yellow sand. If Mr Grosskurth had no idea of his slumbering talent, this is because the events of his life were so overwhelming that they effectively concealed it.

His parents came from Odessa, where they left him in 1905 with his older brother. They came to live in Whitechapel and promised to send for him. His father had been the first to leave, then his mother and baby brother, but there was no money for the fare of the older two. He begged his brother to ask for a month's advance in wages; and with that, they took the train to Frankfurt. There the money ran out, and they lived for some days on the station. He remembers Odessa: 'It was very beautiful, a sort of second Paris, cafés with balalaikas and singers; of course, there was terrible poverty too. My father was an ordinary workman, he made silk cords with tassels that were used for curtains and dresses. I can remember Odessa perfectly, the seaport, where all the wheat from the Ukraine passed through, the dockers loading the ships. Of course, many of the big landowners in those days were playboys – they were too busy visiting Paris or buying race-horses to look after their estates; and they often appointed Jewish people to look after and manage the business. That, of course, was one of the reasons why the Jews were hated. The wheat was being shipped all over the world, and of course the peasants were hungry and very badly off. Later on, after the Revolution, they had to have people who could be administrators, people who had organizing ability, a lot of these too were Jews; until Stalin had so many of them killed. And now, of course, they don't want the Jews to emigrate from Russia, they occupy too many important jobs, there would be a crisis of skilled manpower if they left in any numbers.

'I can remember quite clearly the pogroms, when the hooligans used to come to the Jewish quarters; at night, you would hear the screams of the women, first in one street and then in another. The police did nothing; often they were the instigators of the violence. We knew we had no protection. It wasn't so bad in Odessa as out in the small country communites. In Odessa, some of the men formed vigilante groups; they had electric wires between the houses as telephones, so they could warn each other and summon help when there was trouble. But in the countryside, there was nothing to stop them. They could murder people and never be brought to justice for it.

'The people left Ukraine in thousands. A lot of them walked to Hamburg; from there they got a passage to England, to America; some people disembarked in London under the impression that they had reached America . . . When my brother and I got to Frankfurt, they wrote to my father to send the money for us to continue the journey. I came to where they were living in Whitechapel. I was dismayed. I hated it. The buildings at that time were all black with soot, the air was full of smoke, the streets smelled of dung and hay and horses; there was mud and filth in the streets. I just wanted to go home. And my mother too, she lived to be 95, but she could never settle, she always dreamed of going back. But there could be no return; only the dream, maybe, keeps you going, keeps hope alive.

'My father was working in one of the tailoring shops; and that's where I got my first job; $2\frac{1}{2}$d for machining each pair of trousers. I'd do up to three dozen pairs a day. Oh, how we worked! The cutters cut them out, 50 pairs at a time, you raced through them, stitching without pause. Later, I taught myself to do embroidery, and then beading I did also. That had to be done by hand. The little sweat-shops, they used to send scouts round the big fashion houses to steal other people's designs, see what was in vogue and then do a cut-price version of it, which they could do by paying their workers such low wages.

'When I was young, there was never any question of a child from a poor family having artistic ability. You had to work; and work didn't mean painting. I sometimes wonder if I'd been trained as a child, if someone had seen that I had talent, and it had been encouraged, whether I might not have been master painter. I shall never know. But at that time, there were just the famous artists, the classical painters, and all the others were very poor. I suppose my ability was there, in the designs I made. Then I married, I had three children. That brings other tsores [troubles, worries], you have to survive. I always had a dream of doing something else . . . Now I've been able to achieve it. I don't complain. I have angina; my daughters live nearby; my son died recently. My niece is an opera singer, she lives in Sweden. I'm lucky, I've lived to realize my talents in old age. Not everybody is so fortunate. You can only wonder how many people take to the grave all the possibilities within them that never come to flower.'

Victor, in his twenties, lives in a bungalow on the edge of town, in a quiet cul-de-sac of semi-detached houses with neat front gardens. He is disabled with cystic fibrosis, and has little use of his hands and legs. He has a piercing intelligence and a warm smile. He manages to type by means of a knitting needle which he holds in his mouth. He says that he would have enormous quantities of leisure, except that the basic processes of living take up so much time. In spite of this, he is the secretary of the Cromwell Society in the area. 'I've always been interested in Cromwell and his times, from an academic viewpoint. Not like the Sealed Knot – they're keen on re-enacting the battles of the Civil War; that's interesting, but obviously not something I could take part in.' Victor's mother comes in. She helps with the administration of her son's work, and looks after him; she has to make sure that people who come to the house don't bring even minor infections, to which he is susceptible. She is one of those many hundred of thousands of people – mainly women – who have no leisure, for their life is given up to the service of those they love.

'We research, help each other explore aspects of the period. Some people are interested in the religion, others in the politics; my fascination is with the New Model Army. We have members all over the world – the USA, Europe, Italy particularly. Cromwell led a campaign to free persecuted Protestants in Italy, a small valley where the Catholic church's power never reached, the Valdensi. I'm on the side of Parliament rather than the Royalists, although of course the monarchy has changed a great deal since then. Of course, most people at the time had no choice. The land here belonged to Lewis Divve; had I farmed here, I'd've fought as a Royalist if I wanted to stay, even though I might privately have sympathized with the parliamentary cause. Every year on 3 September we have a service outside Parliament for Oliver Cromwell; a prayer in thanks for him, then finish up singing the National Anthem.

'What we were taught in school about the Civil War was lifeless. History is not about when and where, but about who and why. Most people don't get beyond that because those are not felt to be proper questions at school.

'The society was founded 50 years ago. Its members then were mostly rather more affluent upper middle-class people. They could afford to put up monuments in the battlefields – it's now costing us a fortune in upkeep and insurance. The one at Marston Moor was vandalized recently, and it cost us £1,500.

'My own position is that I favour the Independents' viewpoint. I'm interested in the Levellers' doctrines. Of course, you can read into it what you will: the modern Labour Party identify themselves with the Levellers, certainly people like Tony Benn. But it's full of ambiguities – they still protected land ownership, there was to be no freedom for servants. For instance, John Lilburne, he was a large landowner in Durham, he owned mines and tenant farms. He might have believed in equality for all, but that didn't go as far as believing in redistribution of wealth. Winstanley said more to modern humankind than Lilburne.

'I originally got interested in wargames; only, if you've an inquiring mind, once you get involved, you want to know more. For instance, there's a seventeenth century house in Northampton which they call Cromwell House. People will tell you "Oh, that's where he had his wounds done after the Battle of Naseby." Well, it wasn't actually built then.

'After Naseby, the wounded were brought to St Peter's church. They always put the wounded in churches; I suppose it sanctifies slaughter. They must've known of the victory at about 4 o'clock in the afternoon; and then the wounded were being brought in all night. The A1-M1 link road is scheduled to pass through the field in Naseby which was the site of the battle. I gave evidence at the inquiry.

'What you realize in the study of history is that men and women don't

change, not their passions and their feelings. Even their wisdom too. Much
that was said then you can identify with now. One of the Haselriggs said in
1658 "Never was there a creature born who could rule men without being
responsible unto them." Well, you can't take exception to that. It's like the
present day. Lilburne – his words were more important than his actions:
that's like calling yourself a Christian and not living up to it; it all has a
contemporary ring. The "silken Independents", independent in thought
and religion, but they were still rich capitalists. A lot of money was made at
the time of the Civil Wars, as always in wars. There was land to be bought
up cheap. The City of London didn't lose any of its wealth; merchants and
London businessmen backed political parties.

'It isn't exactly nostalgia; it isn't a desire for the past, but rather the
desire to know what made people tick; and if, and in what ways, they were
different from us. It's interesting to look at parallels – in 1647 the Army
turns Parliament out: badly paid and wanting change in the country. By
1648 that had broken down and it was back to normal with the same
people in charge. Similarly, in 1945, the army voted out Churchill, voted in
Attlee; within a few months that government was in trouble, and was out
by the early 1950s. After the Civil War, soldiers were sent to Ireland
because they didn't know what to do with them; after the First World War
soldiers were sent to Ireland because they didn't know what to do with
them.

'I've written a book about the Civil War. It's called *Parliament's Forgotten General.* I've just finished a second, which is to be published by a small
publishing house in Essex. They put out pre-publication notices in April
1984, saying it was due in August 1984. Then they had cashflow problems,
so they cancelled it. Now it's on again.

'I was lucky in the mid-sixties to have had teachers who taught rather
than minded kids. I had a tutor from the college who came to teach me
maths and English. If you are disabled, people assume you don't have a
mind. One of the hardest things is to bear people's stock responses. One
day when I had been left for a moment in my chair outside a chapel one
Sunday, some of the old women coming out of chapel stopped to have a
look at me. "Can it talk?", one of them said. I said "Yes it can, and if you
throw nuts it does tricks." They were most offended. The careers officer
said to me "You'll never get a job." I said to him "You mean I won't be able
to be a fireman after all?" He didn't know what to say. Once, when mother
was going into the Co-op, one old dear said "I'll look after him', notwith-
standing the fact that the last thing I wanted was to be looked after. She
said "Nice day", etc. Then she said "Has Mummy gone to buy you a nice
bottle of pop?" I said "No, she might get me a lager." "Nevermind", she
said, "it's lovely up there." "Where?" I looked up over the Co-op Hall

where they have the Women's Guild meetings, "No", she said, "heaven. You won't be disabled there." I said "Thank God, I'd hate to be sat in front of a harp and not be able to pluck the strings."'

In popular accounts of these ordinary passions and preoccupations, certain ideas recur with sufficient insistence to suggest patterns of experience. One of these is that even the modest endeavours are subject to professionalization; 'it's becoming big business.' It becomes more competitive and more expensive. Often, the love that people have for their activity is precisely because through it they hope to resist that encircling process: 'You do it for the love of the thing', not to make money. Clearly, the possibilities of turning leisure into business pose a great threat to that commitment, the passionate attachment to doing things for their own sake.

Secondly, there is often a strong sense of escape, of nostalgia. This powerful component of English life remains pervasive. It isn't only that the memories and yearnings for the countryside associated with the industrial period remain strong: the marketing and selling of that form of nostalgia is deeply entrenched; but it also seems that with the passing of the industrial era, that too becomes transformed in popular memory. Where it was once hateful and oppressive, desirable elements can now be detected in it; all the clichés of the testimonies of how people survived, how they triumphed over adverse material conditions – all this becomes the object for a new kind of nostalgia. Conserving and consuming the past become major activities. In part, this may be a reaction to stringencies and uncertainties of the present, the development of the very leisure society that is supposed to be the vehicle of our deliverance. There is a search for a past and passing sense of Englishness; and in this a strong sense that people feel they are not in control of change: something is always being taken away from them; there is a need to stake out something secure that can be repossessed and reconstructed.

Whatever the political implications of this may be, they are far from most people's thoughts. Most leisure-time activities demonstrate an absence of political or ideological consciousness. People want to be left alone. What they want to do, the obsessions and preoccupations, are not the concern of politicians, have nothing to do with them. People want to get on with leading their own lives. This may be a powerful conservative force, one that leads to political inertia and detachment.

There is a recurring sense of unsatisfactory work lives being compensated for through leisure: something unfulfilling, inadequate, about the economic function most of us perform. Many of these elements may be distasteful to the Left; but they cannot be denied or dismissed.

If escape from present time is a major feature of our leisure, equally important is escape from place. Whole areas of Britain, of Europe, indeed, of the whole world have found economic significance because they are places where people do not live; places that invite escape, fantasy and flight. In other words, travel and tourism are major components of the leisure society.

The languor of Sunday afternoons in small towns all over the world can weigh no more heavily than in Clonakilty and the little places like it in West Cork. The elegant Georgian square and the colour-washed, three-story crescent of the main street suggest a much bigger settlement than the little town that soon dissolves into countryside and the steep green hills behind; empty streets, faded holland blinds, old women on the doorstep in the pallid sunshine, wondering at the destination of those passing through. In the Clonakilty Hotel, four girls sit at a Formica-topped table, sipping tea and singing along with the radio 'I Can't Stop Loving You'; an old man sleeps in the window, hands in his lap, head forward on his chest, and the flies settle on the plastic bell-jar protecting the iced buns inside. The town suffers from an absence, the absence of all those who have left over the years. There is something melancholy and slightly shaming for those who stay in places from which migration has been so persistent and continuous, and from where the young still long to go – as many as half the young people have no work – and are further unsettled by the stories that come back from elsewhere. For there is always the presence of returnees, people with the accent of the United States or Australia, walking through the closed grey streets in lightweight raincoats with cameras around their necks, or making their way laboriously through the crowded churchyards, vigilant for connections, memories, roots, clues to an Irish identity which the smooth-worn stones cannot quite adequately provide. Indeed, at times it seems, the whole West of Ireland has become another sort of plantation economy, where one of the most profitable occupations is the cultivation of family trees.

What the Sunday afternoon streets cannot show is the invisible intensity of life behind the sun-silvered windowpanes; where the families gather and hug each other and laugh and cry after separations that have lasted half a century; where they remember the great patriarchal rage, when a grandfather who disapproved of his son's marriage sold the house and the 40 acres of land so that he should not inherit, and the son went off to Cork; and the irony that two generations later, the property had fallen, first into the hands of the family of the rejected bride, and finally into the possession of an Englishman who rents it out as a holiday cottage. Or they talk of those vast scatterings of people over the fancy chocolate-boxes full of photographs: the priest in New Zealand, the wedding of the policeman in

New York, the son in Bahrain working on bridge construction, the labour-ers in London whose children no longer go to Mass and who have grown up to expect the earth; the boys who went to London and became friends with Michael Collins of the Irish Republican Brotherhood.

And this summer has been a time for looking inwards, the worst August in living memory, with the potatoes rotting before they can be lifted, and rousing troubled memories of other, more disastrous, failures of the crop. Skibbereen has been twice cut off by floods, the shops have been selling damaged goods at half-price; some of them will go out of business. In the low-lying parts of the town, sandbags protect the front doors, carpets are hung over the garden walls to dry.

The relentless rain drives the red stars of the wild fuchsia hedges into the puddles, and leaves are torn prematurely from the birch and alder trees. Fires are lighted in spite of the long twilight. If nothing ever happens here, as the young people complain, perhaps this is because enough has already happened. The old can remember the sinking of the Lusitania off the Cork coast in 1915, how they saw the bodies floating in the water, and were tempted to remove the gold watches and chains and necklaces that were washed up with them, but didn't yield, because robbing the dead was sure to be followed by a terrible retribution. Indeed, the people of this rough coast, which is the most southerly point of Ireland, used to thrive on shipwrecks because of the treasure the sea delivered from them. Cargoes of cotton, timber, migrants: they point to the heavy kitchen table and can still name the ship from which it came. Occasionally, during the Troubles – as they are still euphemistically called – guns would be washed ashore; concealed in crates covered by packets of butter or a consignment of fowls; they were sold to whoever would offer the best price.

They tell stories too: how the Brewery at Skibbereen went out of busi-ness on account of a log of mahogany. 'One night after a shipwreck, a fine mahogany log was washed up on to the rocks. It was salvaged by a publi-can who started to tow it up the River Ilen to Skibbereen where he intended to sell it. As he approached the town, the tide turned; so he tied the log to a tree and proceeded on his way on foot. Meanwhile, the wind dislodged the log from the tree where it was moored, and it floated down-river, where it blocked a narrow bridge. The river overflowed and flooded the garden of the brewer of Skibbereen. The brewer was angry, and de-manded compensation from the publican who had caused his home to be flooded. In retaliation, the publican stopped buying his porter from the local brewer, but sent all the way to Cork for it. The townspeople, seeing porter being fetched all that way, thought it must be special, have extra properties. They all began drinking Cork porter, and the brewer was ruined and had to close down his business.'

Nor is the famine completely faded from memory. The very first old man I came across sitting on the wall of the burial ground of the Abbey, where the mass grave and monument to the famine stand, told what is perhaps the most famous story, that of Tom Gairns. 'There were so many dying at that time that they took them to be buried from the workhouse on carts. They used the same coffin with a false bottom, over and over again. To pack them in, the gravediggers had to break the limbs with their spade. They broke one man's legs, and this roused him. He let out a groan. They took him out of the grave, and he was taken home, where he recovered. He was to be seen many years afterwards, walking round the town on his sticks; he was known as the man who was crippled by the hunger.' In 1846, the workhouse contained almost 1,500 people – it had been built to hold 800 – and it had to be closed against any further admissions. In December 1846, 140 people died; early the following year, there were 65 deaths a week in the workhouse. What is also remembered is that there was plenty of food in Ireland; food was being.exported – just as in Ethiopia in our time. The poorest had no money to buy. It took a student from Cork to crystallize what the many people who expressed their revulsion against Mrs Thatcher were actually saying: 'She's all for faith in market forces, which is what Wood and Trevelyan relied on to relieve the famine. You could say it worked; it killed off about one and a quarter million people.'

Pat Cleary, local historian and schoolteacher, says that the town soon recovered from the devastation of the famine. Within 20 years it was a boom town; by the late 1860s, there was a new gas works, a general market, a town hall, a lecture hall, a convent and a new water scheme. Not long after, the railway came. There was even a grandiose scheme to extend the railway beyond the mainland, from Baltimore to Sherkin Island. Only 15 years before, the Griffith Valuation List had recorded the depopulation the famine had caused: most of the dwellings in the poor streets off Vickery's Lane were empty, only two or three occupied. The state of the abandoned thatched cabins where the poorest had lived is not recorded. The aftermath of the famine yielded some early recruits from Skibbereen for the Irish Republican Brotherhood, notably Jeremiah O'Donovan Rossa, Hardware and Agricultural Seeds Merchant, who was arrested and imprisoned for activities connected with the Phoenix Society, a Fenian organization.

In view of the tormented history of the region, it is perhaps surprising that there remains so little bitterness towards the British. 'Without Britain, where would so many of our people have gone for work? I've a brother pipe-laying in London, another in Lancashire. And there is no work here, especially for the young. The Siralux factory is closed, the vegetable canning factory is gone and the animal feeds factory. We depend on tourists now, and a lot of them come from Britain. You can't afford to turn them away by being bitter.'

The windy landscape of changing lights, where the waters are flashes of silver between indigo hills and Friesians graze in the vivid green pastures in the folds of the rocks, has been much transformed since the Irish Republic joined the EEC. The prosperous farmers have built their hacienda-style villas in dominating positions, with arches, terraces and picture-windows. The second most important economic activity is tourism, the service industries associated with the consumption of the landscape itself. Nearly every sizeable farmhouse seems to offer bed and breakfast. If the farm is small, the owner will have a job – council worker, postman, van-driver – while his wife caters for guests from June till September, and they look after a dozen or so cows, some fowls ('I wouldn't touch shop eggs') and grow all the vegetables the family needs. At the weekend, the whole family assembles (the brother from Limerick has picked up the daughter who has flown into Shannon after working in a motel in New Hampshire for the summer) and they sit all afternoon over dinner, which merges into tea, watching the Kerry–Meath match on TV, and teasing the children. Little Mary, who is four, a beautiful child with her mass of red–gold curls, is told she can have the last cream cake only if she goes round and kisses everyone in the room – the lesson that little girls learn so soon, that they must give in order to receive; a prosperous and conservative people, secure in the ownership of the farm that goes back at least as far as their father's grandfather ('And that's far enough for me'). Perhaps they remember, with just a whisper of regret, their own parents, whose work was never done, even while they sat on either side of the square open hearth, the endless scoaiocht by the firelight, the neighbours who came in most evenings, telling stories and gossiping, passing in and out of the language as easily as they went from one room to another; and they may recall the rhythm of those evenings, the tick of the clock against the howl of the wind, and wish they'd paid a little more attention and had bothered about the language a bit more.

'My father was not in the Irish Volunteers. He sympathized with them, but he was a farmer; or at least he thought he was. He used to raise chickens and turkeys for the English market. He'd sit up all night with his sisters plucking them, and then they went out by post. In the end, the increase in postal charges made it no longer profitable. One day during the Civil War, he had been to Cork to buy a new truck. On his way back, he was stopped by some soldiers of the Free State. They wanted to commandeer his truck, but he said no, he would drive them to wherever they wanted to go. They got in, and ran into an ambush on the road. The soldier sitting beside him was shot. He was given a gun and told to shoot his way out. He managed to get out with his new truck intact, and he lived to tell the tale. Earlier, he used to act as a messenger for the Irish Volunteers. He'd leave a message under the second furze bush on the left after the bridge at Bandon; he used to say with that kind of organization, how could the British ever hope to win. He always said the saddest day of his life came on the day when the men who'd fought the British met on the Mart in Skibbereen and split between those who were for the 1920 Treaty and those who were against. Families who'd fought together broke up over it; they were permanently divided by it. Some of them never spoke to each other again.'

Above all, they remember people; like the captain from Cape Clear who had had his coaster requisitioned by the Navy in 1936. He couldn't accept that any government had the right to do any such thing, and vowed to get his own back on them. He had his car put up on blocks and the wheels removed, declaring that the government would never get a penny piece out of him in car tax or petrol tax. He never drove it again. It is there to this day, in his back yard in Skibbereen, just as it was nearly 50 years ago, apart from the rust that has corroded it.

But underneath it is the ache of the separations that remains; part of the physical landscape, visible in the overcrowded churchyard and the depleted towns and villages, the ruined hutments and cottages. Mrs O'Driscoll says 'When the people were leaving, they used to light bonfires up on the cliffs along the coast, so that when the emigrant ships went by, they would see their loved ones waving in the light from them; and that would be the last they'd see of Ireland. They used to come back, perhaps 20 years later, and found their parents had died, and the little house sold or tumbling down.'

'Twelve brothers and sisters belonging to my great-grandfather went to America in the 1850s. They were labourers, tied to a farmer, so they survived the hunger. The ones who starved were the families of untied labourers – they had to pay rent for their lands and for their huts and find work where they could; and when they couldn't pay their rent they were evicted.'

'My father got a job in the creamery and left his brother to farm the homeplace. At that time, it seemed my father had the better deal; he hadn't the responsibility any longer. My cousin still farms the homeplace. He has 30 acres, he raises cows for beef, so he doesn't have the trouble of milking. He has a job as well, he's the local postman.'

As soon as the sun shines, the old come out, leaning on their sticks and turning their faces to the light. An elderly man sits on the stone wall overlooking the graveyard that slopes down to the river. He points to a newly turned grave, covered with everlasting flowers under plastic crosses, paper flowers magnified within a globe full of water. The grave is marked by a surround of white plastic fleurs-de-lis. 'That's the grave of a traveller. He was murdered by his brother. He had an argument with him over some money. The brother took a stone to him, hit him on the side of the head. Those people don't go to doctors, if he had done he might have been saved. It went wrong and got worse, and he died. The brother was charged with murder; he was mad with grief. Life is ours to give, but not to take . . . It's like religion, I was given my religion by my parents, no one can take it from me, but I wouldn't fight over it. I used to work in the cattle-feed factory, but I was made redundant. They've more modern methods of doing it now, so the factory went to Cork I believe. I've 35 acres, 20 cows. My son is a butcher at Bantry, so I leave the calves to suck for beef, and he always has fresh meat.'

At Roscarbery there has been a family reunion: the four sisters who went to London in the 1930s have come home for a month; another sister from Dublin is there. A cousin from America arrives; the family are sent for from where they are staying; they all add a little more to the vast family network which is never completed because it is an organic, still growing thing. They work out their precise relationships, discuss family characteristics over cups of tea, soda bread and fresh butter; astonished to discover traits and ways of being they share with people they have never met before. 'Nobody was ever good enough for her children, she had such pride. In the end, Kathleen married an ordinary seaman, and as a result her mother never spoke to her again. Never; even though she lived only up the road. The youngest also married someone she didn't approve of and went to England.' The enlarged sepia photograph of the mother looks down from the parlour wall, grim and thin-lipped. 'One of the things about us is that we're slow to show our feelings. It doesn't mean the feelings are not there. My boy was going away to Boston for the summer, I wanted to tell him I loved him, I couldn't. Then when he'd gone I sat down and cried my eyes out.'

A few miles to the north of Roscarbery, cousin Tim lives in a nineteenth-century stone cottage against a sheer slope, so that there is no back entrance, shadowed by dripping beech-trees. The house is reached by a flight of irregular stone steps; a dusty whitewashed exterior, plain red-painted door. It remains unchanged, a preserved living-place of at least a century ago, without gas, electricity or running water. There is a plain stone floor, and a huge square fireplace where, in this sodden August, there are the embers of a fire glowing in the mound of ash, half-extinguished by rainwater coming down the chimney. There is a plate of bones for the dog, a smelly, friendly bitch, while a small black kitten plays with the discarded cellophane wrapping from Tim's packet of Sweet Afton. There is barely a concession to the modern world at all – an alarm clock on the high mantel, and a sticky roll of brown flypaper with the carcasses of the flies of many a summer clinging to it. There are two cardboard cartons labelled Kellogg's Corn Flakes; on a piece of string between two nails inside the fireplace, some woollen socks are drying. There is a wooden table covered with newspaper; a low wooden chair with a plain wood seat beside the fire and a higher wooden chair at the table, once painted red, but now worn and greasy. There is a long settle at the back of the room, also made of wood, covered with old clothes; severe and uninviting to indolence. The beams of the rafters are unpainted. There is an oil-lamp on the table.

Tim has always lived here. His father used to own a donkey-cart, and was famous in the district for coming out of the pub in Roscarbery having drunk too much: he would simply lie in the cart and rely on the donkey to find its way home, which it invariably did. Tim's refusal to change from the way he was brought up 60 years ago is a source of exasperated pride in his family. His unwillingness to compromise is fierce and strong; people attribute it to eccentricity. They tell stories about him that seek to diminish the keen intelligence behind the clear hazel eyes and the strong Southern accent: Tim was going to buy a new donkey. When they asked him what he would do with his old one, he said he was going to keep it for spare parts. He was going into the pubs to watch television, and when they asked him why he didn't buy one, he said he hadn't an engine to run it from. He is a gentle man, with a tweed cap permanently on his thick silver hair; he wears oilskin over his trousers and strong studded boots.

Next day he is at Roscarbery Fair. He says the fair is only a shadow of what it used to be, when there would be not only horses and donkeys, but cattle and pigs, sheep and goats, and people would argue and bargain for hours, sometimes drinking so much that they forgot the object of the transaction or it wandered away. The market stalls are all set out in the early morning, ready-made suits in sober colours, strong boots and olive-green wellingtons; booths of plastic toys and novelties for the children; hamburgers from a van with the metal side cut crudely to form a serving hatch. Madam Lisa will tell your fortune for two punt, the crystal ball will cost you five. She wears trinkets around her scarlet head-dress, and the children peep inside her caravan to catch a glimpse of the silver mirror-lenses in her glasses. She tells you that you'll father five children, that your wife will be as true to you far away as she is under your gaze, that you'll live to be 90 and a lot of money will soon be coming to you. The Irish draught horses are tried out around the town square, the children ride the donkeys, swearing noisily at them, the money flows in the pubs. 'The man that owned Mill Pearl, he offered it to the Irish government for 50,000 punt, but the government refused, said they couldn't afford it. It was bought by an American for 100,000, and he brought it back to Ireland to win the show-jumping championship. What a government that couldn't even recognize a gift-horse. Well, they won't last much longer; especially with their indifference towards the farmers in this ruinous summer, and their stupidness in telling us we should become more European and less Irish.'

Even the talk about the present has a faintly archaic ring: the story of the 12-year-old girl, unofficially exorcised this month by two priests because she had seen the devil in the form of a great black shadow covering the shrine that had been built by the parents of a girl who died at 17 in accordance with her last wish; a shrine where the Virgin has been appearing regularly in 1986, telling the people to pray for peace and to go more regularly to Mass.

The memorials to British rule are extraordinarily conspicuous. The church of St Barrahane in Castletownshende remains a dramatic celebration of imperialism and militarism with its funerary monuments to admirals and colonels, and its plaques to the fighters for Empire beside the more touching memorial to the friendship of Somerville and Ross. 'In memory of Sir Joscelyn Coghill Bart. 1826–1905, and of his eldest son Neill Josiah Aylmer Coghill VC, 24th regiment, who was killed in action on 22 January 1879 while saving the colours of his regiment. Having crossed the Buffalo River in safety, he returned to save his wounded comrade and died with him, aged 26 years.'

The descendants of the heroes and adventurers are perhaps among those who return to Ireland as tourists, this time on yachting and boating adventures. They can be seen in the pubs – self-conscious places decorated with anchors and pieces of ancient wreckage, charts of Fishes of the North Atlantic and the lore of Sailing Ships – kept indoors by the northerly gale and driving rain. An English family colonizes the space around the pub fire: three young women, three slightly older men and a middle-aged couple. They spread their oilskins to dry, remove their yellow wellingtons, warm their feet, drink Stag lager and hot whisky. 'How's Sarah?' 'She's in Nepal.' 'Whatever for? Is she trekking?' 'No, she's temping in Hong Kong, earning stacks of money and then just taking off, Outer Mongolia, Taiwan. Then when she has nothing left, she goes back to temping.' 'I'd like to take a year off. I may read English at York, but before that I want to do something really exciting with lots of travel. I got a D for English, I was so relieved, I'd done no work at all.' Johnny is impatient; he wants to get out onto the water. He likes the boat he's on, he feels he could handle her even in this gale. 'Oh come off it, Johnny, it's force ten at least.' 'I've been out in worse. When we were coming back from Spain, everybody was terribly worried about us, because they'd arranged a 21st birthday party for me and nobody knew if I'd make it in time. And last year, when

Charley rang me up and asked me to bring the boat from Baltimore. It was a Second War craft, and it filled with water every three hours, I spent the whole journey across the Irish Sea baling her out.' The young men have fair hair, they wear corduroy trousers, thick oatmeal sweaters; exuding an energy and power that have little place in contemporary life, expending themselves on self-set struggles against the wind and the sea. They sit, bored, on the bar stools, looking to see if the sky shows any sign of clearing; walk disconsolately to the ruins of the Church of Ireland church in Baltimore, where the grey stone is bright yellow and green with lichen, and the grass grows out of the walls; inside the church, there is an old gnarled fuchsia bush ablaze with its tiny red lanterns, and inside each one a bee, with the result that the enclosed space is full of the music of bees amplified against the bare stone.

After the days of rain, the skies finally clear. The water crashes down the hillsides, foams along the grassy channels worn in the side of the road, until it seems the whole landscape is melting into the sea. In the vast dining hall of the Eldon Hotel in Skibbereen, the tables are laid with silver service, although there are no diners; a banquet, set perhaps for the ghosts of the party of Michael Collins who set out from here in August 1922 before he was killed in an ambush; or for the starvelings of the famine; it is significant that all the menus in the cafés and restaurants rigorously exclude dishes suggesting dependency on the potato.

Late in the summer the visitors go away; tables of descent scrawled into notebooks which they will try to make sense of during the course of the winter; many have found cousins, aunts, branches of the family they had no idea existed. Do they know who they are now? Certainly it is impossible not to have picked up something of the sensibility of those poor country people who fled the homeplace in despair and bitterness; only there is little enough sign of it in the bland and modernized countryside that has been newly colour-washed and painted up for the tourists. The version of the past that is on offer must be palatable to the modern taste – one of crafts, of horse-brasses, herbal bags, oatmeal soap and china leprechauns, of pottery and hand-made jewellery and knitwear. ('We're a workers' cooperative', the rather severe young woman from the Clear Island Cooperative said, yet insisting that 'we work together for social rather than economic reasons.') There has been a revision of a tragic and only half-remembered story, which is like those imperfect family histories which are never satisfactorily resolved, but elude the searcher, so that the last clue that will finally tell you who you really are remains tantalizingly just out of reach.

Everything about the Malvern Hills suggests a profound and tranquil conservatism. From the ancient earthworks of British Camp on Herefordshire

Beacon, on one side you can look across the Severn Plain, while to the
West, the Black Mountains are clearly visible. Here, Langland conceived
Piers Plowman, 'in a somer season whan softe was the sonne'. The area
where Elgar lived and worked, and where, as early as 1654, John Evelyn
noted the curative properties of the water for 'King's-Evil and Leaprosie',
at its moment of fullest summer colour and ripeness, evokes deep and
powerful feelings. In spite of the over-walked paths and the erosion of the
hills, the blackberry briars are dark with fruit, the banks of willowherb fill
the air with a gentle blizzard of down. Butterflies have been especially
plentiful this year, Peacocks and Red Admirals flashing across the darken-
ing green of the bracken, and the berries of the mountain-ash are already
scarlet–orange. The wild grasses are bleached by the sun, the tenacious
harebells shake their frail flowers in the exposed places on the ridges. As
the silver-topped cumuli flatten out over the Midland Plain, it is impossible not to feel an intense love of the countryside, a sense of something that
survives alteration and change. As the widow of an army officer expressed
it 'This is where I come for comfort when I want to get away from the
awfulness of modern life.' Many others have had the same idea: in every
sheltered spot there are memorial benches, inscribed with the names of
those 'who loved to walk in these hills'.

Great Malvern, and the small towns that depend on it in the shadow of
the hills, seems to confirm the impression of changeless dignity. At first,
Malvern looks a dramatic example of faded splendour. Its celebrity as a
spa reached its brief height between 1840 and 1860, thanks to the enterprise of a few doctors who developed the water cure; and for a few years it
even rivalled Baden-Baden. The town itself remains a testimony to the cre-
dulity of both the rich and the clever (among them Dickens, Carlyle, Lord
Lytton, Darwin and Florence Nightingale), who permitted themselves to
be wrapped in wet sheets, and packed with blankets in a sitz-bath before a
tour of the wells; drinking at each one and returning to their hotel for an
austere breakfast of porridge. But Malvern's moment of fame was short.
The doctors died or disappeared, the fashionable no longer came, even
though its reputation as a salubrious resort survived and people continued
to come here to retire. They still do – you can see groups of middle-aged
people, a little out of breath on the steep slopes, carrying the local property
guide and wondering if they can afford the bungalow a few miles out of
town.

Malvern retains many monuments to its mid- and late-Victorian wealth;
vast villas with oriel windows and castellations, fretted gables and ample,
dusty conservatories, pink granite terraces and ironwork delicate as lace,
its sedate shops on the promenade, its ornate railway station with cast-iron
pillars along the platform with elaborately wrought foliate capitals.

There are few places so evocative of a superseded social order, still with traces of those who occupied the enormous houses, drove perhaps in their carriages along Lady de Walden Walk, paused along the promenade to buy some *poudre à lavage* or Widow Welch's Pills for Female Complaints. In one of the many bric-à-brac shops, an old lady in knitted stockings and brown boots offers for sale two items which she takes from a paper bag: a black bangle and a necklace of tiny shells. 'I don't know what they're worth,' she says to the shopkeeper, 'I found them in my brother's trunk. He used to send home so many beautiful things from East Africa.' The woman examines the objects. 'I'm afraid this isn't jet, and those shell-necklaces are very common. I can only offer you £3.50 for the two.' The old woman reflects. 'I suppose I shall have to take it.' 'Have you got any Victorian nightgowns or linen at home?' 'I believe so, I must have a look.' 'We can give you a good price for them, up to £12 each.'

In the Nearly New Boutique are the dresses and suits, the jewellery and effects of the recently dead; there is a terrible poignancy about the belongings hastily cleared out by the newly bereaved: a turquoise costume, a string of pearls, a crocodile handbag; so much evidence of all those who go to the resort in retirement and then don't live long enough to enjoy it. The teashops too are crowded with the wraith-like figures of those stranded in this way, bewildered and angry at husbands who have deserted them for death. Not all of them are well-to-do. For there are also memories of another Malvern, of elderly maidservants who can recall having to direct a visiting solicitor from the front door, where he had impertinently presented himself, to the tradesmen's entrance, and who remember themselves, as girls of 14, having to break the ice in the water-jug of their attic room before they could wash in the morning; memories of fathers who drove the big shire horses along the dirt roads, carrying stones from the quarries, which carved harsh contours into the flanks of the gentle hills; and recalling the folk-belief that 'anybody who could get a chimney stack smoking overnight had the right to build a house on the hills.'

But it would be a mistake to regard this prosperous area as merely a place of fossilized social history, as though an absence of industry exempted it from being counted part of the real world. (By that judgement, large tracts of formerly industrial Britain would also have to be excluded.) Its economy is flourishing. The Royal Signals and Radar Establishment is one of the biggest employers, and it is here that the Rapier missile was developed. Another significant source of employment is to be found in the many public schools in the area. The former Imperial Hotel, with its tunnel to the railway station, through which the salt for the brine baths was conveyed, is now Malvern Girls' School; and it has been the fate of many of the luxurious villas to become schools and, increasingly, nursing homes.

Private education helps to sustain many shops which otherwise would not survive in such a small town – art and stationery, several bookshops. In the old-fashioned and sedate haberdashers, where the assistants draw blinds of bleached hessian over the lower half of the outside windows against the sun, the display anticipates the coming term: a metal-edged leather trunk open to reveal the items necessary for a boy starting school: shirts, grey pullover, elasticated grey trousers (age approx. eight years), paisley-patterned pyjamas, fuzzy check dressing-gown, caps in maroon and dark green and blazers with Latin mottoes worked in gold thread. Those private houses which have not become schools have been turned into hotels and guest-houses; a few are converted into flats, where a number of musicians and artists live.

But it is the retired elderly couples who predominate in the town during the daytime. They are present in great numbers in the Winter Gardens on the day of the annual Horticultural Show, held for 150 years on the second Saturday in August.

All the exhibits are laid out on long trestles: vases of splendid crimson and sulphur-coloured dahlias, floribunda and tea-roses, sweet peas and asters; the vegetables too are spectacular – big marrows striped lime and dark green, saffron onions bursting out of their papery first layer, white potatoes polished as eggs, reds with their purple stains, bluish leaves of cabbages, white fibrous roots of giant leeks. Some of the more uncommon produce attracts a great deal of attention. An old lady inspects some bright yellow tomatoes and a plate of wine-coloured French beans. 'Our Marian grew some like that. I don't fancy them, beans that colour. I said to her "I can't eat those. Why don't you grow something I can eat?"' The flowers and vegetables are almost eclipsed by another kind of produce: sponge cakes, stands of rock-cakes and flapjack and date slices, blackcurrant and apricot jam, wine made from wheat, celery, rhubarb, birch sap, parsnips, elderflowers; patchwork covers and cushions, quilting and basket-work, crocheted tablecloths and chair-covers and runners, knitting and mac-ramé, soft toys, formal flower arrangements on themes like Sunset or Siesta in the Shade; and the slides and photographs of suburban gardens ablaze with African marigolds, geraniums and lobelia; everything suggests a vast expenditure of time and energy; even though an 85-year-old former secretary of the Horitcultural Society insists 'People don't put the work into it they used to. When we had the show in the Old Assembly Rooms, you couldn't move for the greenstuff and the flowers.' Another old man, a former farmworker, said 'Three things you need for growing – time, patience and love. People don't have enough of any of them these days. They spend a fortune on it, and it's not half the show it used to be.'

The change that he hints at – a far greater outlay of money on activities that formerly cost virtually nothing – touches that more profound change that has occurred in Malvern, and from which no country town or remote community in the country has been excluded: the extension and intensification of market penetration. And the life of this town revolves conspicuously around markets. It isn't simply that one of the most significant events in Malvern in recent years has been the opening of a vast branch of the International Stores, a building almost as big as the Priory, with its free bus service from Upton-on-Severn and the neighbouring villages, with its crèche and attendants to look after the children while they chalk on the blackboard or watch Mickey Mouse on the video. Nor is it that on Friday the traditional open market takes over part of the car park, with its stalls of cheap fabrics and household goods, locally grown tomatoes and green Pershore plums; this week, the best-selling item was a walkie-talkie set for children, 'to solve the Christmas stocking problem', reduced from £15 to a fiver. One mother, urged on by her seven-year-old, says to him 'I can't give you it for Christmas, it won't be a surprise'. 'That's all right, I'll have it now.' Even the Priory, with its Norman nave, its medieval misericords representing the seasons, and stained glass of rich yellow and cerulean blue, has a sort of elaborate market-stall in the north aisle, where you can buy not only cards and guides to the Priory, but also publications and objects of a distinctly secular nature, natural history and prints of Malvern, pencil-cases and crayons. On Wednesdays, part of the Winter Garden is set aside for an antiques fair, even though Malvern already has several antique shops. There is a display of militaria – daggers, krises and swords, ersatz emergency-issue bayonets of the German Imperial Army, British military Gurkha *kukris* (for £26), fragments of foreign war decorations, combat gear, weaponry, photographs from the First World War. Other stalls offer an Indian hand-made silver tea-blender, tortoiseshell hair-brushes, ivory combs, silver cruets, an epergne, multi-tiered cakestand, china, pottery; above all, the discarded artefacts of late-Victorian and Edwardian households, chafing-dishes and rose-bowls, silver napkin rings, lamps and chandeliers, candle-snuffers and ink-wells, shaving-cases and scent-sprays. Their fascination seems to lie in the fact that they have survived their function; their durability in the presence of the perishability of almost everything in current use. Many of them now ornament the cottages in the hills, plain wooden chairs, footstools, clocks and teapots, stone jars and green glass bottles. Even the celebrated pure Malvern water is marketed now by Cadbury Schweppes, bottled in their plant over the hills at Colwall.

The young people hang round the video shop or sit on the wall of the Priory graveyard, drinking tins of Coke; some in leather motor-bike gear, two with punk hairstyles, some girls with corpse-like make-up. All dressed up and longing to be elsewhere, 'as long as it's not here'. They feel they can't be free here, although it is not labour that claims their energy or takes their time. 'People look down on us. We're persecuted for being different.' To have time without money is a living death. None of them has ever been inside the Priory. 'Have you ever been up on the Beacon?' 'Too much like hard work.' One of the boys grins. 'I went up on my motorbike. I got caught. Fined £25. I thought it was a free country.'

Malvern is by no means the sober and faded place it appears. In many ways, it is a model of modernized, service economy; the realization of one version of a regenerated Britain of leisure and wealth. And just as it is far from being the sheltered retreat it may seem to be, so beneath its surface calm and propriety, there is another, dissenting Malvern. For one thing, the Green (formerly Ecology) Party received one of its highest votes in the United Kingdom here in both 1979 and 1983. There is a vigorous branch of Amnesty International. Very conspicuous in the area was an Oxfam poster campaign, where more than a hundred sites – private houses, schools, businesses – display posters reminding people that it takes millions of women in the world the equivalent of a walk from Hyde Park to Piccadilly Circus every day to fetch water; or that for the price of one Harrier, one and a half million people could be given access to clean water.

Isla Williams, a retired headmistress, has been delighted by the response to the campaign. She has never been able to understand why people are not roused to anger by the spectacle of misery and hunger in the world. The reponse to the famine in Ethiopia shows what a vast reservoir of compassion there is in the British people. Since she has been involved with Amnesty, she says, a shadow has fallen over her life. It is impossible to be happy, knowing what human beings are doing to each other every moment of every day. Dissent here has a strong international dimension. It may well be, as Isla Williams says, that there are no obvious major social problems locally, except perhaps indifference and complacency on a vast scale. 'But we are growing. We had one member of the Peace Movement who gave up his job with the RSRE because he couldn't reconcile the work he was doing there with his conscience. He took a job at half the pay.' Isla Williams grew up in the south of England, a sheltered childhood of boarding school and the security of a family flour-milling business. 'But I always thought it was wrong that we should be able to travel in a motor-car, when there were men in the streets who'd fought in the war, begging or selling matches. But whenever I voiced my qualms, I was always ticked off. I was always told that other people know best. But I always felt very strongly. I was allowed to do charitable work, I became a Sunbeam and befriended a poor family. But it took me years to trust my own feelings, and to dare to think that I might be right.'

Philip Webb grew up on a farm a few miles from Malvern. He, like many other young people, moved away to London, but the tug of the home region brought him back to run an art shop in partnership with an old friend. He is a vigorous campaigner for the Peace Movement. He feels that although nuclear disarmament is the most vital issue, it isn't by itself enough, because it's negative. You need to offer people a positive vision beyond it. He says that although the trade unions and Labour Party express an interest in Amnesty, CND, green issues, they are on the whole too preoccupied with their own internal business and struggles. Guy Woodford, Green Party candidate, says that a lot of people in the Green Party have a Labour Party background. 'The Greens must not be seen as a soft alternative. What we stand for implies something very radical, a global egalitarian and socialist aim. A lot of people feel that the class war within national boundaries is an inadequate formula to deal with world-wide issues. The multinationals represent an evil system that is filtering wealth from the poor to the rich on a vast scale. The Labour Party tends to confuse wealth, resources, with money. The Left is obsessed with slicing the cake, the Right with making it bigger, while we're concerned with the composition of the cake, calling into question its quality and its ingredients.'

None of the growth points for dissent in this prosperous part of the centre of England has any necessary relationship to a party based on labour; the people recognize that the form of leisure society of which Malvern is a paradigm depends upon subordination and impoverishment in other parts of the world. To look beyond national boundaries is not only necessary, but is also liberating and exhilarating.

Looking north eastwards from the hills in clear polar air, you can see the lights of the West Midlands conurbation glittering in the evening sky, but you feel that Malvern – and the many places like it in Britain – far from being a backwater, foreshadows things to come in a way that the old wasting industrial areas do not, both in the pattern of its economy and in the way people react to it. Here, it almost seems as though the longing for a restoration of a pre-industrial Britain is actually going to be realized in a post-industrial, high-tech future. Here, the leisure society offers the illusion that the industrial revolution never happened, that we can escape both its worst horrors and its most baleful consequences.

6

Servicing the leisure society

Leisure and service have been offered to the people of the West as a vision of liberation from earlier and known rigours of industrial manufacture. It is sometimes said that we will have to unlearn the disciplines of the work ethic. This does not mean that we shall transcend it. On the contrary. Not only does 'service' mean the status of servant (and when was there ever liberation in that?), but the necessary and often exploitative labour involved in the production of basic necessities, from which a majority in the West are being freed, is not eliminated. It has simply been transferred to distant places. Only that part that is clean and tidy remains, as industry in the rich countries is 'rationalized', and the service sector predominates. It is easier not to see the subordination, in the eager and smartly dressed workers in the retailing industry, the perfectly groomed and decorous crowds swallowed up each day by banks and offices in the city centres, in the well-scrubbed youngsters in the fast-food outlets, and the uniformed employees of hotels, security or maintenance companies. There remains a half-stifled knowledge that our leisure remains an unequal and dependent privilege; suffused with guilt, it is a commodity (for it is a commodity), not to be enjoyed with whole-hearted relish, but in the shape of a desperate need for *escape*, always contaminated by the sufferings of those at whose expense it has been won.

Nor can leisure be equally available to all. It requires quantities of labour, much of it so low paid that even when those who provide it for the better off are not working, they scarcely have access to the same pleasures. It is a stratified leisure; those who can afford it buy ever more expensive places to escape to: hilltop mansions on secluded islands protected by intense security. ('George Harrison is to sell the £5 million Australian dream home he has been building for the past three years because it has been discovered by sightseers. The 44-year-old ex-Beatle has become one of the pop world's most notorious recluses and was preparing to use the luxury home as the perfect hideaway' the *Sun*, 13 October 1987.) Mass leisure industries will provide more limited and controlled forms of escape, of which the package holiday is perhaps the best example; while for many of those who serve, leisure will be available in cheap and cut-price forms. The leisure of the unemployed remains theoretical because it cannot be realized monetarily; it is therefore not leisure at all, but a sense of permanent exclusion.

This is why even the most rudimentary forms of service can seem like a relief to the young, especially in the early stages; many of them still live at home and are subsidized by their parents. It isn't until they start a family of their own that they realize the nature of the trap they are in. Many young people sell a certain proportion of their time to enable those better off than they are to be free. This can appear as an advantage to those just leaving home. Nowhere is this more true than in the child care and private nanny industry.

Grace came from Ulverston in the Lake District, not far from Barrow-in-Furness, to be a nanny in North London. She is lucky because not only are her employers easy-going and friendly, but she likes the children she is working with. It is the only way she could conceivably have come to London because she would never have been able to afford accommodation. Of her home town, she says 'It's a tourist place, nice to see, but not to live there. It's full of gossip, and I realized that there is more to existence than other people's lives.' Even so, other people's lives are her work.

'My mother died and my father remarried. I don't get on with my stepmother. I liked her at first; but she was a bit too nice. It turned out she is a very jealous person. She can't bear to share my father, even with his children. When he had a heart attack, she didn't even bother to phone till late at night. She said "He's in a bad way, but don't bother to come." When I go home, she goes out. If I go up to stay, I have to stay in a bed-and-breakfast place. She wants to move because it is the house my father shared with my mother. She says to me "This isn't your house any more." My father is a process worker for Glaxo in Barrow.

'My mother died in 1981. I often feel, oh, if only I'd done this or said that to her. Before coming down here I had six months out of work. I tried to look after my Dad at first, but I'd always longed to go south, since I was about 17. After mother died, he got into a terrible rut. He wouldn't go out. I waited on him. I'd more or less taken my mother's place. "You don't do this like your Mum." "I'm not Mum." He carried on as though she would come back at any moment. He'd just sit there, and I felt guilty because I wasn't, and couldn't be her. It had all been so sudden; they'd given her 12 months to live and she was dead within three weeks.

'So when Gwyneth came on the scene, I felt relief. I saw it as my chance to get away. I couldn't bear being tied to the home. I was the only child. My mother was very quiet and reserved, backbone of the family type, traditional working-class wife role. Gwyneth is bubbly and outgoing. She's a very overpowering woman. If you ask my Dad a question, she'll answer for him. I took my boyfriend up. "How are you?" he said to my Dad. "He's all right" chirps up Gwyneth. "Can't he speak for himself?"

'My father just rang up one night and said "I'm getting married tomorrow." I was really pleased. That Christmas Dad said he was expecting me to come home. Later, she rang and said "I don't want you here." She said "If you come, I'll leave your Dad." I went to a bed-and-breakfast.

'A friend of mine had come down and lived in the East End. She worked at the London Hospital. She put me up for a while when I first came to London. When I go back to Ulverston now, everything is still exactly the same, running at the same slow speed, dead slow. Getting drunk is the only diversion. I'm 27 now.

'When I left school, I did a hairdressing apprenticeship. I got a place in college, but I preferred an apprenticeship because, although it's longer, you get more experience. Three years. You get very friendly with the clients. Meeting people brought me out of myself. Women would tell you all about their sex problems. One women, in her sixties, on her third marriage, I was shampooing her one day and she was telling me how her husband wasn't capable any more of giving her what she wanted. I realized I could handle it. It is a great sense of achievement. They trust you with their hair, so they think they can trust you with their secrets and problems. It's an intimate service.

'I left the apprenticeship before I finished because of my mother's illness. I took a part-time job so I could look after her. I went self-employed, doing home-visiting hairdressing. I didn't have my own transport, I had to use Dad's; I was using his car 14 hours a day sometimes. The clients were very relaxed, in their own surroundings. I really enjoyed it. One of my clients always got me breakfast, another prepared lunch. When my mother died, one of them said "I'm your mother now. If you have any problems, come to me." That's the good side of small town life.

'I was self-employed for 12 months. As long as you put the money back into the business, you can make a go of it. But then father needed the car. I went unemployed. First of all, I cleaned up the house, redecorated it. Then I found a factory job – there were too many hairdressers, and to work for somebody else, the money is terrible. So I got a job at Moppy Joe's; they make metal mop-heads, also sockets for cookers, cartridge clips for the MOD. It was a boring job; strip of metal, punch a hole and move it on. I used to watch the clock, see the hand creep on. I did it for nine months, £55 a week. There was a lot of bitchiness in the factory. The gang leader set the tone, she wouldn't speak to new people, so if they weren't strong and independent, they stayed out. She had too much power, she would send people to Coventry, and everybody fell in with her. In factories, the frustration is terrible – if somebody fancies someone else's boyfriend, or if somebody hears what another woman has said about their appearance, it all gets blown up out of proportion.

'Then I went to work in an old people's home. I enjoyed it. I was there 12 months. I didn't get on with the boss. I didn't agree with how she ran the place. The work was in shifts. I worked nights, starting at five in the evening till nine the next morning, $15\frac{1}{2}$ hours. Then in the morning it was "This hasn't been done, that hasn't been done." I'd had half the patients up all night; some were confused, some senile. I enjoyed it because I could help people, but it was too much. I had a final row when I was supposed to do the hoovering. I said I'm a care assistant, not a cleaner. Things got worse, so I left. I was unemployed for six months. That was terrible. I got so that I didn't want to get up in the morning. My father was working 12 hour shifts. When he was on nights, I changed my day, so I was cleaning at night while he was out. I had phases where I'd make washing, so I could wash and iron; I'd make a mess, just to clear it up, give myself something to do. Then I stopped getting up. I stopped living, without dying, if you see what I mean. I didn't eat. I was miserable, depressed, fed up with life. That was when my father met Gwyneth.

'I came to London. I had four interviews, got three of them. Three were nannying, one hairdressing. I accepted the first one, hairdressing. It was Hackney, one of those get 'em in, get 'em out places, wages £55 a week. Then I answered some ads in *The Lady* magazine; one five days a week with £20. I'd had some experience with the children of a friend of mine; they had split up, and I helped her with the children. I'd done that while I was on the dole, not paid.

'The job I have now is good. They're more like friends, not an employer–employee relationship. I work from 8.30 until 7.00. If I need a couple of hours off, I can go. It can be difficult. If I try to discipline the children, they might run to their mother to get her to counter whatever I've said. I call myself a nanny. There is a two-year course in nannying, but I haven't got a qualification.

'I don't think it's hard work. It's the most natural thing for a woman to do it by routines. Dress kids, clean the kitchen, get the kids busy, prepare elevenses, dinner, take them shopping; take them to nursery, then for a walk. I'm tired at the end of the day. I'm very old-fashioned, I believe it's natural for women to bring children up. My mother ran our family; she had all the ideas, but she had to suggest them so that my Dad thought he'd dreamed it up – that's the woman's role. She doesn't get the glory, but she gets the satisfaction of knowing it all depends on her. I had a strict but loving upbringing, and that's what children need. If you've had love as a child, you know how to give it spontaneously to children. I went to visit a friend of mine with a baby. It was bathtime, and it wasn't fun. It was tense and fraught. She didn't know how to cuddle him, how to respond, and that was reflected in the child's behaviour; she had never been shown love as a child.

'When I came south, I was so excited. At first, I couldn't stay in. I kept saying to myself "I'm in London, I'm a big girl now." I thought of London as bright lights and night clubs. I went to these places, where people picked each other up, I liked watching people. But I'm really a home bird: the bright lights don't always show up very pretty things. In Ulverston, there was nothing to do but go to the pubs; there are 30 in the main street. They say that's so that even when it's pouring with rain – which it does a lot – you don't get wet going from one to the other.

'I think being a nanny isn't like it was. They don't live through other people's children. None of this gazing through the railings at the handsome young man you used to dandle on your knee, all repression and tears. To me, it was just an opportunity to come to London. I could never have afforded it if I'd had to live by hairdressing. I'd be in debt. I have a boyfriend, I expect to get married. To me, nannying is a way of getting what I want. And it also suits the family I live with. It's a contract.'

Grace has been lucky, unlike Barbara, who came from Newcastle and lived with the family of a journalist and solicitor in West London. Barbara is an energetic and outspoken young woman of 25, who came to London after two years' unemployment and work as a care assistant in a children's home. 'It was all supposed to be so well regulated. I had weekends off from Saturday lunch-time. I had my own room. It sounded good. But gradually it spread, it began to enchroach horribly. "Could you do this, I've got an important meeting." The woman worked as a journalist on a woman's magazine. In the end, I found myself cooking and cleaning and minding the children, and sometimes being the only one in the house at nights. The marriage was a bit shaky – that is putting it mildly, she had another man who she brought in in the afternoons. And I'm there, supposed to see nothing, know nothing. I was taking the children out to be out of the way so she could have sex with her bloke upstairs, and I'd have to be out in the pouring rain, wheeling the baby and meeting the other one from school, and pretending to take them for a treat to the park, where we got soaked. I was sitting in a McDonalds with baby on my knee, making a cup of coffee last and trying to amuse the little one. I was even reading to her – in McDonalds. I resented it. But they knew I had nowhere else to go. When my mother remarried, my stepfather fancied me – that was the reason I left home. He used to leer and touch me and treat me like a little girl. He kissed me goodnight, a nasty wet kiss on the lips, it was repulsive. I couldn't go back there, so I was trapped. I'd told them about my life in the first flush of gratitude at finding a home; but they knew they could ask anything of me and I wouldn't be able to refuse. I'm not saying that they did it consciously. I used to scheme, I tried to go out and meet boys, I was looking for someone who would give me somewhere to live. If I got chatted up by people, first thing I'd ask would be "Have you got a flat?". I was looking too frantically. I got it all wrong. They must have known. Some thought I was on the game, or perhaps I just made it too obvious it wasn't their body I was after but their roof.

'It got so much worse. I loved the kids, that was the sad part about it. Because there was a bond between us, that was another way in which I could be exploited. The parents were too busy to be bothered, so they took to me, they thought of me as their mother. I was embarrassing and frustrating. I was working up to 16 hours a day, and at weekends. I felt so angry. I was actually being paid £25 a week, and given this little room, so that she could have the leisure to do her job and screw this bloke she was working with. She wasn't even paying me properly; I was doing all this virtually for food and lodging. She prided herself on being terribly elegant and fashionable, which she was. In fact, she could be quite stunning. That didn't make me love her any more. I don't know why they had children. I said so to her one day. She said "Oh one does, Barbara. You'll understand one day." Patronizing. I felt trapped.

'There was a woman who lived three or four doors away. I was waiting at the bus stop on a rare afternoon off. She was standing there, and talking, I must have been looking pretty fed up. I burst into tears when I heard the kindness in her voice. She took me into her house, and I told her how I felt and what was going on. She offered me a room in her house until I could sort myself out. So I went back and gave in my notice. I felt bad about leaving the children. I knew it would upset them. But I felt I'd go mad if I stayed any longer. They behaved as though I had done them the most serious injury. "What am I going to do?" she wailed, "my work". I told her her work wasn't exactly the most vital contribution to society. I really found my tongue, and said all the things that had been burning me up. She couldn't say anything because she knew that I had the knowledge about her and her fellow, while her husband was coming home at 8 o'clock from his legal practice in the city, looking like a wraith for the sake of his 60 thousand a year or whatever it was.

'Since then, I've done waitressing, stripping, casino work. I saved up enough money for a two-roomed flat. It was a funny thing – in the end, it was my boyfriend who moved in with me, rather than my fantasy of moving into somebody else's place. I thought I was going to find some man to look after me, and I end up scraping this guy off the pavement and taking care of him. He now works as manager of a music store; at that time he'd been thrown out by the guy where he was living because he was into drugs. That's life. I've lost touch with my family, I haven't seen them for three years. I resent that my mother never protected me from her man. I still resent it. I think she closed an eye to it because she was scared she might lose him if she said anything. If I call myself a feminist, it's not from theory, it's from bloody bitter and hard experience.'

'They're very kind to me,' says Gail of her employers, 'they're very generous. They give me second-hand clothes for the kids that are good as new really. They're very considerate if any of the children are ill and, of course, they pay me over the odds. But all the same, it's a bit tense. They're a bit snobbish, left-wing snobbish, they think of me as their hot-line to the working class.' Gail is 27 and works as a daily help to a businesswoman and her architect husband in North London. She is representative of a new 'democratic' kind of service, in which the relationship between employer and employee is blurred, covered by guilt and over-compensatory wages. Gail lives in a council block only five minutes away from the Edwardian three-storey villa where she works. Her husband is on invalidity benefit. Gail left school at 16 with no qualifications, was married at 17 and has three children. She says 'The word "servant" would never be mentioned. Mind you, I feel I'm as good as they are. Better, really, if I was to tell you the truth. I'd never give my kids over to someone else when they're only a few weeks old. They earn high salaries themselves, but they don't think the people who look after their children are worth one-quarter of what they get. I worked it out once, it's only a small fraction of their income. Of course, I don't look after the children full-time. It's been a godsend to me. And they are good to me. They took me and Dave out once to a really smart restaurant. It was just before Christmas. The food was lovely, but the evening was a disaster. We talked about their kids all night.'

Chloe is in her early thirties. She goes out at 5 o'clock every morning to travel to one of the two jobs she does for a cleaning contractor. The other job is in the evening. Each involves two hours' travel and two hours' work a day, so that, effectively, she is occupied eight hours. The gross pay is £25 and £30 respectively. By the time she has paid her bus fare, she takes home less than £45 a week. She lives in Dalston, with her children Melissa, who is ten, and Conroy, who is six. Her husband died as a result of an accident on a building site where he was working. Melissa gets Conroy's breakfast, and makes sure they get to school on time. She is a grave and sedate child, troubled by her responsibilities and anxious about her mother's difficult life. Chloe says 'I'd get more on social security, but I'd go out of my mind. I get company. We get on well, all women together. We have a laugh. At Christmas, they had a party in the office. You've never seen a mess like it, broken glass, wine spilt everywhere, crisps and cakes and cream all trodden into the carpet. It was horrible. We refused to touch it unless they give us a bonus. We looked and we said "We not doing that." We got an extra £10.' Chloe thinks about her children's future and wonders. 'The children them, I don't want them to do work like I'm doing. I want something better for them. But what kind of education are they getting? Let them have a good time, and then they come out from school not knowing anything. Will they do better than me? Am I doing better than my Mam? She come here with five pickney, she live in a damp room in Notting Hill, and she work sweeping out the trains them at Paddington station. How is it better? The police just waiting to make the little children into criminals, what chance they got?'

Gina is 30 and does a domiciliary hairdressing service. She is self-employed. Most of her customers are elderly, people who can't get to the hairdressers, disabled or bed-bound. She was trained in a salon before she married; her husband is a gas central heating engineer. Her two children are at primary school. She has between 15 and 20 customers, and takes the equipment to their homes. 'They make me a cup of tea, I chat. They'd keep you there all day some of them, they're lonely. I'm not into being a real beautician and all that. I don't charge a lot. Most weeks I'll make between £40 and £50 a week profit. I only work during school hours, but I love it. It's the social contact as much as anything else, and I feel I'm doing a social service. When I show them how they look, you see them touching their curls, it makes me feel really happy. I wouldn't want to work for anyone else. My friends tell me I don't charge enough, but I think I'd do it even if I didn't get paid at all. That's not quite true, but if it was money I was after, I wouldn't be doing this.'

Janet, in her late twenties, is a waitress for a catering company, which sends out fully prepared menus to people's homes. It is mostly evening work, serving and clearing away at private dinner parties. Janet is one of a team of three who set the table, serve and clear away. She earns £60 for four evenings a week, although it is sometimes 1 o'clock in the morning before she gets home. 'We're ghosts,' she says. 'People look through you. Sometimes they're very nice, but others don't even talk to you. Of course, we go to some very lovely homes, titled people, TV stars. You get good tips from some. Invisible, that's what we are. If they realized what we were listening to, they wouldn't be so free with their mouths. Sometimes, when we go out into the kitchen, we can't keep a straight face. There's other little perks, like little bits of really nice stuff left over, smoked salmon, fruits out of season, things I've never heard of. I take them home. Well, when you're with people who spend more on one meal than you have to feed your family for a week, it sets you thinking. I don't envy them, but I do know there's a hell of a lot of people with more money than they know what to do with. Sometimes they talk about money at their parties. It's nearly always about how poor they are. They can't afford a winter holiday this year. Oh dear. My heart bleeds for them. They'll just have to struggle on till the five weeks they're going to have in Greece in the summer. One day, I might just say something. If I didn't need the job, I would. I let off steam with the bloke I live with. Apart from that, it's see no evil, isn't it, hear no evil.'

Domestic service remains the occupation of a minority. Most of the servicing of leisure in the contemporary world is more regulated and more efficient. Of course, service is nothing new in the experience of the British people. Feudal, military and domestic echoes resonate around the word itself. The only surprising thing is that so ancient and familiar an idea should now be presented in the guise of emancipation. For the sole element that is new in the reconstruction of the lives of people – especially women – in the interests of service is that it now makes its appearance in the form of 'service industries'. This novel combination suggests first of all that this time the service will be more organized: that it should be marshalled into whole industries hints at a factory-like quality. This has the further advantage of reassuring us that what we are seeing is something doubly familiar, the union, as it were, of service with industry; something to inspire a feeling of continuity and of easy passage, in spite of the convulsions of recent years.

Service industries foreshadow a mass-produced servitude; a patterning of subordination on the factory model without, however, the presence of the sullen and refractory industrial worker, the withdrawal of whose skills so easily perturbed the flow of production. This streamlined version of service will ensure that awkward individual hands are supremely dispensable. And this is connected to another aspect of contemporary service: it is, above all, impersonal. This has always been implicit in those forms of service that require dedication to a more abstract or exalted entity – one's country or a deity; but service as labour has always required the existence of a master or mistress. When my grandmother left her village at the age of 11, on the carrier's cart for the house near Eaton Square where she was to live, she was at least in daily proximity to a known employer. And while there are many stories of harsh treatment and indifference towards servants, there are perhaps as many that tell of kindness and of strong bonds of affection between masters (or more often mistresses) and their servants; and some of employers who became deeply dependent upon those who ostensibly served them.

Service industries evoke anonymity, the breaking of all but the most perfunctory and fleeting personal contacts. And this too is perhaps fitting, for it corresponds more closely to the fact that what is being served is an abstraction – the mighty power of money – to which we are all more or less in thrall, and which, in our time, has seemed to become more detached from living flesh and blood, however tyrannical and exacting that may once have been. Indeed, there is something so pervasive and ubiquitous in that power that the 'new' service has taken on something of its earlier associations – the mysterious and implacable authority of a godhead. For even the rich, those nominal and apparent beneficiaries of the new services often express the anxiety that not even they are in control either; they merely occupy a higher place in a hierarchy of servitude, more amply rewarded, it is true, and therefore with a greater interest in seeing that the mechanisms of wealth creation continue to function efficiently.

In fact, it is difficult not to feel that what has been reconstituted in our time is a kind of vast servants' hall, with its distinctions and precedences, and its minutely subdivided tasks, where the power of those at the top can express itself only through intensified pressure upon those beneath them, making them work harder, exhibit a proper degree of deference, a cruel and perhaps despairing passing on of their own feeling of impotence. Economic necessity has taken on an autonomous and unappealable power which can be appeased by the universal service into which we are all being pressed. It is therefore only appropriate that this should, in its turn, be anonymous and depersonalized.

The resonances of the word do not end there. For serving is also what prisoners do, their term, their penal sentence. It carries also the force of duty, to one's superiors, to a sovereign, to one's country. Most telling of all, the word 'to serve' evokes the freely offered labour of women. 'Serving' attracts the idea of wench, infinitely obliging, sexually no less than in other ways. It is no accident that the majority of those in contemporary forms of service are predominantly women, whose pay is destined to remain low because of the ill-suppressed and (to men) comforting notion that they like doing it, that it is part and parcel of their generous nature and their need to give. In this way, 'new' patterns of subordination can be easily justified through traditional cultural practice and prejudice. 'To perform friendly and beneficial actions' is the OED definition of to serve; and since this has been the purpose of women's lives, any money they may thereby gain has something of the discretionary gratuity about it. They are only doing what they would be doing anyway.

The labour thus created to release the better-off for more gracious and leisurely pursuits is increasingly insecure, casual, temporary and part-time, sometimes illegal and often at the mercy of passing market caprice. What in economic jargon is referred to as 'mobile and adaptable labour' means, in practice, that people must be always available, hold themselves in readiness, not permit themselves to become too settled, not expect stability or permanence. It also means that they are often invisible.

Sarah and Judy are both in their twenties; both have worked as temporary short-term catering workers, through agencies who paid them. 'It's slavery. It's heavy, dirty, low-paid work, catering. There's nothing glamorous in it, especially when you're working for big companies, firms that have a core of permanent staff, and temporaries to fill in. They're just providing food for their employees to keep them working efficiently. It doesn't even have the superficial glitz of posh restaurants.'

'Waiting. That's exactly what it is. You have to learn how to stand, how to hold yourself so that your body expresses servitude. I went for one job, there was a chair, so I sat down. Horror. You don't sit down. You're waiting, serving tea, food, you must shuffle your feet, keep your head down and elbows in. It's a self-effacing position; you must expect to be complained to and moaned at. That kind of treatment is part of your job; that's part of the emotional housework women are burdened with.

'The costume itself – frilly pinnies, maids' caps – they've nothing to do with cleanliness, they're a badge of your low status. There are different uniforms that mark out the temporary staff from the full-timers, a different colour, another design. Men have overalls, but women's aprons are pure decoration, a signal that your role is trivial. The women who take the tea-trolleys up to executives' offices at the top of the building are quite different, much smarter, more serious.

'Once you've put the uniform on, you no longer recognize yourself. You become someone else, a non-person, a part of the collective service. When you're out of uniform, people don't recognize you. You might be walking through the building, and people will open doors for you; in uniform, they'd never do that. You see the blankness in their faces when you're not in livery; they just don't know who you are.

'When you're clearing tables, people look through you. One in a hundred may look at you. Somtimes their eyes rest on you, but they're not seeing. The invisible woman, make yourself small. They only look at you when you fail to get out of their way when you're wheeling a trolley or carrying a tray of cutlery.

'You're the human part of other people's wages. You have to absorb their frustrations. If they moan, you must be there to absorb it. You're one of the perks that make their life a little easier. The money you earn is very precisely calculated – it must be just enough to keep your anger down. The pay for temporary staff is appalling £2, £2.20 or £2.40 an hour [in 1987]. I sometimes think to myself "I've just earned 20p, I'd better keep what I think to myself." Of course, if you are treated badly, there are ways, indirect ways, in which you can hit back, you can spit in the soup, the classic thing, or you can take something home, squeeze something extra out of the employers. You can get revenge by not doing the dishes properly. You feel you must get back at that violence to you somehow. If somebody is rude to me, I make sure they get the hottest plate and I don't warn them against it; or serve them the worst piece of food. I had a friend who was a stripper; her way of getting her own back was to let some of the men take her suspender belt, and hanging on to it, then letting go, so it snapped back at them with great force.

'There are always ways of reclaiming your time, a few minutes here or there. People tell you how to do a minimum of work. A lot of it is theatre – you must *look* busy. If there's nothing to do, go dust a picture frame. The art is to stretch out every job; as long as you don't get too cosy so as to become noticeable; keep that cloth moving over the surface. Timing is essential in catering; you're massively busy at certain times of day. It isn't a whole day job; but you've got to make out you're busy all the time or they'll cut staff, then when the real rush is on, it'll kill you. Don't be too efficient, or they'll get rid of some workers. You mustn't sit down, keep moving with a rag in your hand: cultivate a look of modest purposefulness.

'Don't ask questions, do as you're told – that's service. You also have to pretend to know what you're doing; never say you don't know, even if the work is ludicrous. At Barclay's, for instance, there is a conveyor belt taking thousands of dishes. At the end of the day it's washed down, but you're supposed to polish it at night. Service is militaristic – there is the uniform, the coordinated effort, the absurd discipline, the accomplishment of futile tasks for their own sake – the military model makes its appearance in the most unlikely places.

'It's all an extension of housework, therefore always low paid. Women are more and more pressured to take such jobs. Catering is mainly women, many black and immigrant women. Because wages in these jobs are falling, a lot of people are doing a permanent job and moonlighting as well. Some of the temporary catering staff are doing it on top of their other work, or during their two weeks' holiday – some do chambermaiding, silver service waitressing. Some of the work is illegal, off the cards, therefore the workers have no rights. Anything can happen – you can be sent home midday, dismissed on a whim; there's no sickness benefit, you can make no claim against injury, you can't protest about conditions or money.

'The physical conditions are appalling. The level of job-related disability is high: the sheer physical pain of catering is intense – if the labour disappeared, you'd call it torture. The equipment is not designed to make it easier for women: you're standing all day, you have extremes of hot and cold, you suffer from constant cuts and scalds and burns, they don't get a chance to heal so your arms and hands are scarred. You suffer rheumatism from cold water, if you prepare a fruit salad, your hands can be in orange juice for two or three hours and the acid makes your skin sore. You get varicose veins and backache. The work is worse than in the sex industry. A friend of mine who has done it says there is more money and better conditions in it.

'The work is destroying; then at the end of the day, you have to go home and do it all over again for nothing. It is exhausting – fetching, carrying, standing; some of the older women get in very bad shape. Some of the work could quite easily be done sitting down – preparing food – but they're not allowed to. It's heavy work.

'A lot of companies that used to engage their own staff in catering now contract out. Some keep a core of their own staff and make up with casual labour. Then, of course, it isn't the company's responsibility what conditions and pay the people work for. As temporary staff from the agencies you're set against the permanent staff. They see hordes of people desperate for work, and their inferior position is a way of disciplining the permanent workers, makes them keen to hold on to their job. Work intensity is increasing in catering: ten jobs will be reduced to eight, then six; people are racing round, working harder. If you can't cope, you just drop out, you're nobody's responsibility. The unions have been undermined by privatization, fragmentation.

'These companies are very hierarchical. You can pick out where they stand in the system when they come to eat – look at their shoes and dress, see what they eat, listen to what they talk about. It can be quite shocking – because we are invisible, people don't modify their conversation in our presence; a lot of it is shocking because it's so vacuous. Because you're bottom of the heap, some people who think they have a slightly better deal than you try to lord it over you: it's the have-littles against the have-less. You can see how even those who are way above you in the pecking order are beaten down, and how they pass it on to those below them.

'The directors eat at the top of the building, whereas the caterers are in the basement or even the sub-basement, the lowest of the low. In some places, you are completely cut off from daylight, you never see the sun. For months you can go to work in the dark, work all day in artificial light and come out in the dark.'

Sara says that both her mother and grandmother grew up in the tradition of domestic service in the USA. 'Being able to make the links, to see the reconstitution of old forms of service in the contemporary world, helps to keep you sane. Even to name it to yourself is a victory, to be able to understand what is happening. When I first saw myself in uniform, it looked outrageous. You have to say to yourself "That is not me, that has nothing to do with me." You split yourself as women always do, and always have done.

'It is violence, selling yourself and splitting your real self from it, even though the real self still gets oppressed by it – health, morale, exhaustion. As wages go up, so subservience goes down: those on the bottom rung of pay must always assume the most servile manner.

'When agencies were first set up, women used them to move easily from job to job – not only catering, but cleaning, other services; and they could walk out if conditions were bad, just as secretaries temping can. But now, with unemployment and lower wages, the agencies are ripping off the employees. They handle the money, they are taking a higher proportion of the gross pay than they used to.

'Because all this is happening to women, it isn't seen as important or serious. Women have always sought flexible work; because of their families, they've tried to fit their life round the job. But now the jobs are not so flexible, and it's women who are taking the strain. You go to an agency, there's 200 people there, they can pick and choose. You know that women do two-thirds of the world's work, have 5 per cent of the income and own 1 per cent of the wealth. The leisure society belongs to men.

'A day's work: you set out early, 6.30, to go to an agency. Many specialize, deal with cleaning, chambermaiding, secretarial. As soon as you come out of the tube, if you see a crowd in a doorway, you'll know that's an agency. You go and register, see what jobs are going. Then you go to the address to start, usually at eight. You have to pay your fare to the agency, your fare to the job, and then have to go back to the agency to pick up your money – all those hidden expenses are incurred before you even start to earn. The clothing you must provide – appropriate shoes, supportive tights. Sitting in agencies is like sitting in the dole office. A lot of the people are poor and desperate. The staff can be rude, racist and insulting. They pick and choose. They may well send you to the company nurse when you get to the workplace for a health check. Look at your skin and your teeth – like horses, to see if you're healthy enough to work. A lot of people are in poor health, but they need the work, so they suppress the cough, hide what is wrong – they're sick because they're poor. The quality of food is bad for those who are actually serving others: at one insurance company, the lowest permanent staff and the temps had to have something different from the rest: they weren't allowed fruit or juice, they had baked potatoes or chips. The food we eat is greasy, dirty, full of dyes. Some people would eat three plates of food at lunchtime to get something for nothing, but it was junk food.

'If you have a cough, a cold, you try not to sniff, say you're fine. You can't afford time off, space to be ill. It gives you a great insight into people.

It's the classic story, the slave knew the slavemaster better than he knew himself. Servicing people, you learn the kind of things about people that market researchers are paid extravagant sums to find out – what kind of food someone will eat, social attitudes. A lot of social information is accumulated. But you're not seen and not considered.

'Then there's the whole trip of emotional housework; people treating you as though you were their personal servant. You might be in a cafeteria. Someone will come to you and say "I want a bun, but I'm on a diet, what sort of bun would you recommend?" You don't want to know. They want to chat, they want advice, they want reassurance. What is really offensive is those who say to you "Are you enjoying your work?", "Happy in your job?" or "Having fun?". I say to them "Do you think I'm so much less a person than you are that I'll be satisfied wiping this table?" They might just want to chat – but that's emotional housework, that's women's work also, making the wheels run more smoothly, interceding, being emollient and obliging. Sod it.

'It is the same relationship as in the home. The only difference here is that it is all more stark; in industrialized services it is all so much clearer, there isn't the pretence that conceals exploitation in so many marriages, personal relationships. All you can do are minor acts of industrial sabotage. At one place, it was always the youngest women who had to go and get the tea. Once every two or three weeks – not too often – there'd be a crash on the stairs and everything would go flying; then the young woman would come in, holding her leg and pretending she'd tripped. Well, it creates a diversion. It lets them know you exist.

'The food that is thrown away is sickening. You're not allowed to take it home, it must go into the waste-bins, and there it goes – by the ton. It's generally poor quality. It's rubbish. People are being poisoned. It comes in great tin vats, cans, it's powders, liquids, dehydrated, reconstituted; it isn't packaged like goods on sale to private consumers: this is behind-the-scenes stuff, full of additives and colourings, for industrial use, nature-identical flavouring – that means chemical formulae. The contempt for those who eat it is there, just as the contempt for those who serve it is.

'For executives there are different menus altogether, different cutlery, separate kitchens; they have wholemeal bread, fresh vegetables. There aren't many black waitresses up there. The women on tills are mainly white – wherever there is contact with the public. I was making sandwiches in one place. There was a vacancy, and a black woman applied for the job. The white staff started saying "We're not having coloured women here, they're dirty; not black women making sandwiches."

'You see the other side of the façade; you realize the whole society is a front, two-dimensional. Behind, it's exploitative and destructive and corrupt. And that is what you are servicing. Only you know it. Women know. We're watching it all, we have no illusions.'

Laura is a croupier. Now 28, she lives in a small flat in the shadow of Westway in an elegant Victorian house. She has two cats, called Lucifer and Jesus. At home, she wears jeans and sweater. She goes to work on her bike through Hyde Park. A croupier on a bicycle sounds a little incongruous, but not half so incongruous as what she calls her uniform: a bottle-green, low-cut evening dress, close fitting with a ruched panier-effect at the waist. The uniform is the emblem of her subordination. After seven years as a croupier, she is now an inspector in one of the best-known Mayfair casinos.

She grew up in South London, and wanted to be a graphic artist, but was advised by her mother to do a secretarial course as something to fall back on. She was bored with it, and saw the advertisement for croupiers in the *Evening Standard*. 'There is nothing glamorous about it.' After seven years, any delight in the rather exotic employment has long faded. 'You have no rights as staff. Whatever the punter wants, you have to be compliant. That is the secret of the work. You are not allowed to solicit anyone into gambling, but you have to be alluring. You entice them without any overt advances.' Laura feels it is the ultimate contradiction: woman as sex-symbol but also as comforter to those men who lose their money. At the same time, they are not allowed to 'fraternize', a term borrowed from the vocabulary of warfare; it means they are not allowed to make assignations with punters. 'You see such a greedy side of life,' says Laura. 'It makes you cynical. You might think there's glamour in it, for the first week. I started work in the Golden Nugget, which is the down-market side of the business. It's a bit more relaxed in some ways because the stakes aren't so high; you can answer the customers back. But as you go up-market, you have to become more discreet, more perfectly behaved. I was amazed when I first started. You see punters fighting; the management used to bash them up, dump them outside on the pavement. It was a bit like the image of the Wild West. The only thing is, the people I work with are some of the nicest I've ever met.

'The best clubs are like Aspinall's or Crockford's, that's the old Wedgwood building with the beautiful Wedgwood ceilings. I now work for Mecca. They've changed their name now to London Clubs; they say it was changed because of bomb threats, the association with Mecca, I don't know how true that is. There are so many casinos now in central London, it's the punters who are in short supply. We have to be friendly to the punters, learn to smile, but not entice them to gamble. The

Gaming Board is very strict. The thing is, though, you recognize the inspector when he comes in; he goes round writing things down.

'There is a training room over the Golden Nugget. We spent two weeks learning the games, without pay. They teach you roulette, how to cut chips. After a time, you can tell how many chips you have in your hand without counting them. You have to learn the tables; each table has its own design of chips so they can't be transfered.' She gets out her *American Roulette Procedures Manual.* 'We play a mixture of French and American roulette; in French, the croupier places the bets for you; American roulette is very brash and fast. Each punter has his own personal maximum. If a punter has a personal maximum of £500, that means he can put £20,000 on a forty-piece bet; that would win up to £196,000. We had the Sultan of Brunei in the other day, Scotland Yard detectives were there, with their walkie-talkies, protecting him. He is allowed £1,000 maximum.

'It's nothing to see people lose a million in an evening; and then maybe win it back. As a dealer, punters blame you personally sometimes when they lose. Then they'll swear at you; quite often in Arabic or Japanese, so it doesn't sound so offensive. Most of those in our club are foreigners – Arabs, Japanese, a few Indians, Malaysians. There is a *salle privée* at the club, where most of the big players go. The Saudi royals, Kerry Packer, Kashoggi, people like that go to the various clubs in our group.

'My duties as a dealer are to start roulette; deal the games, make sure they don't cheat, whether by stealing each other's chips or putting a late bet on the winning number. You spin the ball, and make sure no more bets go on before it drops. You put a dolly on the winning number, a black and white stopper. They sometimes claim they had bets that weren't there before the ball dropped. That's why you have to have an inspector at each table.

'You'd get the sack if it was discovered that you met any of the clients out of work; although of course in practice you do meet some of them: they might own afterhours drinking clubs, or you see them walking round Bayswater. You're not allowed to go to other casinos as a punter; and your relatives are not supposed to come in either. It is very strict, at least in principle.

'I've been doing it for seven years. I've had enough. It shows you how people with money can do as they please; they can get away with behaviour that you or I never could. They can do what they want, and nobody checks them. Other people humour them; in fact, those who hope to make something out of them actually encourage it. A lot of punters think women are there only to be abused or insulted. You have to become thick-skinned. It wouldn't do to burst into tears. You learn control. Fortunately, I'm fairly placid, and although I do get angry, I don't show it.

You have to take abuse from them, anger, swearing. That's part of the job, that's the service isn't it? It's their way of relaxing, it's their money, it's their leisure to use you as they choose.

'If you did answer back, you wouldn't get any back-up from management. I'd never get support if I leapt to the defence of a woman being insulted. And, what's more, nobody is ever promoted on merit; it's all at the whim of the directors. If they like you, if you play golf with them. It is very chauvinistic. The directors employ women to stand in low-cut dresses to attract the punters, then to smile and be generally yielding and compliant. I get very angry, but I don't give them the satisfaction of seeing that they can provoke any emotion in me. I get satisfaction from thinking, "Well, they're losing." I'd never do it, even if I had their money. I would never gamble. They have no perception of reality; the sort of money they have distorts their perceptions. They only ever meet people eager to serve them, to maintain the fantasy they want to build around themselves. We had one wealthy punter who took exception to one of the inspectors. He said he wouldn't come back to the club until this guy was fired. And he didn't. The management moved him to another club to satisfy the punter. They would have sacked him if they hadn't had that option.

'I'm paid at a monthly rate. £14,000 a year; that is including the maximum for long service. You get more if you do certain games – so much for roulette, for blackjack, for punto banco – that's a form of baccarat. The general manager gets a percentage of the profits, so naturally he wants to keep everything moving as fast as possible. You know the roulette wheel must be kept constantly spinning – from two in the afternoon until 4 o'clock the next morning.

'I keep out of the way of the directors. I've never had any problem with them. We're not allowed to start a union. Some have tried, but everyone would have to join to make it effective. I'm not saying I'd go on strike all the time; but you need protection at work. The women would be better treated if there were a union. They don't respect you.

'It is different from other jobs. Working at night for one thing. You're not allowed off the premises once you arrive for your shift. A lot of people see the work as instrumental to doing something else; one I know is working to go round India, another is building a boat with her boyfriend. They don't regard it as permanent.

'Most gamblers are addicted. You see people ruined, it's pitiful. Some have vast debts; they can get credit up to a point, but when they don't pay, they're jumped on. Sometimes you see people who are broke; they'll be scrabbling through their purse to make up £1 in loose change to make a last desperate bet. Others have lost all their money, yet they can't tear themselves away; they just stand and watch, the look on their face so forlorn. The atmosphere can be very tense. I don't know why they do it – they're not happy. We have to be happy, but not too happy – management say we mustn't smile too much, otherwise the punters think you're laughing at them. That happened to me once, when a guy was losing. I smiled at him, and he did his nut. "How can you smile when I'm losing, get out of my sight." He was desperate. I made myself scarce, what could I do? You learn to assume a sympathetic smile, not too amused; that's the extent to which you are manipulated. Once a punter tried to attack one of the dealers with a big glass ashtray. He climbed over the table to beat her with it. Management did step in then: it wouldn't be good news for the club to have a croupier slain by a demented punter.

'They're very superstitious. There's one punter who always kisses his tie before playing; some have their own private rituals. I go onto automatic pilot. Nothing surprises me. There is something rather pathetic about a majority of punters. Like any addicts, there's something missing from their lives – apart from their brains that is. Occasionally, prostitutes come in, looking for business. One Saudi prince kept asking me out. I had to refuse, otherwise I'd have lost my job. There is a woman who owns a string of boutiques in the Mayfair area. She employs a lot of young girls working for her who are on the game. She introduces them to fabulously rich men. They date them, take them to hotels or wherever. Then the girls ask them for presents; they get the men to buy them clothes from these boutiques, really expensive stuff. Then when the men have splashed out, the girls give the clothes back to the boutique owner for a certain percentage, commission. A girl can have the same garment bought for her several times over. She'll come in sometimes, bringing girls for these princes and businessmen; they'll look them over, decide which one to have. We get a few pimps in. There's one who comes in sometimes with his wife, other times with his mistress. The management know them, chat with them, because the customer is always right, of course.

'Some gamblers can't stop themselves. It's a way of losing control. You have so much power with all that money, you want to give control of your life to chance. There are of course many people who are very nice. There is one Arab who is very pleasant; only when he lost a million last week did he become almost rude.

'At the time of the famine in Ethiopia, there was a group of Africans who came in, and they spent several hundred thousand pounds. They weren't Ethiopians, of course, but I still found it hard to be civil to them. At one point I had to walk out of the room. Spending all that money on nothing while others are starving. On nothing. It is such a joyless activity. Some women can't take it, and they leave; they find the work too stressful. Others get hardened, cynical. They hate it, but are trapped, because their family depends on the money. They can be very bitter. There used to be a lot of male dealers, but now they're nearly all women.

'I'd like to study ancient history. I'm taking some O-levels now. If I'm not careful, I'll stagnate. Those people at the casino are happiest who've got something else going for them as well. Those who haven't will go home at five in the morning, sleep all day, then back to work at night. That can be very destructive. People who work there can be terrified of losing their jobs from one day to the next. For a woman who's getting older, it's frightening. I'm doing psychology, English literature. I'm interested in occupational therapy. I feel I've some insights into these things from my work. Child psychology, especially – you see such juvenile men.

'Physically it can be very tiring; an average of 40 minutes to an hour on, then a short break. You get backache, standing all the time, taking abuse, doing all the mental arithmetic, keeping vigilant for cheating. Glamorous it isn't.'

Laura's friend Julie had also been in the gaming industry, but she managed to get out and start up her own business. I met her in a flat in a heavy cul-de-sac of ponderous Victorian houses in Kensington, oppressive six-storey buildings with *portes-cochères* and wrought-iron railings. Julie and her partner Dale have just redecorated what used to be a series of cheap rooms and bed-sitters into a luxury flat. Redecorated is an understatement: it has been sculpted out of the interior of these rambling and rather ugly houses. For Dale and Julie leisure and work merge; to be working on something you enjoy, and to be rewarded so well for it – that is an integrated life, a desirable balance from which most people are excluded.

The flat consists of a big front room on the ground floor, a smaller bedroom behind from which you pass a minuscule kitchen, through an arch, down a step into a sizeable bedroom with squat bathroom – oval sunken tub – beyond. The kitchen is so small because in luxury flats people spend little time cooking: either they eat out or they buy ready-made meals in. Kitchens are for snacks, making tea or warming through a prepared meal. Luxury kitchens are, it seems, a contradiction in terms – archaic institutions for the petty bourgeoisie; for the rich, the kitchen is withering away. Julie and Dale have been buying flats and modelling them after their own design and selling them at considerable profit. Today, a friend is taking photographs of the finished work, in order to submit them to *Interiors*: a feature in such a magazine will guarantee even more work.

The front room, spacious and well proportioned, has been tiled with black and white squares. The wallpaper is hand-painted, each beige stripe executed separately. Over the big fireplace, ornamental and beaded panelling, with carved swags of flowers and foliage. Some of this is wood, some is papier mâché. There are two Doric columns framing the window; at the corners of the room bosses with lions and crossed spears. In the grate is a metal casket with coals glowing in the hot August afternoon. There is a *chaise-longue* with regency-style stripes, and on it, a violin, some pages of music, with heavy books with marbled covers stacked on the floor. There is a rosewood table with a bowl of green grapes, and a vase of white lilies. Everything looks cool and contrived. The photographer sets up his equipment, and takes pictures from all conceivable angles. In the bedroom there is a four-poster bed with lacy drapes, a Victorian marble washstand. The dado is painted and combed to give a marbling effect.

Julie is in her mid-twenties; a woman with delicate features and dazzling smile; a cascade of blonde hair. She wears a black track suit. During the course of the afternoon, she opens three bottles of white Mouton Cadet. Dale, the photographer, Julie's friends arrive: we cannot disturb the perfection of the room that is being lighted for the pictures; so we sit on mock-antique footstools in the back room. Julie started renovating and decorating flats three years ago; having started with a flat she bought for £10,000 in Lewisham. Since then, she and Dale have progressed: this one will be sold for £150,000. If it were on the other, more fashionable, side of Kensington Gardens, it would fetch a quarter of a million. Dale has been living here. Now the flat is sold, Dale has to be out within a few days. He jokes about being homeless. He never lives in comfortable places: he is always moving into derelict property, then when it has been renovated, and made comfortable, he has to go.

Julie lived as a child in a small town in the West Country. She came to London to do a foundation course in art. She dropped out after one year because 'My tutor thought Andy Warhol was the ultimate artist.' She bought her first flat with her grant money. 'That was the down payment.' She says 'I'm very manipulative. I wrote to the DHSS saying that I would commit suicide if they didn't pay my mortgage, and that I needed £40 for myself. I said it seemed a shame that someone so young should do away with herself for the sake of such a paltry sum. It worked. I spent six months enjoying myself. I went to Greece. I don't know how many other people have tried that one with the DHSS, but you can imagine the headlines in the paper if anyone did actually top themselves after threatening the DHSS.

'That Christmas I went home, and the pressures from the family to get myself a job, to conform. It was unbearable. I have a mother who is a Nazi and a brother who is a Buddha. She has a problem with happiness. That is to say she doesn't know how to find it, which is as well because if she did she wouldn't recognize it, and if she could she wouldn't know what to do with it. Suffering is her element. Then my brother can do no wrong. He is perfection in every way. So what chance is there for me? My father is bitter and twisted; so is everybody's father I daresay. He has worked for the Civil Service all his life, well not all his life, I suppose he didn't as a baby. So I left but I bowed to pressure, and two days after Christmas I got a job. I went to be a croupier, and that is where I met Laura.

'The interview was wonderful; 500 people queuing outside the Sportsman Club. I was interviewed by this tubby man whose fake suntan stopped at the neck. A lot of the directors gambled. There was one man, charming person, he ran away, took the company car to the airport and jetted off into fantasy. Two months later, he reappeared, re-instated at the casino. I enjoyed being a croupier: you meet interesting people, but also the flotsam and jetsam of the world. One man who worked there was 19, and already had been divorced, had children, had had two or three careers. This guy looked like Cliff Richard. A lot of the punters own horses, they gamble on the Stock Exchange, they exchange tips about the races or stocks and shares.

'I worked at Aspinall's. John Aspinall is an interesting if weird man. He loved wild animals, his zoo was his obsession. They said to me "When he sees you, he's going to freak"; I was dressed casually, it was a small, very select club. But he never complained about me. He'd bring his chimpanzees into the staff room to have us baby-sit for them.

'I had a cushy time. I worked at the best clubs; some people become very bitter, then that's how other people treat them. A lot of the staff blamed the job. I think it's up to them, if they don't like it they shouldn't be in it. I wouldn't go back. I got out.

'I'm not an acquisitive person. I collect beautiful things, not diamond rings and fur coats. I like money, but as security, not for its own sake. I think I was dominated through money, because of my mother controlling me, and whatever I had – food, clothing – depended on her. Money gives you freedom to be who you want to be. You can only go so far with money though. Anyway, I got a mortgage and bought my first flat while I was still on Social Security. I thought I'd like to do up flats – not go into property. I like the actual work of doing them up, seeing them improve. You can express yourself through your imagination in the decor. I did up my flat, sold it, had enough to buy a better one; and then I could buy two, sell one. It's absolutely easy once you've done one – you're on your way. We haven't looked back.

'When you're a croupier, you have to understand that as soon as people come through the door of the casino, they metamorphose: they revert to childhood. A lot of them are letting out the caged infant within. They spit, they throw things, they change their personality completely. The worst I've ever met was a well-known Tory MP. I have never been so abused in my life as I was by him. He called me an effing bitch. When he used to come in, everybody tried to get as far away as they could from his table. Even the manager would say to me after one of his sessions of abuse "Are you OK?". That was solicitude indeed. I took no notice, so I really didn't mind. I've never been physically hit, but I had to endure this MP shouting at me for three-quarters of an hour. It was a little wearing. You just have to switch off when they swear at you. You do tend to see the punters as your enemies. The punters are always right, management will always back off, will never stand up for you. You're caught in the middle. Some of the punters of course don't even notice you, they keep their minds on the money. Others like you to chat to them. They're very superstitious, gamblers: one woman always wanted me to wear a particular necklace because she was convinced it helped her to win; another always carried garlic as a charm.

'Money is the pure driving force. And you see sexism. It's like society in general more concentrated. It goes money first, men second, women third, that is the order of precedence in gambling. Those evening frocks we wear, they burst into flames if anybody holds a ciggy too near them – what does it matter one or more croupier or less incinerated, as long as the rest continue to look decorative.'

Conroy Blaise has had very direct experience of servicing the rich. He has worked for 20 years as chauffeur. A tall and soft-spoken man from Barbados, now in his late forties, he is still a handsome and attractive figure; self-contained, somewhat enigmatic, he says from having learned to remain buttoned-up in the livery of driver – uniform, peaked cap. When he was younger, he was married to a white woman from Manchester. They had two children, but his wife drank; at that time, he was driving a lorry, and he dreaded coming home from work to find things missing in the house, furniture sold, the room wrecked on one of Valerie's drinking bouts, the children missing. When they were taken into care, he left home, and became, after a number of driving jobs, chauffeur for an executive of an international pharmaceuticals company. He lived in a small flat over the garage. 'The garage was the most important place, it had to accommodate a Rolls and a vintage Cadillac and a Volkswagen. The garage had been the stables, and it was all covered with red ivy. It was very nice. But the house was a big mansion in the country, a long way from London. I used to be very lonesome. I was always being told to drive to Heathrow or to Gatwick or to meetings up and down the country. And then I think the woman was getting very lonely. Their children were grown up; they had staff in the house; she had nothing to do. She was involved in a drama group in the town, she did work for charity. I had to drive her to London to do shopping, where she met her friends. I could be on duty day and night; I had no fixed time, I must have been at their disposal all the time. I had everything in the flat, TV, video, it was warm and comfortable. But I noticed that the woman didn't like me to have girls there. She couldn't really say anything, but she didn't like it. I had a girlfriend for about a year, we used to drink and play music and party a little with some of her friends; the woman told me the noise was disturbing her, and would I stop doing it. Well, she slept about a quarter of a mile away at the other side of the house, no way could she have been upset by it; at least, not in the way she said. Then she started coming to see me; like before we would go on a trip, she went to see her mother who was in a nursing home in Surrey, and she'd come and have a drink, and I knew then she was interested in me.

'She took me to a hotel in London. She bought me some clothes, so I could go with her out of uniform. It wouldn't do for her to go to a hotel with a chauffeur; so she bought me a suit of clothes. I didn't want to, but she was my employer, I felt I didn't want to lose what I had. Once you've been well off, it is very hard to go back to being poor. The poor can always learn how to be rich, it's the easiest lesson in the world; but the other way, it don't work. When me and my sister were kids, my mother used to take us to this church; and she was so strict, we never had anything. She worked and worked machining in a factory and didn't earn much, then on Sunday it was church all day. We never had much of a childhood, we knew what it was not to go hungry, but we always had cheap food, goat meat and oxtail, and stringy chicken with rice and peas, only the spice did give it any flavour. So I went along with it. I felt bad when I saw the husband. He had no idea. He used to talk to me about his wife, he thought he could say anything to me; he didn't think of me as a person that had any feelings. He said she was spoilt and selfish and didn't have enough to do with her life. I didn't say anything; and then it come to me, he was giving me her, as a present; he did know. It was like she was one of the perks of the job. I knew he had women when he went away on trips abroad because when I met him from the airplane he sometimes was with a young woman in a fur coat and he kissed her goodbye.

'You have to be careful because rich people are treacherous. One day, he decided to find us together; so he came into my flat one night when he should have been away, and we were drinking; and she was half undressed. He gave me the sack. He had had a quarrel with the wife, and he wanted to punish her. So after seven years, I was to be her punishment, just as I had been her gift when things were going all right and he didn't want her to make any fuss about what he was doing. So it makes you feel you're not a person. You're something other people do to each other. They buy you to use with one another, to gift, to punish. They're buying you. It's all right to be a driver, a chauffeur, to wear clothes somebody else chose for you; but that isn't where it stops. They own you. Well, I had never thought much about what it was to be a slave. But I knew; even though I wasn't kept in shackles, not ones that you could see. But I was bought and then I was abandoned; and money can do that to you just the same as you could be bought or sold on the plantations of long ago. What people do to one another when they have too much time and too much money; they play with other people. My body was servicing her, driving him, making their lives easier. But what does it do to you who are used like that? And what does it do to them? They think they are better people for it?

'They gave me some money. I bought a truck. I do cheap moving in the East End. I don't know what happened to my wife. If I saw my kids I wouldn't recognize them.'

Brighton suggests a town built for and upon leisure; the fantasies of the Prince Regent embodied in the Royal Pavilion, once the privilege of the rich, have been replicated on a mass basis in our time. Almost without industry, it serves pleasure and escape as few other places in the United Kingdom do. With its marina, casino, entertainments, hotels, English language schools, museums, shops, it is dominated by the service sector. It is also a place of beautiful façades, elegant stucco, ornamental ironwork, and of hidden squalor. It is also a place of great energy; a dynamism that comes perhaps from a curious contradiction at the heart of rich Western society which recognizes neither material sufficiency nor spiritual peace.

Around the Jobcentre are lean and shabby young men in denim suits and dirty trainers with two or three days' growth of beard: the jobs on offer include live-in servant to help with child, take swimming, babysitting etc.; banquet porters at £2 an hour; cooks in small hotels from 7.30 to 10.30 and 6 to 9, all day Saturday; nannies and temporary Christmas staff, packing in a furniture warehouse, cleaning at £1.63 an hour; a woman is wanted for topless modelling of underwear and swimwear, £150 a session.

It is also a place of great enterprise; house-cleaning companies that will do your flat from top to bottom for £40 a time, private meals-on-wheels services for 17 per cent of the population who are over 75 in Hove; the games rooms and pleasure arcades, with youngsters playing computer games, fruit machines, whirring and bleeping noisily; a few old women eagerly feeding 10ps into the Cascade machine, where the coins pile up but never spill over the edge that pays out; shops that have opened and closed in a season; dusty kebab houses and burger joints; gun-shops and military memorabilia, a stamp emporium; little shops making soft toys with electronically controlled voices which hold real conversations – only the children have to adapt themselves to the programmed dialogue; shops selling costumes for masquerades and fancy-dress balls; carnival novelties, fireworks; joke-shops selling plastic shit and plastic hamburgers and horror masks with eyes gouged out.

Brighton is also the 37th most deprived borough in Britain. It is equal to Wigan in the proportion of take-up of free school meals. The cost of living is well above average here, but wages are 87 per cent of average. Concentrated pockets of poverty are hidden away on estates that are concealed in the folds of the Downs behind the town, or in substandard, multi-occupied properties. Much of the work is seasonal and casual; people are employed and discharged with the rhythm of the year. The town has the third highest house prices in the country – it is cheaper to buy a house in Ealing than in Brighton. In early 1987, the DHSS allowed £42.30 for a single bed-sitter, £65–70 for a double. This involves a distortion of the market because people who earn enough to pay £42 for a bed-sit can afford to buy a one-bedroom flat. Many landlords are kept in business in seedy bed-sitter accommodation through housing benefit, which at £9 million a year is a form of generous out-relief to landlords. The £9 million could provide Brighton with all the council housing it needs; but that would go too far in the relief of distress for this government's taste. Only 17 per cent of the houses are council owned; home ownership stands at 60 per cent. The rest are privately rented and, at 23 per cent, this is much higher than the country as a whole. Because there is little money to be made out of fair rents, people sell or convert their properties; there seems to be a very high proportion of one-bedroom flats. Most of the advertised rented property is holiday lets.

In Brighton you can see more clearly the nature of those glamorized occupations into which young people are being directed. What is less clear, but may be happening, is that this is a gently meandering avenue of downward mobility, a process of even greater depowering for people. Manicurist wanted at £2 an hour; experts in eyelashes, synthetic nail-building parlour. What is there to learn about society when your competence is with nails or eyelashes or hair? Perhaps the romance that haloes these jobs (not for the practitioners) has to do with the power of image-changing; a similar kind of magic to that believed to be practised by those witches into whose possession your nail-parings or locks of hair fell.

I visited the Technical College and met many of the students being prepared for the new job opportunities. In a hairdressing course of 15 students, it was revealing to learn that the occupations of their parents were of considerably higher status than those they could be expected to attain: PR consultant, insurance salesman, computer programmer (mother in school cafeteria), district nurse and inspector at Ford's, British Telecom engineer, pilot, English teachers (both mother and father), chef (father), British Rail worker (father), self-employed builder, electrical maintenance worker.

First of all, the students are overwhelmingly women. The idea that they are filling in before marrying into the status they will presently occupy dies hard. The head of department said that the only one likely to own a salon is the sole male because the women will be expected to get married and drop out. It is, of course, only to be expected that this extension of 'caring' should be serviced by women.

The beauty therapists and technicians are compelled to adopt a severely clinical 'nursing' model of beauty care and massage because the only other profession in which women touch strangers is prostitution. This leads to a great ambiguity about the industries for which they are being trained. They do not, on the whole, admire the unnatural and synthetic beauty of the women in *Dynasty* and *Dallas*, even though they have a keen eye for those who are naturally attractive, such as Priscilla Presley. There are too many occupational hazards for the workers to be dazzled by the public perception of what they do: dermatitis, backache, varicose veins, foot trouble, infections, dry and cracked skin, allergies, fear of Aids were some of the things cited by the trainee hairdressers. Because it is an elaboration of traditional caring, they philosophically accept that low pay will be inevitable. After two years' training, many will earn little more than £50 a week. Another common complaint is that they long to be actually working, not learning theory. But most sensibly point out that the best way is learning on the job, the traditional apprenticeship. But what salon owner is going to pay wages to apprentices when YTS will provide it for nothing, and then can employ fully trained people at 19 or 20, with no need to invest in the time and effort spent teaching. The dearth of apprenticeships is seen as a consequence of YTS. The studying, in most cases, prolongs dependency on parents, and this is seen as reinforcing a sense of low status. 'It is humiliating having to ask your parents for money all the time.' In order to study, many of the young women are also working, mostly in other low-paid service jobs, especially in cafés and restaurants. One woman, aged 19, and with a daughter of ten months, is working in a Bingo Hall each evening. She goes straight from college to Bingo Hall, gets home at 10.30, puts the baby to sleep, and is up at seven the next morning. Her husband is working part-time, and Support Income makes up their income.

They are also keenly aware that hairdressing is a very crowded profession. Salons open and close regularly; you have to have something special to make a go of it; yet a majority hope to run their own salon in due course. They expect to work for someone else for two or three years at least before being able to start up on their own. They also know that it is the kind of work that can be done from home, so that even when they have children, they won't necessarily have to give up work completely. It is also a skill that is always going to be needed. Those who have already worked in the industry have had Saturday or holiday jobs, sweeping up and occasional shampooing or 'just handing out the rollers as they're needed'; in other words, they feel they haven't been allowed anywhere near the real work. The subjects they study have a rather grandiose sound: communications, business organization, art, wig-making, hygiene, biology, manicure, men's hairdressing. It is difficult not to feel that a great deal of the course is mystification, the transformation of something so functional as hairdressing into a major profession. On the other hand, the young women have a real sense of satisfaction and creativity in advising people on how to make the best of themselves, to improve their appearance. It is an ambiguous feeling: the elaborate instruction feels to many like being lost in a maze of only faintly relevant knowledge. The common sense of those who haven't yet learned that being wise means accepting everything, sometimes ask 'Why do we have to do all that, when we're here to do hairdressing?' It places them in a very subordinate position to which the theoretical expertise is going to be handed down in very small parcels.

That this in part places them at a disadvantage in the wider world soon becomes apparent. Without exception, they expressed their lack of interest in political or social issues. 'I don't know anything about politics', 'I don't understand it', 'It's boring'; pleading, as it were, an ignorance that earns exemption from responsibility. Political responses vary from complete disaffection 'My parents don't vote', to vague gut-feeling either that 'Thatcher is doing a good job' or 'I'd like to shoot her.'

Because these refinements of service depend absolutely upon the superfluity of wealth available for image-making, for the enhancement of appearances, this is necessarily a dependent area of work. In that sense, it is bound to be conservative, requiring the maintenance of existing patterns of power and wealth. This is reinforced by the labyrinths of esoteric knowledge and learning through which they must pass; for instance, 'You must never say varnish when speaking of nails; it is enamel.' The feeling that it is subordinate to the wealth-creating economy means that in the event of any serious recession, this would be one of the first areas of employment to be squeezed. This also reinforces the 'women's work' aspect of it; the latent notion that in the background there will exist a 'breadwinner' to fall back on in later years if the lean times come. This perhaps helps to account for the parents' acceptance of their daughters' choice of profession.

There is a widespread feeling that you have to be hard, at least publicly. You must look out for your own interests because nobody else is going to do it for you. This is the way the world is; it would be absurd to pretend otherwise. On the other hand, you're not really like that underneath. 'We're all soft and a bit scared; only you must never let your vulnerabilities show, or other people will take advantage of them.' The sensitive, more spontaneous, self has to be suppressed; it is the cynicism and the keeping up of a cool and tough exterior that matters. 'Everything depends on appearances, and that includes yourself,' one young woman said. 'You must never get involved with the clients.' Because hairdressing salons are places where you touch strangers, this can lead only too readily to mistaken intimacies. It must have a clinical aspect, even though it is at the same time, very tender. One woman, speaking of when her friends do her hair says 'It is a very pleasurable and intimate experience. When it is being done by someone you know, you can admit to the pleasure; but not when you are dealing with people you don't know.' 'It's another extension of the cherishing woman's role; but at the same time it's impersonal. That sets up contradictions within yourself.'

Hairdressing salons are places where the customers feel safe. This means they can tell you what they feel and think. They can let themselves go. You mustn't. You have to learn to be able to say 'Oh yes, oh no, oh dear, isn't that a shame?' But without getting too involved. 'When she tells you her husband has gone off with somebody, or they haven't slept together for ten years, or they've got this worry about their health, you mustn't take it to heart.' 'On the other hand, when they say their husband's gone off and left them, you don't say "Oh yes" and then go on to tell them about the wonderful time you had at the disco last night.' You must listen, and let them know you've heard what they're saying to you; only don't try to sort out their lives. The caring role has strict limits.

The concern with appearances also uncovers another dilemma basic to the lives of young women: there is no way a young woman can satisfactorily be in the world that will win approval from everybody. If she doesn't bother with her appearance, she is dismissed or made fun of. If she is ugly, then she has to try extra hard with her brains or her personality or her extreme good nature, to make up for it. If she is always concerned with her appearance, strives too hard to be glamorous, she's a slag. Because there is no agreed model, this discussion generates enormous energy; some of it vehemently anti-feminist.

The students of beauty therapy and hairdressing are in their third year. They are even less starry-eyed about their profession. 'It's the people coming out of the salon whose fantasies you're servicing, not your own.' Most of them do not get grants; but nearly all of them work. One is in a bowling alley, Saturday 10–6, and gets £15.75. 'Serving people and looking after their smelly shoes.' One works in the bakery of a restaurant, cooking scones and custard tarts. 'There's no real training. You just copy what the others do – it all comes ready-mixed anyway.' She works 8–5 on Saturday, and on Thursday 8–2, and gets £19.75. One works in the restaurant of British Home Stores. 'It's a grannies' eating-place, where people who are nervous of eating in public go: rubber peas and chips. I get £6 for four hours' work.' One young woman is working each evening in a Bingo club, 20 hours a week, £38 a week. Another works at Bejams, £11 a day; yet another gets £15.50 in a café, and another £13.72 in Superdrug. An enterprising young woman is doing hairdressing from home. 'I can't advertise because I don't pay tax. Some weeks I might get £50, others only £15.' 'I work on Saturdays at American Express, on authorizations, £2.55 an hour. Each department has a limit to the amount of credit you can have on one card, and if they exceed it, I have a computer and I can authorize it or not.' 'I'm working in an old people's home, £1.77 an hour.' 'I'm in McDonalds two nights a week: £2 an hour, £2.20 after 10 o'clock, £2.50 after midnight. I work till 1.30. It's very clean, they wash the floors every hour, wipe the menus and tables, it's obsessive.' 'I work two nights a week in a private rest home, £2 an hour.'

Some of the new salons that have opened up in Brighton are, they complain, more like discos. 'They're very shiny, but there's never anybody there, just the stylists nodding their heads to the music. They're expensive and they do weird haircuts. You can't have a fantasy hair-do for the workaday world; you can't get up every morning and style it and curl-tong it and mousse it, not unless you stick your head in a bird-cage all night, or sleep bolt upright to preserve it.'

The images of beauty promoted by models and advertising and TV are, they insist, not intended for copying, but 'just to give you ideals of what might be suitable for yourself. Those ideas of glamour are plastic, they're not real.' 'You couldn't look like that while you were working – it's not for the workers in the beauty salons, it's for the customers.'

'You have to look well groomed, smart, and look as if you know what you're doing. You can't look too glamorous yourself. You can't have a wild hairstyle, otherwise it'd get all mixed up in the oils and massage lotions and creams.'

'The work we will be able to do as beauty therapists could take us into a salon, onto a health farm, in hotels, on liners. In Canada and Australia, and of course in the USA especially, it is all much more developed as a profession. Here it's only just beginning and there is a lot of prejudice.'

'You have to have money to afford the services. For instance, a body massage would be £12, a facial £8, manicure £6. If you were, say, a woman of 35, and you wanted to look after yourself, you'd have one facial a month; at 45, perhaps two and, as you get older, a daily fix.'

'The trouble with beauty therapy is that it is felt to be a bit tarty. If you say you are a masseuse, you're ... you know ... not quite respectable. My father didn't want me to do it. You have to learn to give male body massages, and one slip and they may think you're trying to touch them up. So the way you have to react is to take the medical model, it has to be a semi-nursing sort of job. You have to be the tart or the nurse; women's roles are already mapped out in advance. And even when you take the line that it's a sort of nurse role, you're never quite free of traditional associations. Nurses are supposed to be easy; and all those hospital books about romance in the operating theatre. I mean, 60 years ago, nursing was not considered respectable.'

'When I went to the careers officer at school, *he* said "Yes, but what do you want to do for a living? That's all right for a sideline, a hobby, but it isn't a living." And I knew exactly what it was I wanted to do, I spelled it out for him. But they have these stereotyped ideas of what constitutes a career.'

'I was at a private school because my parents were abroad. They more or less thought all girls would be secretaries and all boys accountants.'

'It's a serious programme of study. We have to do anatomy, science, biology, diet, figure correction, teaching exercises, electrolysis, art. We're designing our own salon at the moment; and we have to do communications. And first aid. In case anything goes wrong.'

'We have to learn to apply cosmetics to hide birthmarks, moles, acne, scar tissue; we have to do camouflage make-up, pigmentation, cysts, loss of pigment. We have to get medical permission to do some of those things.'

'We're not beauticians. You get quite snobby about that. Beauticians are the people who stand behind the make-up counter in Boots, display make-up. Ours is a much more technical and scientific job.'

'A lot of people who could benefit from our skills don't know that such skills are available. People who have blemishes that could be corrected, go round feeling self-conscious and unnecessarily unhappy.'

'When we get away from college we hope to have experience in a beauty salon. Here we can practise – massage, hairdressing: we do styling and hairdressing for £1 a time, for old-age pensioners who couldn't afford to go anywhere else. They have to sign a form saying they accept responsibility if anything goes wrong; not that it ever does. There is a very quick turnover of staff in beauty salons because they don't pay very well. We shall be lucky to make £60 or £70 a week when we begin. There is no beauty in the wages. You can work for yourself, though, do it from home, have your own kit, your own folding table, go round people's houses or have a do-it-yourself salon in your front room. You can have a family and work at the same time.'

'In fact the only day you don't work is the day you give birth. That is a great advantage. For the rest, you're leaning over fat rich women who want to be 20. You have to smile while you're massaging her, even though you're stinking hot and you know that all your efforts won't make much difference.'

'They think you can perform miracles. They think you can transform them; you have a kind of magic that will make them perfect.'

'There is a lot of acting, smiling, pretending. There can be a lot of bitchiness in salons. It's different for men – they can charm women and persuade them to have this style or that treatment. It isn't so easy for a woman, especially a young woman who is quite attractive, when so much of the clientele is older and richer. The worst are those who think they know it all, who are experts in all aspects of beauty, and try to tell you your job. Of course, you might make a mistake; then you just have to apologize or, if you can, bluff your way out by carrying on as if you knew what you were doing all the time.'

'They also think we're doctors; we can "cure" them. You have to be quite intimate, ask personal questions. In doing electrolysis, for instance, you have to know if they have facial hair whether it comes from a hormone imbalance, or if it is a side-effect of taking certain kinds of drugs. You also have to know what is socially acceptable, what kind of bodies do have hair growth, whether they are racially acceptable or not. In some cases, you have to get permission from the GP before doing any work on them.'

'When we've finished our training, there are other possibilities that touch on alternative medicine and forms of therapy – like aromatherapy, essential oils which through massage relax or stimulate the individual. This is not part of our course, but there is enough to make some of us want to branch out later. We can do reflexology because we have quite exhaustive anatomy lessons.'

'What is good about it is that you are helping people. You get job satisfaction. You meet people, and you can actually see the results of what you do. It's creative, it's flexible. You can work from home. It's a *happy* job; you are offering something positive to people.'

'The disadvantages are only too obvious – low pay, hard work, long training. You get backache and varicose veins.'

Several of the young women had wanted to do nursing, but they felt they would not be able to overcome their fear of blood. 'There was no way I could deal with dead bodies and blood', 'I can't be quiet, so I'd be no good,' 'I wanted to be a vet', 'I wanted to travel, go abroad.' Two or three felt they might emigrate, Australia or Canada, where the profession is more special and has higher status.

One young woman said 'It's the old story of women having to pretend. *Putting on an act*, something you don't feel. Not, in this instance, directly for men. But, of course, most of the women that you are dealing with are wanting their image burnished for men, so really you're serving strangers, strange unseen men. You see the women smiling at themselves seductively in the glass, and you know the look is not for you, or for them, but for their men. So you're servicing ghosts. We are expected to be an advert for the job, without being tarty. You must make the customer feel good. You have to be extremely efficient and professional so that no one mistakes what you are doing. You are manipulating other people's fantasies, massaging not only their bodies but their images too; playing with appearances – something changing and fugitive.'

There are, as in all aspects of women's work, contradictions which the individual woman must somehow reconcile. Servicing the rich is not as crude as it sounds, for there is also the element of healing, making whole, hiding blemishes, giving people back their self-respect and confidence. In some ways, there is a collusion between the fantasy of the customers and the fantasy of the workers: the young women are, on the whole, not interested in society or politics. They say 'I just want to get on with *my* life and be left to do so in peace.' They say '*I have chosen this*', and therefore accept that they must take responsibility for all the negative aspects of it, the wear and tear on the body, the occupational risks, the constant pretence. There is something very poignant in the using up of the youth and energy and beauty of these young women in the grooming of other women to render them more acceptable to men. But, at least, this form of labour brings their work into the public domain: there is always the potential for struggle there, in a way that was not possible when the labour of the vast majority of women was enclosed within the sequestered cell of the family.

Leisure, for many people, involves buying exemption, if only occasionally, from the tyranny of some of the recurring and necessary labour of living; among these, the providing of meals is one of the most irksome. Accordingly, the feeding of people becomes increasingly the responsibility of big business. Meals are replaced by 'eating episodes', whereby people eat increasingly in the streets, on public and in private transport, in shopping centres; sit for a snack here, snatch a bite there. There is no clearer example of what the leisure society means. The ability to buy becomes the most fundamental activity, an ability that eventually supersedes all others: there is nothing like money for erasing the memory of how to do things for ourselves. This opens up vast new markets for the sale of foods that become more and more expensive, more and more wasteful. The global spread of McDonalds' burgers gets children accustomed to tastes that have disastrous consequences in the Third World – subsistence giving way to ranching, with subsequent exhaustion of the land. Armies of nutritionists, psychologists, chemists, agronomists, technicians, salespeople, market researchers, advertisers are employed in the confection of new products, many of them 'nature identical' in their taste and texture, but in fact created in the laboratories of the food industry. It is clear that leisure in the rich world is a vortex which involves altering patterns of eating, processing and ultimately farming all over the world, to the detriment of the poorest.

One group of workers almost exclusively employed in the catering industry in Britain is the Chinese community. Indeed, London's China-town has become that most saleable of all commodities, a major tourist attraction. This grubby, and otherwise profoundly unappealing, corner of London now has a significant role in the promotion of the capital as a place of fascinating and colourful diversity. People come here to buy tasteful Chinese kites for their children, to enjoy the spectacle of the Chinese New Year, to buy souvenirs and, of course, to eat in the res-taurants that bring a breath of Hong Kong to the heart of London.

Those who live and work here do not see their lives in quite this benign and cheerful light. Indeed, many feel that to be a kind of living museum involves the imposition upon them of an alien purpose; the more so, since many families have been subjected to the dissuasive pressures of immigra-tion laws for what turns out to be the privilege of falling victim to racial abuse and harassment. The image of a peaceful and docile community that is sold as part of a tourist package is beginning to crack. Years of being moulded to stereotypes is making more and more people impatient and angry.

A case in 1987 of what is seen as blatant injustice against four Chinese waiters drew many of the discontents of the community to the surface. The Diamond 4 Defence Campaign marked the beginning of resistance to wrongs and injuries that have long been part of the Chinese experience in Britain.

Late one evening in June 1986, four men and a woman went into the Diamond Restaurant in Lisle Street. They had been drinking. They ordered wine, but since it was after licensing hours, this was refused. They asked for Coke, spring rolls and spare ribs. When they were told the spare ribs had run out, the party rose to leave. They were presented with the bill for what they had consumed and became abusive; one of the waiters was knocked to the floor, kicked and punched. Others went to his assistance. During the fight that followed, both customers and waiters were injured. One of the waiters phoned for the police. The customers were taken to the back of the restaurant and given coffee.

The police took statements only from the customers, and then sent them to hospital. The waiters were taken to the police station, where they remained overnight before being charged. Only then did they get medical attention. Throughout their time at the station, they had access neither to an interpreter nor to a solicitor. The trial took place in June 1987; all four were convicted of affray and sentenced to two years.

Jabez Lam, who works at the Chinese Advice and Information Centre, has a copy of the police interrogation: the questions refer to 'the Chinese' and 'the Englishmen', as though it were a war report. 'Witnesses said they saw you hitting an Englishman. Is that right?' 'Tell us who some of the Chinese were.' Press reports echoed the prosecution counsel who said the 'victims were clubbed like seals'. The Chinese community was shocked and angered by the verdict. 'People want to know why the police took statements only from the white customers, while their bill still remains unpaid, and why it never emerged that the violence was initiated by them. When Chinese victims of assault are forced to defend themselves, they become the accused, and the troublemakers their accusers.' It seems, says Jabez Lam, that the police have discovered that they are more likely to get a conviction if the defendants are non-white, so they must be presented as the aggressors. So much easier to turn a conflict into white and non-white, without any awkward questions of justice intruding. The judge even congratulated himself on his own leniency in sentencing the men to 'only two years'.

One Chinese waiter, who has worked for many years in a provincial town, expressed the feelings of many people. 'We've always had to put up with racial abuse. Chinese restaurants are the places to go to after the pubs close. If people are in a bad mood, or they've had too much to drink, they start an argument, insult you, refuse to pay. Some of them only come into the restaurant to carry on drinking. You can tell they're not even hungry – you only have to see them throwing up in the gutter outside on Friday and Saturday nights. Their whole attitude shows contempt.'

The Chinese Advice and Information Centre is monitoring examples of racial harassment and injustice. The Diamond 4 Campaign triggered the reporting of many cases, the kind of incident which people had previously accepted, believing there was no remedy. In December 1986, a waiter was out in his car with his three children. One of them wanted to go to the toilet, so he stopped near his place of work. As he slowed down, there were three pedestrians in front of the car. He sounded his horn to warn them. When he had taken the child into the restaurant, the three men started banging on the car, rocking it and frightening the children by poking their umbrellas through the window. The father heard their screams and rushed out. During the scuffle, he was kicked in the groin.

When he got home he felt ill and fainted, and had to be taken to hospital. He was arrested in the hospital bed, charged with assault and given a two-year suspended sentence. Another man is selling his take-away in a south coast town because it has been attacked and wrecked several times; the police have done nothing to protect him or to find the criminals. In another case, a group of young men went to a take-away after it had closed for the night. They banged on the door, and when there was no response, kicked it down. The son of the owner came to see what was happening. Forced to defend himself against them, he was arrested when the police arrived.

'It is very alienating' says Weibi Zheng, worker at the Advice and Information Centre. 'People feel they don't belong. You can't go on for ever, just smiling at all the abuse and insults. You can never win because the stereotypes are contradictory: from "stupid Chink" to "wily Oriental". The violent mythology of the kung fu cult coexists with that of the inscrutable Chinese who never say what they think.

'Last week, a woman came in with an official letter she had received from Wandsworth Council. It told her to stop cooking smelly food. There was no investigation – the assumption was that a complaint by a white tenant must be justified. Then, of course, there are the periodic rumours – there's one at the moment in Tower Hamlets – that, under cover of darkness, neighbourhood cats and dogs are being stolen and served up in Chinese restaurants.'

The Chinese community has also been able to observe in practice the government's dedication to 'family life' in the working out of the immigration laws. People have been required to prove that their marriage has not been contracted for the purpose of immigration: this exposes their relationship and conjugal habits to the kind of scrutiny that would destroy the most stable of couples. 'It's such hypocrisy', says Weibi Zheng, 'a government proclaims its devotion to the virtues of the family, and then actually sets about undermining it. What they really resent about so many Asian people is that for them family life has a real meaning which has been lost in British culture: we are a reproach to the official ideology because we practise what they preach. No wonder they resent us.'

Chinese people in Britain have always been scattered, a few families in each town, operating a take-away or a restaurant. There has been little opportunity for people to come together to celebrate their community, although in recent years Chinatown has begun to act as a focus. 'People have always worked long hours. Most restaurants are family businesses, and it is the women and children who get exploited. The young people have no choice. In addition to that, racial abuse is just part of the stress of work. And then Chinese employers like to project themselves as pals of the workers: being given a job is seen as a favour. Everything conspires to keep the people quiet. Quiet and divided.'

The sentence of the four waiters was reduced on appeal to nine months each. This is seen as a partial victory, but scarcely an adequate response to such an injustice.

Mrs Chu is the wife of one of the imprisoned waiters; a reserved but articulate woman who has been the object of unwelcome but, she feels, necessary publicity in the fight to have her husband's innocence acknowledged. She worked with him in the Diamond for two years. 'He was always good-humoured: he was the one who went to serve rough or rude customers when the other waiters wouldn't. He worked from 4.30 in the afternoon till two in the morning, six nights a week. His net wage was about £80. He had worked there for five years, had never been in any trouble.' Mr and Mrs Chu's first baby was born during the trial in June. She has had to go to Social Security. So far, she has received nothing, living off loans from friends and family. 'The whole case was so unfair. Three of the men have young children. Their wives are now isolated, frightened and without resources. The case was headlines in my local paper. The neighbours now avoid talking to me.'

Jabez Lam says that the feelings of the people can be gauged by the fact that the fund collected £9,000 towards legal costs within two weeks of being set up. 'We've accepted all the rubbish that's been thrown at us for too long. If you conform to the docile stereotype, you take all the violence inwards, it destroys you; and you still get called cunning, secretive. If you resist, you'll be called vicious kung fu thugs. But our days of being a set-piece tourist attraction are over. Britain likes to claim that equality before the law is a distinguishing feature of a civilized country. That hasn't been our experience.'

It is only when we begin to look at some of the working conditions, experiences and practices of that sector of the economy that services the leisure society that the extravagant claims of the rich which we discussed at the beginning of the book can be seen for what they are. Their pretensions to be the bearers of the true burden of labour are shown to be nothing more than part of that elaborate preoccupation with appearances, surfaces and façades of this rich society which has elevated the worship of wealth into the highest form of duty: a false decor, pasted over an unchanging and harsher reality. Those now being pressed into service, particularly women, ethnic minorities and young people, are increasingly unorganized, scattered and casual workers. The intensity of their work and conditions of labour are often damaging and destructive to both body and spirit. That a weakening of working people's resistance to the power of capital should be seen to be the most urgent necessity at this time is a strange distortion of the truth. But then, if we continue to look upon the wealthy and their model of economic development as both a source of hope and an inspiration to the good life, the world will remain as it is, turned upside down. The self-attributed heroism of their labour only distracts from those who are doing the real work of society, unnoticed, uncelebrated. The fact that the new working class does not have the familiar form of those who worked together in pit and mill and factory should not alter our perception of their needs and struggles. It is a strengthening of their resistance that is most necessary at this time; and if that strength is not to be found among those who consider that they are beyond the need of it in Britain because the forms of their service appear benign, there is no dearth of people in the rest of the world who understand only too well that resistance to patterns of expropriation and loss can no longer be local, but must be on the global scale.

7

Beyond the leisure society

The promise of leisure is industrial society's response to all the contesting visions that have been evolving since the 1960s. It belongs securely to the growth-and-expansion dynamic of capitalist society and it is an appealing prospect to people whose lives have for so long been shaped by labour. This is why those of us who are sceptical of its liberating possibilities – who suspect that it is yet another mechanism whereby economic processes that are increasingly disarticulated from human need may survive – must be able to offer living practice and example of how we propose to transcend these plausible versions of a future leisure society.

To suggest that the people of the rich countries of the West might respond to a call for social and political (as distinct from the many available kinds of personal) liberation appears, at first sight, a quite outrageous project. After all, everybody knows that liberation movements are for the poor, the dispossessed, the excluded. It would be absurd to claim that the rich should want to be free of anything; indeed, persuading us that more, much more, of what the rich already have is all that is required to make human life a paradise on earth has been the universal (though not uncontested) object of politics in our time. For these are the most privileged people in the world; they enjoy a standard of living which the rest can regard only with wistful envy or violent rancour. Their societies are capable of the most prodigious technological achievements – from intricate life-saving surgery to dramatic thrusts into the remotest regions of the galaxy. Who would dare to suggest that their people might, in some nebulous way, be 'better off' if they had less of what they have so single-mindedly struggled for?

These rich societies do indeed find meaning and purpose in the need for more; but whether that need is the need of the people, or the need of an economic system that must for ever grow and expand, has become confused. It is the merging of these two quite separate things, the apparent interchangeability of them, that has caused political discussion to become so narrow, yet at the same time, so opaque.

It is not so much that capitalism has delivered the goods to the people, as that the people have been increasingly delivered to the goods; that is to say, that the very character and sensibility of the people have been re-worked, re-fashioned, in such a way that they assort approximately (and who can measure with what distortions?) with the commodities, experiences and sensations (of which leisure is one of the most refined), the selling of which alone gives shape and significance to our lives.

It is certainly not by fulminations against material things (nor indeed against the plethoric marketed immaterialities of capitalist societies) that anyone is likely to be convinced that all is not for the best in the richest regions of the world. It is only when we look at the great social and moral scourges that afflict those privileged places that we begin to see that the price paid for their coveted advantages far, far exceeds that marked on all the goods and services for sale. But, by a curious process of dissociation, all the cruelties and barbarities of our contemporary life – those horror stories that are the staple fare of TV, newspapers and consequently of popular daily discourse – appear to occur in a different sphere, almost another dimension, from that in which the abundance of precious and eager things on display exists, tempting us or taunting us, according to the income we have at our disposal. We do not care to reflect on what the relationship might be, for instance, between rising crime figures, on the one hand, and an economy which is flourishing, we are assured, as never before. We seldom wonder at the connections that might exist between all the marketed excitements and sensations that are the object of everyday transactions, and the unstoppable spread of prohibited stimulants, such as psychotropic drugs, which are such a short step away from all the other fantasies of escape and transcendence indispensable, it seems, to those blessed and opulent populations which the rest of the world cannot wait to catch up with. Perhaps the reluctance to examine any possible links between such things is because we might uncover the most profound and unremarked addiction of all, that from which all the others flow: that most mysterious and protected dependency, that most solitary and sacred bond that exists between us and our money.

This is how it is that we have come to view social evils as if they were phenomena of nature, impenetrable in their origins, that have to be supported, no matter what violence they do to people. They are consigned to a quite separate realm of experience from that of those normal daily exchanges which can nevertheless transform everything – from the most prosaic of necessities to the most sublime abstractions – into hard cash. This is a quite artificial separation. For many of those evils are nothing more than an extension, or perhaps a consequence, of the seemingly limitless extension of market relationships to more and more areas of human experience, a growing subjugation of the freely given service, the generous thought, the charitable impulse, the spontaneous feeling to money-determined transactions and expressions. It is not difficult to see why we have erected such an impermeable barrier between the sanctified processes of marketing on the one hand, and the moral and social ills on the other: that collusive disseverance, that institutionalized schizophrenia, is a bargain, nowhere made explicit, but which saturates our social, economic and political life with the pervasive and nauseating odour of blackmail. The good things, this unspoken covenant implies, are available, and will remain available, only on condition that we accept all that accompanies them, all the indignities and humiliations, that public spectacle of human disgrace that is paraded before our mesmerized and powerless gaze – the crimes of unspeakable violence, the rape and molestation of women, the injuries to children, the attacks on the elderly, the fear on familiar streets, the home neighbourhood haunted by those who wish us harm. All this is beyond our control; and must remain so, for to look at its roots and origins might expose connections and causes in those things which we hold to be the most cherished and elevated manifestations of our famous freedoms, which, alas, we seem no longer able to distinguish from the freedom of impersonal market forces. In other words, we fear too close a scrutiny of our riches, and the consolations they can buy because this might cause them to vanish, to be snatched away from us. Indeed, the dishonouring of humanity and the exaltation of things creates an equilibrium which none dares disturb. In this way, the official and public humanitarian concerns of the society, with its commitment to welfare, its solicitude for the individual, are increasingly ritual, its promise of enlarged freedoms and limitless leisure, illusion. Underneath, it is all so different.

Any project of liberation would dare to look clearly at this relationship, and no longer accept the separation currently in place; would require to reject this as a Manichean division between false opposites – between material progress on the one hand and unregenerate human nature on the other, between wealth and wickedness. Such a liberation would assert that we can indeed be free of many of the cruelties in which we now acquiesce; not all of them, of course, for no social, economic or political transformation can eliminate injustice, wrongdoing and brutality (and any which claims to do so will certainly finish by aggravating these things). But as it is now, the silences, the hypocrisies and the willed unknowing, mean that however we may fret and fume, the streets continue to become less safe, people feel more insecure, the march of daily violence is unchecked.

What has to be stated with the utmost clarity is that the shaming and ignoble features of our rich society are not merely manifestations of human wickedness; many of them have a dynamic relationship with all the advantages, benefits and privileges that are supposed to be such a source of hope and striving to our people, and a model of developing to the poor of the earth.

Then it may be seen that a movement of liberation would not mean loss, renunciation or impoverishment. Quite the contrary. To be able to rest in a sense of sufficiency, to be sustained by a feeling of security – a possibility well within the reach of all humankind – would release us from the anxieties about our individual means of 'salvation' (impossible, anyway, in this world), from artificially prolonged strivings, from wasteful illusions of scarcity. It would set us free to dwell on satisfactions, discoveries of what we can give each other freely, conviviality and gladness that are at present suppressed, indeed, denied in the increasingly monetized realm of our social existence. For in such an easily imaginable condition, other people would cease to be rivals and competitors for inadequate funds, for insufficient means of subsistence; they would become part of our resources, companions in the sharing of a moment of calm and peace, in which to reflect, to nurture the next generation, to retrieve a sense of human purpose from the economic machine. The possibilities of a modest and equitable plenty have yet to be explored; in which leisure would not be something cramped and threatened, dependent on money, and would cease to be a commodity.

Of course, it will not do to urge people to come out of the cities in the manner of St Bernard of Clairvaux (we do that already in our way, seeking private solace in our ex-urban fortresses, crouching jealously over our sterile booty), nor by exhorting people to relinquish the prize and treasures which they have stored up on earth. It is by looking at the other side of our infantile dependency on money, that compelling, fearful addiction, that we may begin to understand the origin of so many of our unnecessary sufferings. We would then perceive the threats and evils that shadow our lives, not simply as the perverse and incomprehensible actions of deranged individuals, but as pains and penalties that are, in large measure, socially determined; and that may well lead to a felt need for emancipation. The sense of relief and well-being would be overwhelming. We would see ourselves delivered from the fear of one another, from the isolation and mistrust of false rivalries. We would see the public spaces suddenly emptied of their bugbears and monsters, of the predators, junkies, muggers and vandals and rapists who have colonized our imagination and haunted our spirit. It would be a kind of social exorcism. We might also be astonished by the chords of sympathy and assent in others. It would be the beginning of perhaps the greatest liberation movement of all.

There are already many hundreds of groups and thousands of individuals practising such possibilities. The people of the Life Style Movement ask what is the point of proposing other models of development to the poor of the earth when we do not have a living alternative ourselves. Conceived in 1972 by Horace Dammer, its members seek 'to live more simply that all may simply live'. It evolved out of conference of church leaders on man's stewardship of God's world, on proper concern for the world's resources. 'But no one could be expected to take any notice of such pious utterances unless we tried to align our lives with them.' It isn't simply a Christian movement; nor is it ascetic. It is not for heroes or martyrs. It ties to be a commitment to modifying our own use of the world's riches, so as to inflict the least possible damage on the poor.

John took early retirement from his metallurgy lectureship at university to take over the rather loose organization of the movement because the members are scattered all over Britain and beyond. Dilys, his wife, gave up paid employment because of ill health. She says 'I am a hedonist. I don't want people writing to us saying how much they've gained because they are free from materialism. That may be all right for some people, but that isn't the point of the movement. Integrity and honesty are more important than heroic acts of renunciation. We lead comfortable lives. The fact that our income halved when John took early retirement was frightening, but it does show you how much of your money is wasted on things that add only very marginally to your store of happiness.' John says 'That's not to say I'm giving away all my possessions. It's a balance between stewardship and selfishness.'

Horace Dammer is Dean of Bristol. He says 'It affects what I buy. Before I buy anything I say to myself "Do I really *want* it?" Not need, want. This has a moderating effect on what I buy. It isn't painful. In any case I was brought up to be careful with money. As a child I had a choice of jam or butter on my bread.'

Max has given up paid employment. 'I get great pleasure out of circumventing useless expenditure rather than forgoing things. I'm very keen on keeping fit, preserving my health. An obvious thing to do would be to use a squash court, but when you think of the expensive equipment, the high material inputs for two people – you can get the same exercise, fitness and camaraderie running through the park; and that costs nothing.'

Horace: We have a member in Bristol, a woman in late middle age, very smart. She decided she would cut down the amount of money she spent on clothes. She saved £500 in a year, which she

gave to Christian Aid. The point is, she still looked very good . . .
It's a question of taking thought before you make decisions. So
for her, it wasn't a question of saying 'It's wrong to look nice.' . . .
There is a Balinese proverb, quoted, I believe, by Schumacher:
'We have no art; we just do things as well as we can.'

Jeremy: A kind of joyful austerity?

Jean (who lived for a time with the Iona community): That word
worries me. I'd say a joyful simplicity.

Dilys: I'm still not happy with simplicity.

Max: I like the word *voluntariness*: a conscious awareness of the way
we live. When I gave up full-time employment, I never considered
it as a drop in income. My living expenses remained the same: I
was living on a basic income. I simply gave up the ability to earn
more and gave the surplus to Oxfam, in the sense that I work for
them, give them my time instead.

Horace: By forgoing from choice a higher monetary standard, you
give time, which has become demonetized for you. That is a
liberation. We are talking about what we can give to each other
freely, without entering the market place.

Max: We are not a movement of the retired or of the unemployed.
We are finding a way, trying to show a way towards different
kinds of fulfilment that don't depend upon rising income.

Horace: In fact, we are profoundly subversive. Of course, I don't
look like a subversive, being a Dean and looking rather respectable. But what we're doing is taking on the way the whole
economy works – rising expectations, living standards. It really is
very radical indeed.

Jean: We are a movement for global peace and justice; and within
that framework, also a movement for personal change. So you
combine the two. You don't drop out, you don't embrace self-
punishment; and you don't turn your back on the poor. For me,
care over the stewardship of time is also important: it's easy to
spend so much time being busy, wasting the scarce resource of
time.

Dilys: The opposite is my problem. I've had to learn to live with
enforced leisure. I can identify to some extent with the unemployed. Increased leisure is a worry for me!

Max: Leisure for most people means the space between work. The
unemployed have a very particular experience of it – one that
can't be recommended. The leisure-promise is yet another way of
trying to disguise the fact that we live in a post-scarcity world; yet
the illusion has to be maintained that we don't, for the sake of

keeping the economic and social structures in place. The unemployed are the socially excluded, unemployment the ultimate nightmare. All that would change if we declared a basic income the right for everyone, take the stigma and the sting out of not doing paid work. The unemployed are the human sacrifice to the maintenance of the illusion that we have to go on in the growth economy. They're doubly exploited.

I worked in a bank once. My job was checking the bonds of one bond issue. I had to check each one, because they are negotiable instruments; that meant looking at it intently, turning each one over as they came from the printers. There couldn't be any error. The supervisor said 'You're doing that awfully quickly.' I had to slow down, and do each one at what was deemed the right speed; an absurd form of make-work.

Jean: You have to separate your value and self-worth from that which can be measured in financial terms. If you're not in paid employment, like a woman working at home, who has no project because she doesn't appear in the measured economy, it is easy for her to feel she has no worth. We need to valorize the non-monetized. The question that excludes you is always 'And what does your husband do?'

Horace: Of course, many women are claiming there should be wages for housework. It ought to be the reverse process: bringing the informal economy into the money market cannot be a liberation for people.

Dilys: We should be thinking of other forms of value – value each other for what we are; being rather than doing. Fromm talks of the primacy of being over having; I think being is more important than doing also.

Jean: Awareness of the things we do and their consequences, not only for our immediate circle, but in the wider world. If I think of the effect of what I buy on the world, I'm taking responsibility.

Max: It's important to say 'Yes I will take personal responsibility.' It *does* matter what I do, not 'What can I do about it?' The aggregate of the changes I've made and the changes other people have made will have their effect. I was listening to the radio at the time of the Live Aid concert. A woman phoned in and said 'I've bought the record, I've been to the concert, I've bought the T-shirt, I've bought the book. What more can I do?' I was thinking, 'Yes that is actually the problem.' If there wasn't all that razzmatazz of wasteful living that industry requires, some of the things people are collecting money for wouldn't be necessary. What you're trying to cure is aggravated by the method you use.

Horace: We easily become a party to it. For instance, I've been to Australia a few times, where we have quite a few members. I think, 'What am I doing, jetting across the world to advocate a simple life?'

John: Everything is flawed. You can't, as individuals, resolve all the contradictions. We talk of liberating needs from the way they are structured by this society, yet this society provides many real comforts and consolations.

Jean: Greed is a powerful motive. I'm not greedy for material things, but I'm greedy. I want to go and visit this community, go and see what that initiative is doing, what's happening somewhere else. It's a form of greed.

Horace: It's called sin. (*Everybody laughs.*) I think laughter is important, to save us from being too pompous or self-important. On the whole, the criticisms we get are teasing rather than harsh. People say we're naive; which is far from the truth.

Dilys: As though living simply had something to do with being slightly simple-minded.

Horace: Actually, it is intensely practical; and its purpose is to save the world in a peaceful way.

Dilys: People have attacked us far less since Ethiopia happened. We can say to them that we are trying to prevent events like what happened in Ethiopia from happening at all.

Jean: Those who talk about conserving the resources of the earth seldom draw conclusions for their own lives; and that is what we're trying to do. In a way, we are trying to show a way forward. We're saying 'Look, we can live like this. It's imperfect, but we can say it's a joyful experience. It isn't a question of asceticism and renunciation. It's fun.' I came to London today and I got a kick out of looking at the shops and not needing anything that was in them.

John: It isn't always fun. I don't want to lead a saintly life; and nor do most other people.

Max: You can't moralize. But you can show people that your life isn't deprived without all the things that we're told we need. The unhappiness of going without certain commodities is not balanced by the unhappiness that the striving and tension and effort that goes into the getting of them, nor by the social tensions and cruelties that are a byproduct of the getting of them – the violence and crime and sickness.

John: The pressures in commercial enterprises are all to raise status – new car with this year's registration plate, latest clothes, holiday in more exotic locations. Parents work longer hours for the sake of the family, which then requires an au pair and whatever; and, in fact, the family life, for the sake of which all this is done, becomes damaged and inhumane.

Horace: You have to face the fact that people enjoy making money.

John: Yes, and we have to understand that people have things, buy them, invest in them because so many of them have been poor, and that represents security. But if they lose their job, all that can be swept away. It keeps up illusions of stability, even though in fact, it's very fragile.

Jean: I know a man of 60 who, when he lost his job, said he didn't feel he was a man any longer. That's what it does to people who've been schooled to labour, and nothing else.

Horace: We need to change the meaning of the word 'wealth'. That's what Lifestyle is about – changing the norms, the expectations, free ourselves from the dominance of money.

Dilys: Why is it that men like money?

Horace: Power. The ability to get things done that you want done.

John: Power to choose and fulfil your wants. No needs. You have no choice without money. You can manipulate people with it; that's why it seems to have a life of its own. I'm in favour of a basic income, a scheme that would look after basic needs. Everything that was earned on top of that would be according to the energies and desires of the individual. There's no point in trying to stifle people's impulse to get more if they want it.

Horace: Choice is essential. But it's like with children in our society – they are overwhelmed with choices, more than are agreeable or meaningful to them. Choices can be a burden. But to have no choices is a sign of severe deprivation. What was decisive for me was working in India, seeing the abjection of that poverty in the world. That was when I came to the conclusion that unless we lived our own lives in sympathetic accord with the help we wanted to give, then giving itself is inadequate.

Max: Simplicity of living has always appealed to me. It was through my children that I became aware of One World, the finiteness of resources. Through them I realized that if we were enjoying something, it was because others were going without. In the end, it is because you love your children that you want other children to survive in the world, not for them to have whatever's going at someone else's expense; because that is the way the world will destroy itself, and those you love along with it ... I realized that the words 'I can afford it' don't mean 'I'm entitled to it.' If I can afford it, why can't others?

Jean: It goes back to when I was younger too. Going to the Iona Community was a revelation.

Max: The average Swiss earns 40 times the pay of the average Somali. The United States, with 6 per cent of the world's population uses 36 per cent of the world's resources. The model of the North is an impossibility for the rest of the world. You don't need a calculator to tell you what kind of resources would be needed for the rest of the world to catch up with the United States.

Horace: On the personal level it is essential because it will help to make the world inhabitable; yet you have to be very humble at the same time, not think 'Oh we're doing this', not be proud and self-inflated. At another level, we're pretty powerless and ineffective. You have to balance these two conflicting attitudes.

John: A decent humility. I'm upheld by a sense of witnessing. Unless our voice is heard, and a humane way is found through, then the outlook is bleak. Yet it isn't *only* a personal witness. You can't pressure people into joining through guilt, that is the wrong way.

Horace: And yet the forces arrayed against us are so powerful that it has to be a movement.

John: The membership is on the whole middle-class.

Horace: Well, all revolutions are started by the bourgeoisie. If you adopt a simple style of life, that presupposes that you have the choice. That must also start with the bourgeoisie. This is to be expected – you must begin with those who have the choice to control consumption.

Jean: The life of the poor is also simple, but it's simple in a horrible way. Involuntary poverty and market dependency is a cruel combination. We're actually talking about disengaging as far as possible from that dependency. We seem genteel and unthreatening because we're so respectable; but the implications are awesome because we are running counter to the whole motor that propels the economy of rich societies.

John: The poor are daily subjected to models of wealth; to be poor in such a society is to be dispossessed.

Jean: Eventually there will have to be legislation for resource allocation unless we can find voluntary alternative models. We must find a way, how to live. Self-reliance rather than self-sufficiency. Self-sufficiency implies the creation of an environment that is inward turning and excluding. Self-reliance implies that the community has strength to look outside and give back the strength it has gained within. Self-sufficiency is cutting off, isolation. Self-reliance implies strength, an equal interchange.

For me, it's a question of finding a space 'to be'; but you have to be careful you don't turn being into just something else to do. 'Doing' in the world implies feats, exploits, monuments; it's macho. Being is sufficient.

The people who respond most vibrantly to calls for liberation are those who are the most oppressed and excluded; and this means, in particular, black people. Melanie and Kyle, young people in their early twenties, have a clear idea of what needs to be done in the complacently racist Midland town where they live.

'I don't have leisure', says Melanie. 'It isn't leisure we need in this society, there's too much work to be done. And that work means demanding more for black people, asking for what has been denied us. It means reclaiming our history and experience, our dignity and all the other things that have been taken from us.

'My grandmother came to this country in the fifties. She worked in a little sweat-shop till she finished, just a year or two ago, getting only £50 or £60 a week. When she talks about what she went through then, it would break your heart. She was going to send for her daughters, but she could never afford it; only my mother came. She kept herself to herself because in those days they put "No Blacks, No Coloureds" in the windows of their houses. Racism was advertised as if it was a commodity. Since then, they've become more subtle about it. My grandmother never spoke to anyone unless she was spoken to. She did years of unpaid overtime because she daredn't protest. My mother was brought up not to make a fuss, she though "Maybe it'll be all right for our children". Well it won't be all right for us, until we make it known that we won't settle for the injuries and humiliations they suffered.

'My mother became a Jehovah's Witness. She had kidney disease, kidney stones. But because they don't allow anyone to have blood transfusions – they believe it is consuming the blood of another person and that is against the commandments of God – the operation which the surgeon had to do was very difficult and complicated. It left her kidneys permanently impaired. She had to go to Oxford three days a week for dialysis. It was wearing her out. What they've done now is set up the dialysis machine in the spare room at home, the room that used to be mine. My father has to do shift work, so that he can help her three days a week on this machine. It makes me angry. My mother became a Jehovah's Witness, she needed the faith when she was walking through the wilderness and, boy, was this town a wilderness for a young black woman in the 1960s. I'm never going to let my daughter go through that. She is two; and I live with her in a flat. My ambition in life is to make sure we get justice and a decent life; leisure would mean doing nothing about it. I couldn't accept that. What makes me mad is that living in this parochial town, the black community here have taken on the attributes of the place itself. They are inturned and indifferent to the outside world: it's funny – all the things that the place itself is known for – the black people have got some of those qualities as well.

'All the official legislation just makes racism more subtle. It goes underground. It doesn't go away. All the signs and signals that people use to express racism, what they really feel. When they say "It used to be lovely round here", they mean "It's gone down since black people moved in". Or if they say something anti-black, they say "Present company excepted" or "You're different", or "It's not you, it's the others". Or "Why have you got a chip on your shoulder?" As soon as you go into a shop, you know who the store detectives are because their eyes are on you straight away. Then at school, when the summer term comes, the teachers were always extra nice to the black girls because they wanted us to be in the sports, running, athletics, netball; so they would be friendly to us. Then their friendship waned with the summer. It was a seasonal friendship because they wanted us in the teams. It implies black people are all right for sports; but they didn't pressure us to do well academically because everybody knows that isn't our strength. But you try and tell them they were being racist, they wouldn't know what you were talking about.

'My teacher, she called me into her study one day and she said "Melanie, you're one of my best girls". Hand on top of mine, condescending, controlling. "You're one of my best girls. Why have you got this chip on your shoulder?" She phoned my Mum, and when I got home, my Mum was in tears, "Why have you got a chip on your shoulder?" It was at the time when we had to decide whether to do exams, and a lot of my friends were saying "Why bother?", they were dropping out. They could see there was no work, it was a waste of time. They knew what a hard time their parents had – they told us they had only put up with it for our sake; and we could see that it wasn't going to be better, but would be worse for the next generation. That was the last thing our parents expected for us. That's what made me radical.'

'I came from Barbados when I was 13, to my mother,' says Kyle. 'I was looked after in Barbados by my grandmother. She was one of 13 children, so there were always a lot of people to help look after you, bring you up. I went to school. The first week a teacher asked me something about English history, I said I didn't know anything about English history, and I didn't care either. I asked him what he knew about Barbados history. He told me to shut my mouth with my big lips. Well, I knew what to expect before I came to England. There's a lot of white people there. But what happened to me, the racism just made me shut up; for about six years I didn't say a word of what I was feeling to anybody. They say in Barbados small island, big mouth, Barbadians are supposed to be arrogant. But I didn't say anything. I'm not ambitious for myself, I don't want to be a big star, but I'm ambitious for my people, people's power, that's all that matters. That's what I'll work for. You don't need paid work. The work that needs doing, there's nobody in this society going to offer you money to do it. A lot of the things we have in Barbados, like the family, like being self-sufficient, we have to build up the strengths black people have, not try to imitate what the whites have done. I'm officially unemployed; but I'm working all the time. It just goes to show you that what they call work – paid employment – has no connection with what people need. I don't believe in work. I'm not saying I want leisure. You've got to have something to do in the world that gives your life meaning.

'I'm not a very religious person, but a lot of things in the Bible make sense. The black people were the oldest civilization; the whites came and conquered them. It says in the Bible "The first shall be last"; to me, that means that black people will have their proper place again. Black people lack confidence. There's so many experts and professional people telling you that you can't cope with your own life; that just reinforces the feeling that you're not competent, you're incapable. It undermines your faith in yourself and each other; and that's where we have to find the strength. All the images in the society devalue you. Like the papers are full of the Stockwell strangler. They publish his picture before he comes to trial. Why? Because he's black. Look at the terrible things they do. Do you know, it makes me afraid to open the papers in the morning because I think oh what horrible stories will there be. When something like this happens, there is a wave of hatred ripples through white society, you can feel it. When I see an old person crossing the road in this town, my mind goes back to Barbados, and my instinct is to put out my hand to help them – I think of my grandmother, my aunts. But because of all the racial stereotyping, I can't do it; that helping hand is frozen. If I do, I know they'll probably throw their arms in the air and scream that I'm attacking them.

'It's like when you see what is happening in South Africa. Mrs Thatcher's actions are watched and judged by black people. They know that what she says is all in code, it's for domestic politics; she's talking to her racist friends in Britain; "Oh no, sanctions will hurt the blacks." She has so little sympathy for black people in Britain, it seems a miracle that she should have such tenderness for them on the other side of the world.

'A lot of black people don't realize how much they suffer. They try to forget, put it out of their mind, turn their back on white society. Others try to be good, set out to prove to the whites that black people are decent, law-abiding. That way, they'll never win because the stereotypes are stronger than individual actions.

'For me, liberation doesn't mean leisure. It's something that white people need as well as black. Their lives are crippled by fear and hatred, they are gluttonous for vanities; they worry if they miss the next episode of *Dallas*, while people in the world starve. Who do you think needs liberating?'